"So heartened to see these true fund-raising sages sharing their distinctive approaches with a wider audience. Three elements make The Generosity Network remarkable: the core partnership approach (we've all heard it, but they embody it); the importance of genuine self-reflection regarding your own attitudes about money, wealth, and giving before soliciting others (which nobody talks about and is such a fundamental and enlightened starting place); and the spiritual element to fundraising (which is central to all real giving). I'm not only a better fund-raiser, but a far better person from having learned from them."

—Laurence Jahns, senior vice president of Advancement
at Robin Hood Foundation

"Jennifer McCrea and Jeff Walker have personally guided me through the process of building a nonprofit organization, and this book only adds to the wealth of knowledge they have shared with me over the years."

—Barbara Bush, CEO of Global Health Corps

"Jennifer McCrea and Jeff Walker have written a seminal new chapter in the history of the fund-raising profession. The Generosity Network exponentially broadens the dynamic range of the profession. It will make fund-raisers weep with ecstasy at being understood. It will transform the entire way those looking to hire them think about what they should be looking for. It elevates the profession from the province of begging to realms of joy and artistry. Why should tech entrepreneurs be the ones having all the fun? Is it possible that raising the funds to end malaria or cure breast cancer could be every bit as fulfilling as building the first electric car company? The possibility has never before been considered. It has now."

—Dan Pallotta, author of Uncharitable

"Jennifer and Jeff have captured the great joy of fund-raising. Their book will prove to be inspirational to many volunteers and staff."

—Suzanne Helm, vice president of Development at the
Council on Foreign Relations

The Generosity Network

*New Transformational Tools
for Successful Fund-Raising*

**JENNIFER McCREA
AND JEFFREY C. WALKER
WITH KARL WEBER**

DEEPAK
CHOPRA
BOOKS
NEW YORK

Published in the United States by Deepak Chopra Books, an imprint of the
Crown Publishing Group, a division of Random House LLC,
a Penguin Random House Company, New York.

www.crownpublishing.com

Deepak Chopra Books and colophon are trademarks of Random House LLC.

Library of Congress Cataloging-in-Publication Data is available upon request.

ISBN 978-0-7704-3779-4

eISBN 978-0-7704-3780-0

Printed in the United States of America

Book design by Maria Elias

Jacket design by Jess Morphew

Authors photograph: © Mark Jason Photography

10 9 8 7 6 5 4 3 2 1

First Edition

To Jack Maley, whose creativity, vision, energy, encouragement, and wisdom helped to launch Exponential Fundraising. Also to my beautiful stepkids, Abby and Jake. And to my wonderful, supportive, and loving family: Mary, John, Robbie, Michael, Noreen, and Christopher McCrea; Judy, Steve, Andy, Ben, Emily, and Carolyn Dobies; and Janet, Tom, Katie, Tommy, and Alex Luketich.

—Jennifer McCrea

To my beautiful and amazing wife, Sue, whose idea it was to write this book, and to my ever-energizing kids, Courtney, Ryan, Morgan, and Hunter, who I am so proud of. And gratitude to the Cahill family, with whom we share all the ups and downs of life . . . we are blessed to call you our friends. I love all of you.

—Jeffrey C. Walker

To my wife, Mary-Jo Weber, whose work and life have taught me the meaning of the word "generosity."

—Karl Weber

SOME OF

OUR GENEROSITY NETWORK

NEW PROFIT (newprofit.com)

Josh Bekenstein
MANAGING DIRECTOR, BAIN CAPITAL, AND CHAIRMAN, NEW PROFIT

Vanessa Kirsch
FOUNDER AND MANAGING DIRECTOR, NEW PROFIT, INC.

Tripp Jones
MANAGING DIRECTOR, NEW PROFIT, INC.

Amanda Clark MacMullan
HEAD OF DEVELOPMENT, NP

Darrell Hammond
CEO AND CO-FOUNDER, KABOOM!

Eric Greitens
FOUNDER AND CEO, THE MISSION CONTINUES

Shruti Sehra
PARTNER, NEW PROFIT

Kirsten Lodal
CEO, LIFT

Elizabeth Riley
PROFESSOR, BABSON

Pam Cantor
PRESIDENT AND CEO, TURNAROUND FOR CHILDREN

MDG HEALTH ALLIANCE (www.mdgha.org)

Alan Court SR
ADVISOR TO THE SECRETARY GENERAL'S SPECIAL ENVOY FOR MALARIA, UNITED NATIONS, AMELIOR FOUNDATION

Ray Chambers
AMELIOR AMELIOR FOUNDATION, SPECIAL ENVOY TO THE UN SECRETARY-GENERAL FOR MALARIA AND HEALTH FINANCE

Naveen Rao
MERCK, MATERNAL MERCK; MATERNAL HEALTH PILLAR, MGD HEALTH ALLIANCE

Phyllis Heydt MDG
HEALTH ALLIANCE, CHW MDG HEALTH ALLIANCE, CHW PILLAR

Cathy Calvin
PRESIDENT, UN FOUNDATION

Suprotik Basu
CEO, MDG HEALTH ALLIANCE

Leith Greenslade
CHILD CO-HEAD, CHILD HEALTH PILLAR, MDG HEALTH ALLIANCE

John Megrue
CO-CEO, APAX CEO, NORTH AMERICA, APAX PARTNERS, LLP

Blair Miller
VICE PRESIDENT, MDG HEALTH ALLIANCE

Alan Batkin CO-HEAD, MDG HEALTH ALLIANCE, CHILD PILLAR; EX-CHAIR, INTERNATIONAL RESCUE COMMITTEE

Anna Levine,
PRESIDENT, BUSINESS LEADERSHIP COUNCIL FOR A GENERATION BORN HIV FREE

MUSIC TO KIDS K–12

Richard Foos
CEO, SHOUT FACTORY, LITTLE KIDS ROCK

Shelly Berg DEAN, FROST SCHOOL OF MUSIC, UNIVERSITY OF MIAMI

Madelyn Bonnot
EXECUTIVE DIRECTOR, QUINCY JONES FOUNDATION

David Wish
FOUNDER AND CEO, LITTLE KIDS ROCK

Quincy Jones
QUINCY JONES PRODUCTIONS

Cynthia Albert Link
VP, EXTERNAL AFFAIRS, BERKLEE COLLEGE OF MUSIC

Roger Brown
PRESIDENT, BERKLEE COLLEGE OF MUSIC

Peter Muller
PDT FUND, MUSICIAN

MIT MEDIA LAB

Seth Godin
AUTHOR

Redi Hoffman
EXECUTIVE CHAIRMAN, LINKEDIN, AND PARTNER, GREYLOCK PARTNERS

June Cohen
EXECUTIVE PRODUCER, TED MEDIA

Peter Gabriel
MUSICIAN AND HUMAN RIGHTS ACTIVIST

Joi Ito,
DIRECTOR, MIT MEDIA LAB

Susan Schuman
CEO AND CO-FOUNDER, SYPARTNERS

Keith Yamashita
CO-FOUNDER AND CHAIRMAN, SYPARTNERS

Michelle Kydd Lee
DIRECTOR OF THE FOUNDATION FOR CREATIVE ARTISTS AGENCY (CAA)

BLUE SCHOOL

Matt Goldman
TREASURER OF BOARD OF TRUSTEES

Blakely Braniff
DIRECTOR OF DEVELOPMENT

Renee Rolleri
CHAIRMAN, BLUE SCHOOL

UNIV. OF VIRGINIA CENTER FOR CONTEMPLATIVE STUDIES

Paul Tudor Jones
CHAIRMAN AND CEO, TUDOR INVESTMENTS CORPORATION, AND FOUNDER, ROBIN HOOD FOUNDATION

Sonia Jones
CO-FOUNDER, CENTER FOR CONTEMPLATIVE STUDIES

David Germano
PROFESSOR, UNIVERSITY OF VIRGINIA

FILMMAKING

Teri Schwartz
UCLA SCHOOL OF THEATER, FILM AND TELEVISION

Kalyanne Mam
FILMMAKER, A RIVER CHANGES COURSE

BRIDGE BUILDERS COLLABORATIVE (MIND TRAINING)

Jud Brewer
MEDICAL DIRECTOR AND ASSISTANT PROFESSOR, YALE THERAPEUTIC NEUROSCIENCE CLINIC

Scott Kriens
CHAIRMAN, JUNIPER NETWORKS, AND FOUNDER, 1440

Dinabandhu
NATURAL YOGA

Jim Gimian
MINDFULNESS MAGAZINE

Scott Beck
TANGO GROUP

Tim Ryan
CONGRESSMAN

Austin Hearst
CHESTNUT HOLDINGS

Charlie Hartwell
HARVARD BUSINESS SCHOOL

Gary Weber
HAPPINESS BEYOND THOUGHT

UNIV. OF VIRGINIA

Governor Gerald L. Baliles
DIRECTOR, MILLER CENTER OF PUBLIC AFFAIRS, UNIVERSITY OF VIRGINIA

Alison Traub
DEVELOPMENT & PUBLIC AFFAIRS, UNIVERSITY OF VIRGINIA

Gordon Rainey
HUNTON & WILLIAMS, EX-RECTOR

Carl Zeithaml
DEAN, MCINTIRE SCHOOL, UNIVERSITY OF VIRGINIA

Bob Sweeney
UNIVERSITY OF VIRGINIA

Henry Skelsey
PRESIDENT, DARDEN FOUNDATION

Terry Sullivan
PRESIDENT, UNIVERSITY OF VIRGINIA

Bill Fryer
IRON TREE CAPITAL, UVA LAW SCHOOL FOUNDATION

Harry Harding
DEAN, FRANK BATTEN SCHOOL OF LEADERSHIP AND PUBLIC POLICY, UNIVERSITY OF VIRGINIA

John Nau
CEO, BUD TEXAS

John Griffin
PRESIDENT, BLUE RIDGE CAPITAL, AND PRESIDENT, MCINTIRE FOUNDATION

Bob Pianta
DEAN, SCHOOL OF EDUCATION, UNIVERSITY OF VIRGINIA

Lily Bowles
ALUMNI, UNIVERSITY OF VIRGINIA

MINDFULNESS MEDITATION

Adam Engle
EX-PRESIDENT, MIND LIFE INSTITUTE

Goldie Hawn
MIND UP

Joe Loizzo
NALANDA INSTITUTE

Sharon Salzberg
INSIGHT MEDITATION

Vivian Kurz
SHECHEN

Jonathan Rose
JONATHAN ROSE COMPANIES

Deepak Chopra

Diana Rose
GARRISON INSTITUTE

Matthieu Ricard
PRESIDENT, KARUNA SHECHEN

MONTICELLO

Alice Handy
PRESIDENT, INVESTURE, LLC

Dan Jordan
RETIRED PRESIDENT, MONTICELLO

Leslie G. Bowman
PRESIDENT, MONTICELLO

Liz Blaine
DIRECTOR OF PRINCIPAL GIFTS, MONTICELLO/THOMAS JEFFERSON

DRAPER RICHARDS KAPLAN

Anne Marie Burgoyne
DIRECTOR, DRAPER RICHARDS KAPLAN FOUNDATION

Christy Chin
PORTFOLIO DIRECTOR, DRAPER RICHARDS KAPLAN FOUNDATION

Jenny Stein
EXECUTIVE DIRECTOR, DRAPER RICHARDS KAPLAN FOUNDATION

HARVARD

David Gergen
CENTER FOR PUBLIC LEADERSHIP/HARVARD SCHOOL

Nitin Nohria DEAN, HARVARD BUSINESS SCHOOL

Jim Bilder
ADJUNCT LECTURER IN PUBLIC POLICY, HARVARD KENNEDY SCHOOL, AND SR. RESEARCH FELLOW, HAUSER CENTER

Cathy Coyle
HARVARD KENNEDY SCHOOL

Nathalie Kylander
ADJUNCT LECTURER, HAUSER CENTER FOR NONPROFIT ORGANIZATIONS

Aviva Argote
EXECUTIVE DIRECTOR, HAUSER CENTER FOR NONPROFIT ORGANIZATIONS

Ellen Levine
PROJECT COORDINATOR, NGO LEADERS FORUM AND COURSE IN EXPONENTIAL FUNDRAISING, HAUSER CENTER FOR NONPROFIT ORGANIZATIONS

Chris Letts
RITA E. HAUSER SENIOR LECTURER IN THE PRACTICE OF PHILANTHROPY AND NONPROFIT LEADERSHIP

Marshall Ganz, SENIOR LECTURER, HARVARD KENNEDY SCHOOL AND HAUSER CENTER FOR NONPROFIT ORGANIZATIONS

Jim Honan
SR. LECTURER AT THE HARVARD GRADUATE SCHOOL OF EDUCATION AND ADJUNCT FACULTY AT HARVARD KENNEDY SCHOOL

FILM SOCIETY OF LINCOLN CENTER

Dan Stern
PRESIDENT, RESERVOIR CAPITAL GROUP, LLC

Rose Kuo
EXECUTIVE DIRECTOR, FILM SOCIETY OF LINCOLN CENTER

Ann Tenenbaum
WOLFBOMB PRODUCTIONS

Bennett Goodman
CEO, GSO CAPITAL PARTNERS

PHILANTHROPIC COLLABORATORS

Noa Meyer
TEN THOUSAND WOMEN, GOLDMAN SACHS

Melanie Schnoll-Begun
MANAGING DIRECTOR, MORGAN STANLEY PRIVATE WEALTH

Scott Harrison
CEO, CHARITY WATER

Pauline Brown
CHAIRMAN OF NORTH AMERICA, LVMH

John Kluge
CO-DIRECTOR, PEACE AND PROSPERITY ENDEAVORS

Tom Tierney
CHAIRMAN AND CO-FOUNDER, THE BRIDGESPAN GROUP

Chris Stone
PRESIDENT, OPEN SOCIETY FOUNDATION

Andrea Kerzner
FOUNDER, LALELA PROJECT

Chris Anderson
CURATOR, TED

Terry Torok
CEO, LIVE FROM EARTH, AND BOARD MEMBER, LALELA PROJECT

Katya Andresen
CEO, EPALS

David Ferguson
PARTNER, PERELLA WEINBERG PARTNERS

Maggie Doyne
EXECUTIVE DIRECTOR, BLINKNOW

Sue Lehmann
INDEPENDENT MANAGEMENT CONSULTANT

Amy Herskovitz
EXECUTIVE DIRECTOR, PERSHING SQUARE FOUNDATION

Dan Pallotta
FOUNDER, ADVERTISING FOR HUMANITY AND THE CHARITY DEFENSE COUNCIL

Bill Mayer
CHAIRMAN EMERITUS, THE ASPEN INSTITUTE, AND PARTNER, PARK AVENUE EQUITY PARTNERS

David Bornstein
CO-FOUNDER OF THE SOLUTIONS JOURNALISM NETWORK

Aedhmar Hynes
CEO, TEXT 100

David Saltzman
EXECUTIVE DIRECTOR, ROBIN HOOD FOUNDATION

Robert Sherman
EX-PARTNER, NOVO FOUNDATION

Gunther Weil
FOUNDER AND CEO, VALUES MENTORS

Chris McConnell
THE MCCONNELL GROUP

Darla Moore

Meg Garlinghouse
HEAD OF LINKEDIN FOR GOOD

Tracey Durning
SOCIAL ENTREPRENEUR AND ADVISER

Jerry Colonna
HUDSON HEIGHTS (LIFE COACH)

Ann Ornish
VICE PRESIDENT, PREVENTATIVE MEDICINE RESEARCH INSTITUTE

Dean Ornish
PRESIDENT AND DIRECTOR, PREVENTATIVE MEDICINE RESEARCH INSTITUTE

Peter Reiling
EXECUTIVE VICE PRESIDENT FOR LEADERSHIP AND SEMINAR PROGRAMS, THE ASPEN INSTITUTE

Chris Wearing
PRESIDENT, TENEO CONSULTING

IDEO.ORG

Joceyln Wyatt
EXECUTIVE DIRECTOR IDEO.ORG

Patrice Martin
IDEO.ORG

Tim Brown
CEO, IDEO.ORG

MORGAN LIBRARY

Richard Menschel
THE GOLDMAN SACHS GROUP

Bill Griswold
DIRECTOR, THE MORGAN LIBRARY AND MUSEUM

CONTENTS

Epilogue

Recommended Resources

Exponential Fundraising Participants

Index

The
Generosity
Network

LOVE IN ACTION

by Deepak Chopra

I first met Jennifer McCrea back in 2005 when she attended the Alliance for a New Humanity conference, which I was hosting in Puerto Rico. That conference addressed a long-standing passion of mine and a question of vital importance to the future of our planet: How can we get people from around the world and from disparate arenas, from politics and entrepreneurship to science and philanthropy, to forge alliances that can help humankind move in the direction of a more sustainable, just, peaceful, and healthy world?

This is a very big vision, and big visions require the combined efforts of many dynamic networks. So it was only natural that Jennifer would be drawn to our campaign, since Jennifer is one of the world's most persistent and effective networkers for good. She attended the conference with the financier and philanthropist Ray Chambers, who is, like Jennifer herself, a great example of what I can only call "love in action." And that's how I came to know Jennifer and her work.

It was the first of many meetings that Jennifer and I have since enjoyed. Whenever I check in with her, I find that she is working to raise money, awareness, energy, and resources on behalf of some vital project, whether it's helping the poor in one of our planet's most underdeveloped regions, reforming the American educational system, finding treatments and cures for epidemic illnesses, or helping to ensure that some of our vital cultural and artistic institutions continue to survive and thrive. Jennifer's interests and energies know no boundaries. As long as it's a worthy cause, she is ready to step up to the plate, and the world is a much richer place as a result of her efforts.

As for Jeff Walker, I've known him for a number of years. We too met initially through Ray Chambers (who is yet another master networker), and I got to know Jeff well when he attended a retreat that I hosted in Taos, New Mexico. (Jennifer was also there.) This was a gathering that was centered on getting in touch with the higher, expanded levels of awareness where we humans experience intuition and creativity as well as big, Platonic realities such as goodness, joy, equanimity, altruism, compassion, and love—the great and eternal truths that are referred to as "divine attitudes" in the Eastern traditions.

It's typical of Jeff that he would be drawn to such a gathering. He was a very successful businessman before he began donating the bulk of his time to philanthropy and the promotion of social causes. But even during his years as a financial executive, Jeff was always devoted to seeking deeper, more humane, more creative ways of relating to the world—quite different from the stereotype we may have of the "cutthroat businessman." And I've found that when Jeff and Jennifer collaborate on a project—and activate the network of creative, passionate individuals they have discovered and partnered with over the years—there's very little they can't accomplish.

Since that retreat in Taos, Jeff, Jennifer, and I have frequently met, shared ideas, and worked together. A year ago, for example, Jeff attended the annual conference I host under the title of "Sages and Scientists." This is a gathering of evolutionary thinkers from many fields—cosmologists and neuroscientists, geneticists and psychologists, statesmen and entrepreneurs, physicists and poets—with the goal of elevating the global conversation. People tend to talk about what's wrong with our world: environmental problems, persistent poverty, ethnic strife, violence. These are important discussions. But we also need a forum where we talk in very concrete, practical terms about what we can do to bring about sustainability, peace, and well-being, defined in the broadest way possible—not just physical well-being but emotional and spiritual well-being, and not just these but also financial well-being, career well-being, social well-being, community well-being, and even global well-being. To achieve these goals, humankind must experience a new kind of evolution—not physical evolution but evolution of the mind, soul, and spirit.

In fact, I think that this notion of evolutionary consciousness is close to the heart of what Jeff Walker, Jennifer McCrea, and millions of others like them are doing. Whether they fully realize it or not, they are helping to usher in the next phase of human evolution through the ideas they are generating and sharing, and through the spiritual connections among countless people their work is helping to spark.

Here I think about a phrase coined by the great scientist Jonas Salk: "the survival of the wisest." Salk had the vision to look beyond materialism. He saw that evolution, as it applies to modern human beings, isn't Darwinian. We no longer live in a state of nature in which organisms are competing for their share of limited resources. Rather than involving a struggle for the survival of specific gene pools, human evolution now focuses on the assimilation of new information, the creation of deeper and more agile ways of thinking and reacting, the use of technology to overcome our physical limitations and achieve greater power over nature, and above all the development of a higher vision of humankind and its spiritual capabilities.

Now our progress has reached a tipping point. Our technological knowledge is capable of destroying us, and in an age of information, anyone can access that knowledge to use for either catastrophic or creative purposes. The choice isn't left to governments, churches, corporations, or isolated geniuses. It's in the hands of everyone. But putting technology in the hands of everyone will yield progress only if our spiritual vision of ourselves evolves at least as quickly as our intellectual and technological prowess.

So where is human evolution taking us? This is where people like Jennifer and Jeff come in. Over the past several years, I've seen the emergence of what I call self-organizing, dynamic networks of creative and intelligent people. These networks are facilitated by technological connections such as Facebook and the Internet itself, but ultimately they are social, intellectual, and spiritual constructs. Even more interesting, some of these self-organizing, dynamic networks are formed from groups of karmically connected people—individuals who share similar intentions and who are pooling their intelligence and other resources to bring those intentions to fruition.

So human evolution is no longer about competition—it's about cooperation, and about the emergence of a new level of consciousness, one that is highly complex yet elegant in its simplicity, and entirely self-organized. If you have an intention, evolution now organizes around that intention. Of course, our intentions vary as widely as human passions themselves vary. But what they all have in common is a spiritual essence that I define using a phrase I've already mentioned: "love in action."

Every great religion emphasizes the importance of love. But as I've always maintained, love without action is irrelevant, while action without love is meaningless. However, when you combine the two, what you can achieve is almost limitless. And this insight is at the heart of the philanthropic work that people such as Jeff and Jennifer are doing, as well as at the heart of this wonderful book they have written.

My wish is that *The Generosity Network* will serve as a catalyst for the thousands of self-organizing networks of dynamic, creative, and karmically connected people who we see springing up all around the world. I hope it will inspire the millions of individuals who are pulse points in these emerging networks to share even more of their wisdom, creativity, energy, and spiritual gifts for the ever-expanding benefit of all humankind.

Deepak Chopra
New York, New York
February 2013

READ THIS FIRST

The Generosity Network is for all those who are deeply committed to a cause and want to attract others to join them in partnership. That includes those charged with raising funds and attracting resources of other kinds for charities, nonprofit organizations, foundations, universities, hospitals, and many other worthy causes. It includes anyone who works in one of the 1.8 million organizations that make up America's nonprofit sector, or the 10 million nonprofits around the globe, since virtually all of those associated with nonprofit organizations have important roles to play in attracting the support (financial and otherwise) of people they come in contact with.

It also includes the millions of Americans who devote part of their time to a favorite organization or cause, whether it's a local charity; a church, synagogue, temple, or mosque; a beloved alma mater; an artistic or cultural institution; a service organization; or the community PTA, Girl or Boy Scouts, Little League, or library.

For all these readers, this book will provide ideas, tools, techniques, and approaches that will make attracting and working with partners easier, more effective, and more fun (for some samples, see the list on pages 6–7). Not only will you be able to raise more money than ever before, you'll also succeed in attracting more resources of every kind—including time, talent, connections, and institutional support. And this in turn will make it easier for you to achieve your organization's goals, bringing personal and social benefits to everyone you touch.

ELEVEN OF THE SECRETS YOU'LL LEARN

by reading The Generosity Network

1. Why reshaping your relationships from the transactional to the transformative is the crucial secret to creating generous, long-term connections.

2. Why the jazz band is a powerful metaphor for a nonprofit organization and its partners—and the simple steps you can take to build your own band (and produce some truly amazing music).

3. How to identify the psychological and spiritual obstacles that are keeping you from being an effective fund-raiser—and how to overcome them, once and for all.

4. How to conduct a first meeting with a potential donor that moves from "that was nice" to building a deep and growing relationship—a totally new approach to connecting with people who can help any organization build an impressive roster of partners.

5. Straightforward, little-known methods to defang the monster most dreaded by every nonprofit fund-raiser: The Ask.

6. How small, inexpensive dinner events can spark more partnerships—and yield greater long-term financial benefits—than the traditional fund-raising gala.

7. How a trip around the world—or around the corner—can transform an indifferent acquaintance into a passionate lifetime partner.

8. Direct from your favorite video game: how avatars are forging profound, real-time links between nonprofit organizations and partners halfway around the world.

9. Specific steps you can take to turn a disengaged board into an energized source of ideas, talent, networking links, and financial support.

10. How today's social media and technology tools can help even the smallest organization create personalized connections with enthusiastic supporters from around the block—or around the globe.

11. The most powerful and effective communication tools you can use to connect with partners—and the horrific language and messaging turn-offs you've probably committed.

KNOW YOURSELF, KNOW OTHERS, KNOW HOW TO ASK

First, a word about the overall approach and perspective of this book.

There are dozens of books about nonprofit fund-raising. Many are interesting and well-written, offering tips and techniques that we're sure have proven useful to numerous readers. But there's a significant gap in the fund-raising literature that we aim to fill. Practically all the existing books are strictly *transactional* in their orientation. They treat fund-raising as a branch of salesmanship and so focus on strategies and tactics analogous to those used by salespeople. The goal: to close the deal, which in this case means to get a check from the donor.

We find this view of fund-raising woefully inadequate—and ultimately ineffective. We believe true success in the nonprofit sphere requires a complete shift in the way we think about fund-raising, from the transactional to the transformative.

The traditional approach to fund-raising is one of the main reasons why most of us in the nonprofit world think of fund-raising as a necessary evil— something separate from the mission of our organizations, something to endure for the sake of a greater vision of the world in which we want to live.

But when it's viewed properly, fund-raising is not a necessary evil. It's sacred work, a beautiful practice characterized at its best by compassion, joy, commitment, and partnership.

It grows from the core conviction that we all want to make a difference with our lives and that, with the unique resources we each have to offer, we can tackle some of our planet's biggest challenges and opportunities. There is beauty in that conviction and in the prospect of living our lives in accordance with it.

Part of the reason for our misunderstanding lies in the very word *fund-raising*, which places the spotlight on money alone. And while of course money is a critically valuable resource in the good work we all seek to do, there are other resources that are equally underactivated: time, creativity, networks of relationships. *The Generosity Network* uses the broadest possible definition of fund-raising, referring to the activation of *all* resources in support of worthy goals, projects, organizations, and visions.

There are other common ways of thinking about fund-raising that blur reality and hamper our effectiveness. One is to talk about it in terms of "asking for help."

That's the language of dependence. It transforms the fund-raiser into a supplicant on bended knee, seeking assistance in a world of scanty resources from a wealthier, more powerful donor.

In *The Generosity Network*, we invite you to shift from "asking for help" to exploring how all of us can work together in pursuit of a common vision using the unique resources we each have to offer. When we think in those terms, we soon find that the sense of dependence and scarcity disappears. Instead, we discover that we are living in a world of abundant resources, and that we are simply waiting for a team of partners to arrive who will call upon the floodgates to open.

So this is not just another book about how to be a more persuasive salesperson, another book about tactics and strategies for more effective fundraising, or even another book about how to find and tap into your donors' passions. Our message is a new one: *True generosity is rooted in relatedness.* Fundraising is, above all, a form of connection. And the greatest gift we bring to our partners is not just the chance to support important work, but rather the opportunity to join and build a community of people who are joyfully discovering their unique gifts and applying those gifts to meet specific challenges. That's how we *really* move the needle on the most urgent challenges of our time.

The process starts with three common elements that we'll urge you to delve deeply into:

1. FIRST, *KNOW YOURSELF!*

"Know yourself" is the classic teaching of ancient philosophy, the elementary practice from which all wisdom starts. It's also an extremely *practical* piece of advice. In *The Generosity Network*, we'll urge you to get to know much more about what makes you tick, beginning with one of the topics people in our society find most difficult to address: your relationship with money. We'll ask you to consider a series of challenging questions about money—questions you may never have dared to explore:

- What is money's role in my life? Am I comfortable talking openly about it? Why or why not?

- Do I think of money as a scorecard, or as a resource to be used for things I care about?
- Is my attitude toward money shaped by my fear of being dependent on others?
- Do I ever use money to control others or to buy their respect or affection?
- Am I willing to redefine what "wealth" means to me?

We'll also ask you to consider how you spend your money. And we'll invite you to reflect on what it feels like when someone asks you for money. Does it provoke fear, anxiety, gratitude, anger, or joy?

Whether you're a full-time fund-raiser or otherwise engaged in a non-profit cause, the answers to challenges such as these are critically important. Otherwise, money is going to continue to be used as a tool to manipulate us rather than as a resource to advance our work and enrich our lives.

Your relationship with money is just one of a number of inner spaces we'll encourage you to explore. Others include your need for control, your willingness to open up to other people, your deepest beliefs about the meaning of success and failure, and the unspoken values that shape your most powerful drives. No, this is not a psychological self-help book. But to be truly effective—and satisfied—in your work as part of a cause-centered team, you must start by fully understanding yourself. We'll offer activities and questions that will help you on this journey.

2. SECOND, *KNOW OTHERS*! (ESPECIALLY THOSE WHOSE PARTNERSHIP YOU SEEK)

Fund-raising is often considered hard and scary because we believe that asking for resources will make us vulnerable. We fear rejection and dependence. This causes us to put up walls that prevent us from seeing our partners and potential partners as what they really are—human beings like us who want to make a difference.

Many philanthropists we know feel fear that fund-raisers (and other people) are nice to them only because they want their money. "They see me as a walking checkbook" is the common complaint. Isn't it ironic how anxiety about money poisons both sides of the relationship, making it more difficult for both donors and recipients to be open and genuine with each other?

Only when we begin to recognize this dynamic—and learn to avoid it—can we treat the work we're doing as it deserves to be treated, as beautiful and sacred.

Our goal in *The Generosity Network* is to help you get to the point you can honestly look at your organization's partners and say, *I respect and love you for who you are. I want to know you deeply and to trust in the process of our friendship.*

Out of that trust, we can create incredible results.

3. THIRD, *KNOW HOW TO ASK*!

Asking someone to become your partner is a source of enormous fear for many in the nonprofit world. But at its core, it's truly a simple proposition if you put your faith in the vision of your work, if you see yourself and others as a true team, and if you see and respect the unique value each of you has to give.

Many great fund-raisers, like great salespeople, succeed because they are confident. This is about more than confidence. It's about *confidence with an open heart.* Confidence that you can work with others by developing a real, authentic relationship with them, inviting them to shape a collective vision that gets refined and defined over time.

This kind of asking feels good. There's no rejection—just passion that seeks a different channel than the one you are seeking to fill. Asking for money (or any other resource) when you are standing up, not on bended knee, is a joy—an invitation for people to relate to their resources in a new way.

To guide you toward this new way of asking, we'll challenge you to consider questions such as:

- Am I willing to take a risk with others? To become vulnerable with them? To enter a true relationship with them?
- Am I willing to see my partners and potential partners as fully human?
- Am I willing to allow others to find their own passions, even passions I may not share?
- Am I willing to be the kind of person who finds continual opportunity, growth, and community as part of a team working on a common cause?

These three themes—know yourself, know others, know how to ask—are the keys to a transformational style of fund-raising. They also offer the best possible summary of *The Generosity Network*. All the rest, as the saying goes, is commentary.

◀┈┈┈┈┈┈┈┈┈┈▶

The two lead authors of this book, Jennifer McCrea and Jeff Walker, bring very different but complementary backgrounds to this project. Jennifer McCrea has spent twenty-five years as a fund-raiser, consultant, coach, and advisor to CEOs, fund-raisers, and board members from a wide variety of nonprofit organizations, ranging from the Acumen Fund, Grameen America, Teach for America, and Columbia University to the Quincy Jones Foundation, the Rhode Island School of Design, Creative Commons, and many others. She's also a senior research fellow at the Hauser Center for Nonprofit Organizations at Harvard University, where she designs and leads the Exponential Fundraising course—a groundbreaking course on the practical, psychological, social, and spiritual aspects of nonprofit fund-raising, team building, and network creation, attended by founders, CEOs, and top executives from some of the world's leading nonprofit organizations.

Jeff Walker came to the world of philanthropy from a successful career in business. In 1983, he and a partner created the first venture capital unit at Chemical Bank, which evolved over time into a highly successful $12 billion investment powerhouse. At the same time, Jeff was active in the nonprofit world, serving on the boards of nonprofit organizations including Monticello, the University of Virginia McIntire School, the Big Apple Circus, Millennium Promise, the Berklee College of Music, and many others.

So Jennifer and Jeff started their lives' journeys in very different places—Jennifer as a fund-raiser and a nonprofit consultant, Jeff as a business leader and philanthropist. But by the time they met in 2005, they found themselves in amazingly similar places—professionally, psychologically, even spiritually. Both had discovered that the driving force in their lives was the passion to support particular causes that were near and dear to their hearts. Both had begun exploring and experimenting with more effective, innovative ways to connect other people to those causes. And over time, both had escaped the sometimes constricting walls erected by their prescribed professional roles. No longer simply "the fund-raiser" and "the philanthropist," Jennifer and Jeff and evolved and grown to the point where they were . . . well, just Jennifer and Jeff. Being themselves. Doing cool stuff. Working and building together.

Like a pair of explorers leading an expedition, Jennifer and Jeff found themselves in little-known territory—the resource-rich continent where generosity thrives and potentially world-changing seeds are sprouting, blooming, multiplying. They found themselves encountering more and more people who wanted to join the exploration: nonprofit founders, cause-driven social entrepreneurs, researchers and experts, philanthropists and foundation heads. "How can we join the party?" these newfound friends were asking. And so the original Generosity Network was born, grew, and expanded, throwing off sparks of invention, discovery, and change in many directions.

In the years that followed, Jennifer and Jeff have collaborated on a wide array of projects. They've worked together to conceive, launch, and manage campaigns for nonprofit organizations in fields from economic development and health care to education and the environment. They've helped build powerful teams behind nonprofit organizations as varied as the MIT Media Lab, the Quincy Jones Musiq Consortium, the MDG Health Alliance, the Harvard Kennedy School, and Millennium Promise. They've worked with nonprofit leaders to improve their team-building skills, energize their boards, redefine their brands, refocus their missions, and redouble the effectiveness of their programs. They've helped organizations attract financial gifts ranging from $100 to $100 million and orchestrated fund-raising efforts at the multibillion-dollar level.

Now Jeff and Jennifer have teamed up with writer Karl Weber to share what they've learned with you. We invite you to read on in the spirit of the Guidelines for Band Members that we offer to students in Jennifer's Exponential Fundraising course (see page 15). This is the approach that will enable you to get the most out of the book.

The Generosity Network is always looking for new recruits. Welcome to the team!

Jeffrey Walker and Jennifer McCrea with Karl Weber
New York, New York
February 2013

GUIDELINES FOR BAND MEMBERS

You're invited to read this book—and share its contents with friends, colleagues, and partners—in the following spirit:

- *An open mind.* Learning happens when we are willing to consider new ideas. Take the perspective of a learner, not a knower.
- *Courage.* The quality required to put new ideas into practice in face of opposition, bias, or sheer inertia.
- *Humor.* The lubricant that makes groups more creative, mutually supportive, and productive.
- *Curiosity.* Young children learn continually because they are interested in almost everything.
- *Daring.* If you're willing to think big and dream great dreams, there are no limits to what you can achieve.
- *Persistence.* Be ready to *start,* knowing there will be setbacks along the way, but that you will grow and learn in the process.
- *Humility and self-awareness.* Know yourself—and always remember, with relief and joy, that you are *not* the center of the universe!

PART ONE

GIVING, GETTING, GROWING

1

THE NO "OTHER" WAY

*The Radical Transformation at
the Heart of Generosity*

The journey of discovery

begins not with new vistas but

with having new eyes.

—Marcel Proust

When Jennifer teaches her Exponential Fundraising course at Harvard University's Hauser Center, she begins by asking a deceptively simple question: "What is fund-raising?"

A simple question—but the answers that are called out from every corner of the classroom are surprisingly varied. And many of them imply a lofty, ambitious vision of what fund-raising is all about:

"It's relationship building."

"It's matching what we do with people's passions."

"It's making communities—tribes of people who share our values and want to change the world together."

"It's opening up networks."

"It's getting access to all kinds of resources—money, time, commitment, and creativity."

"It's about telling our story."

"It's giving our donors a new way of expressing themselves."

And perhaps most idealistic and ambitious of all: "It's a vehicle for individual and organizational transformation."

Wow. That's a lot of grand-sounding meanings to attach to one simple, humdrum, business-as-usual word! But perhaps that complexity—and that lofty sense of ambition—helps to explain why some of the world's busiest NGO leaders and managers would steal several days from their overcrowded schedules to attend a course called Exponential Fundraising in the first place. For these practical idealists, fund-raising isn't just about meeting a dollar quota or achieving a certain rate of return on an annual appeal campaign— it's about making a difference in the world through creative human connections.

But then Jennifer asks her second question: "How do you *feel* about fund-raising?" The answers to this question are highly charged—and not nearly as lofty-sounding as the answers to the first question:

"I hate it."

"It scares me."

"I avoid thinking about it."

"It's the worst part of my job."

"I'd rather do almost anything else."

Finally, Jennifer asks the crucial question: "What makes fund-raising so hard?" And the answers to this question are very personal—and quite revealing.

One student replies, "It's because of the stigma around money. People say that money is the last taboo—that talking about money is harder than talking about sex, religion, or politics."

Another comments, "It's all about the power relationship between giver and asker. I hate being in the position of a supplicant, coming on bended knee to beg for a few pennies from some donor's overflowing coffers. It makes me very anxious, and it feels . . . I don't know . . . degrading, somehow!"

Another says, "It's the fear of rejection. Asking for a donation brings up memories about every time I've been turned down—every girl who refused to go out on a date, every college that rejected my application, every job interview that didn't produce an offer. Just thinking about that litany of disappointments reinforces the deep-seated fear that says, *You're just not good enough!*"

Still another comments, "It's the uncertainty. What should I ask for? How much is too much? How much is too little? When should I ask? What words should I use? How will people react? Do they have some kind of hidden agenda? It's not like any other relationship, and it just makes me so nervous!"

And yet another complains, "The fund-raising situation is so ambiguous. The potential donor and I get to know one another—we talk about our lives, our work, our dreams, our values. But then we have to talk about money, and to quantify our commitment in terms of dollars and cents. Which makes me wonder: Is this supposed to be friendship or business? It's confusing!"

Our friend Lars Jahns, a senior vice president of advancement at the Robin Hood Foundation, summarizes these two sides of fund-raising with this little story:

Fourteen years ago, when I did my first training program with our board, I wanted to get them enthusiastic about fund-raising. So I used the line, "Always remember what the first three letters of *fund-raising* are!" Without skipping a beat, one of the board members interjected, "Lars, remember what the first *two* letters are!"

Sad to say, reactions like these are all too familiar—and very understandable in the context of how people traditionally think about fund-raising. People tend to hate and fear fund-raising. The phobia rises, at times, to the level of organizational dysfunction. One very distinguished, venerable nonprofit we know actually went several years with its vice president for development position completely vacant. When we asked one staff member why this leadership vacuum had been tolerated, she told us, "There's a sense here that fund-raising is at best a necessary evil. We've got to do it, but it's really beneath us. After all, we're doing God's work—why should we have to lower ourselves to ask people for money?"

Weird, isn't it? Many of the same people who are capable of thinking about fund-raising as an idealistic quest for partnership, community, and even self-transformation can also see it as a soul-sucking source of fear, anxiety, and shame. No wonder those of us who live in the nonprofit space sometimes fall into the trap of thinking about this essential activity as "the fund-raising demon"—a frightening specter of unpredictable shape that we'd give almost anything to avoid.

TAMING THE DEMON:
Fund-raising and Transformation

A big part of the reason we sometimes feel haunted by the fund-raising demon is the way we lose sight, in our day-to-day work lives, of what fund-raising is really all about.

On the most obvious level, fund-raising is about asking people for money. And that helps to explain the emotions we associate with fund-raising. Many of us have painful relationships with money. So the idea of talking about money with someone you barely know—particularly someone who may well have more money and therefore more prestige, power, influence, and self-confidence than you—can feel intimidating or even frightening.

But is money the focus of your life, your aspirations, your career, or your work? Is money the reason you've dedicated yourself to promoting a particular organization and the cause it addresses?

Of course not. It just takes a moment's reflection to realize that money is simply a means to an end. And what is that end?

One answer is the particular goal or goals to which your organization is dedicated. The immediate, short-term goal may be very specific: to meet next year's operating budget, to create an endowment fund, to build and furnish a new headquarters, to provide scholarships. But the short-term goal is often subservient to a bigger, more ambitious long-term goal: to alleviate world hunger, to mitigate the impact of global warming, to educate the next generation of Americans, to provide health care to those in need, to foster appreciation for music and art, or to improve public policies concerning human rights, immigration, incarceration, or scientific research.

Being continually aware of this much bigger, value-laden context for the work we do is one big step toward taming the demon. "Asking for money" evokes scary, unpleasant emotions, but "working to make the world a better place" is exhilarating, inspiring, and energizing.

The approach to fund-raising that Jeff and Jennifer have discovered is still more expansive than this—and that's because it places fund-raising in an even bigger, broader context. Fund-raising is not just "asking for money"; it's not even merely "a step toward making the world a better place." Fund-raising is *a vehicle for transformation*—personal, organizational, social, even global.

Does that sound a bit *too* grandiose? Maybe. Maybe it even feels slightly overwhelming: "Are you telling me that my job is to make people transform themselves? I thought it was scary just to ask them to write a check!"

But here's a paradox: this big, expansive, grandiose vision of what fund-raising is, or should be, doesn't need to overwhelm you. Just the opposite, in fact. Broadening your perspective on fund-raising to embrace the need for personal and social transformation can be amazingly liberating.

THE GAME CHANGER

Jennifer herself knows exactly what it's like to feel trapped by the challenge of fund-raising. Her first job out of college back in 1988 was as a college fund-raiser. She was excited to go to work for her liberal arts alma mater, which had given her so much in life. But she knew nothing about fund-raising or about nonprofit work in general.

Her first day on the job, the college president, himself a former fund-raiser, told Jennifer something she's never forgotten. "Jennifer," he said, "always remember that money can't be raised sitting behind a desk."

He said this sitting behind his desk.

Jennifer's boss made it clear she was expected to make three hundred face-to-face visits that year for the college. So she dutifully hurled herself out into the field and started to call on alumni.

Six months later, she was walking down New York's Fifth Avenue telling herself that she had picked the wrong profession. Her legs and arms felt like lead weights as she dragged herself back to her nonprofit-sized Manhattan hotel room. She'd been making one call after another, talking with scores of perfectly nice people about the good work of their mutual alma mater, asking for a financial donation, and getting one friendly, polite rejection after another.

Jennifer was deflated, confused, and despondent. What to do next?

Jennifer made a decision that night in her little hotel room—a decision to try something different. The next day, at her scheduled breakfast meeting with a successful young banker named Peter, instead of selling the college's latest plans, hauling out the blueprints for the proposed new science building, or repeating the statistics demonstrating why a liberal arts education is so important, she decided to concentrate on finding out how Peter wanted to make a difference with his life.

Suddenly it wasn't about money. The meeting became the start of an open-ended, unfolding journey. Jennifer discovered that she was interested in learning what Peter cared about. They talked about his life, his work, his dreams, and his passions in a way few people get to do in the course of an ordinary week. In the process, Peter learned some things about himself. The meeting was alive and creative and more joyful than any Jennifer had experienced before.

It led to a donation, yes. But more important, it led to many more meetings between Jennifer and Peter, and a co-creative partnership that made a big difference for the future of the college and for both their lives.

That call was a game changer for Jennifer. She has since made some six thousand face-to-face visits with prospective partners on behalf of organizations large and small. And in essence, they've all followed the same pattern as her conversation with Peter. Two people sit down together and have a deep conversation about their lives and about what they can do together that might be creative, exciting, rewarding, and fun. In most cases, the two are able to come to a shared commitment to make something happen together—often not something they can define in that first meeting, but that they discover mutually in the days and years to come.

That's the kind of difference a simple change in perspective can make.

FUND-RAISING AND THE UNIVERSAL QUEST FOR MEANING

As Jennifer first sensed in her hotel-room epiphany so many years ago, fund-raising is not just about money—it's about energy, creativity, human connections, and joy. And that means it touches desires, dreams, and yearnings that are much bigger than your personal goals, ambitions, and challenges, or even those of your organization. They are *universal*—the shared inheritance of every human on earth—and ready to be tapped.

This truth helps to explain some of the most confounding realities of fund-raising.

Why is it that getting people to give money can feel so difficult—even when we have a watertight, logical case to make that demonstrates the importance of our cause, the effectiveness of our program, and the value of our work? It's because people don't give money (or anything else they value) for purely logical reasons (see the sidebar "Four Realities of Giving," below).

FOUR REALITIES OF GIVING

1. *Giving is emotional.* People are inherently generous, and they are driven to give by emotional factors—specifically the activation of "mirror neurons" in our brains as a response to our observation of the experiences of other people. Shockingly enough, this familiar truth is often ignored by nonprofit organizations when they design their outreach programs (which tend

to focus on data, statistics, and charts rather than human faces and real-life stories).

2. *Giving is personal.* Social psychologists tell the story of a tankful of brine shrimp being neglected in an elementary school classroom. The kids ignored the slow deaths of the shrimp until only one survivor was left—whom the kids named, anthropomorphized, and eagerly began to care for. This seems illogical, yet it reflects human nature: people want to help one person, not a mass. The good news: modern technologies, from social media to mobile communications, make it easy to connect would-be donors to individual recipients and so trigger the instinct to help.

3. *Giving makes people happy.* When we help other people, our brains release endorphins, producing an emotional sensation often called "the helper's high." This encourages people to give again, a beneficent form of "addiction" that nonprofits can help to reinforce by providing tangible evidence of the positive results generated by giving.

4. *Giving is social.* When a clear plastic donation box is displayed in a museum lobby, people tend to make the same kinds of gifts they see. If the box is empty, they give nothing; if it is filled with coins, they give coins; if it is filled with bills, they give bills. (There is a limit to this effect: if the box contains only hundred-dollar bills, fewer people give, because they feel that ones and fives may not be welcome.) Similarly, public radio stations find that listeners become donors when they hear stories about people like themselves making contributions.

Source: Katya Andresen, chief strategy officer, Network for Good.

Research shows that people connect themselves to a cause overwhelmingly for emotional reasons rather than objective, logical ones. This is why the fact-based appeals many nonprofit fund-raisers rely upon are generally ineffective. Merely providing statistics about the millions of individuals whose lives are impacted by a problem, data demonstrating the effectiveness of a particular approach, or a numbers-heavy business plan outlining a strategy (however impressive) is unlikely to touch people where they live.

People become dedicated to causes that change their self-image and make their lives feel rich with meaning. It's a dynamic we're familiar with from everyday consumer behavior, where drivers buy cars not to fill basic transportation needs but to enhance their self-esteem, where people choose clothes and computers based not on functionality but on the "cool" factor, and where, as cosmetics mogul Charles Revson famously said, "In the factory we make lipstick, but in the store we sell hope."

Rather than fighting against the innate human yearning for emotional fulfillment, nonprofit organizations and those of us who love them need to appeal to it on behalf of the world-changing causes we serve. If you want to turn people into passionate partners for your cause, you shouldn't focus on creating yet another slide show laden with statistics that validate your arguments (though, as we'll discuss, a strong case for support is an essential tool in the fund-raiser's kit). Instead you need to focus on providing a promise of partnership and personal growth, along with an avenue for achieving them.

This is the crucial link between the universal quest for meaning in the life and the work of the nonprofit organizer, partner, and fund-raiser. And this is why a dramatically new attitude toward other people, your work, and yourself is the essential first step to becoming a truly effective advocate for the causes to which you're dedicated.

When people hear about the work Jennifer does, they often comment, "Fund-raising sounds like incredibly hard work. Yet you seem not only to be good at it but actually to *enjoy* it. What's your secret?"

Her answer is always the same: "I know from the bottom of my heart that people *want* to make a difference with their lives and with their money. They *want* to work together and to share their passions with like-minded individuals. And that's why philanthropy grows from deep-seated human needs. That's the only secret." Once you understand that people want to make a difference on the planet—even if they aren't aware of it yet—you realize that the act of fund-raising not only is not difficult, painful, or frightening but is, in fact, deeply meaningful work.

OVERCOMING THE OBSTACLES THAT BLOCK THE FLOW OF RESOURCES

We sometimes hear fund-raising defined as "harnessing resources." This definition isn't a bad starting point. At least it broadens the conversation beyond money to include the entire range of resources that our organizations need to thrive and grow. But the concept of "harnessing resources" makes it sound as though the resources required are limited, hard to acquire, and eager to escape—like wild mustangs that resist being tamed.

In reality, the resources we need to drive our world-changing work are abundant; when they are connected through human networks that link the individual passions of dozens or hundreds or thousands of people, they can be leveraged and magnified until their power is virtually immeasurable.

So if you think in terms of "harnessing resources," you are trapped in a perspective that is shortsighted and inaccurate. Instead, we're going to help you think in terms of *unleashing* resources—multiple forms of energy that are just waiting to be freed.

Remember Jennifer's secret: People *want* to make a difference. They *want* to channel their time, energy, creativity, and, yes, their money toward worthwhile causes that will enrich, lend meaning to, and transform the world and their own lives. So resources will tend to flow naturally toward you when you focus on the most important aspect of the fund-raising process: *creating human connections*.

When you make those human connections, you automatically see and clear away the obstacles that stand between you and the flow of resources—obstacles that, in most cases, you've helped put in place yourself. Once the obstacles fall, resources naturally tend to flow toward good ideas and worthy projects.

Let's talk about some of these obstacles. What follows is just a partial list—there are many more obstacles, as we'll discuss throughout this book. But these are some of the biggest ones that it's useful to address at the very beginning.

Obstacle #1: Scarcity Many fund-raisers are hamstrung by the false belief that money is a scarce commodity. Let that one go.

Yes, it's true that we live in a time of economic uncertainty, that the global recession of 2008–9 has been followed by a recovery that (as of early 2013) remains slow and fitful by the standards of recent history. But the fact remains that nonprofit organizations today have access to an incredibly vast pool of financial resources, real and potential.

Did you know that during the first half of the twenty-first century, individuals are expected to contribute to private foundations more than ten times the amount of money they contributed in the preceding one hundred years combined?[1]

Did you know that, during 2011 alone (the last year for which data are available), Americans donated $298.4 billion to nonprofit organizations?[2]

Did you know that the baby boom generation—today's middle-aged adults, often described as "cash-strapped" and unprepared for retirement—

---

1   Thomas J. Tierney and Joel L. Fleishman, *Give Smart* (2012), 218.
2   See www.charitynavigator.org/index.cfm?bay=content.view&cpid=42.

are projected to receive $8.4 trillion in inheritance monies from parents and grandparents, and that when lifetime gifts are included, the total intergenerational transfer expected balloons to $11.6 trillion?[3]

There is plenty of wealth in our society, much of it *eagerly seeking* a positive outlet—like water from a mountain ice melt, naturally drawn by gravity toward the channels that will let it flow downhill.

The same is true about other resources: time, networks, creativity, ideas, passion—there's plenty of all of them out there. For example, during 2009, volunteers in the United States alone contributed a total of 15 billion hours of their time to nonprofit organizations, worth $279 billion at average wages.[4] There's no shortage of resources. Our job is to identify the obstacles blocking our receipt of them.

The doctrine of scarcity fosters an attitude of anxiety, fear, and needless competitiveness among nonprofit managers and partners. So not only is it inaccurate, it's also harmful. Let's jettison it.

Obstacle #2: Despair The challenges we face are big—but we mustn't let this fact drive us to despair and inaction. Despair convinces us that the problems in Africa are too big; that global warming is so far advanced there's nothing we can do to reverse it; that our educational system, our health care system, and our economic system are so dysfunctional that we might as well give up. Despair is the mind's way of keeping a safe distance, of telling itself that nothing can be done.

Of course, it's true that our species faces serious problems that will take enormous efforts to fix. That's one reason so many of us have chosen to devote our lives to addressing them. But it's also true that humankind has surmounted incredible challenges in the past, from eradicating smallpox to lifting hundreds of millions of people in China and South Asia out of poverty. And no one individual, or any single nonprofit organization, is sad-

---

3   See www.metlife.com/about/press-room/us-press-releases/index.html?compID=32895.
4   See www.urban.org/UploadedPDF/412209-nonprof-public-charities.pdf.

dled with the responsibility of resolving any of our greatest problems alone. Rather, each of us carries the burden of making things better in our own chosen sphere, in whatever corner of the planet we've picked to focus on. Defined in that narrow way, the tasks we face are eminently manageable—and the results, multiplied by hundreds of thousands of nonprofit organizations and millions of individual volunteers, can be truly impressive.

So face up to despair. Look at it, examine it from every angle, and you'll find that it wilts under the bright, searing light of scrutiny.

Obstacle #3: Fear of the Unknown Reaching out to make real human connections—the prerequisite to letting resources flow downhill—can be intimidating at first. A common reaction is to flee from spontaneity and authenticity into a world of regimentation, planning, and control. Rather than speaking from the heart and with an open mind, we take refuge in the comforting concept of "the thirty-second elevator pitch." Borrowed from the craft of salesmanship, the elevator pitch is a canned, pre-scripted mini-presentation of the case for your cause, supposedly designed to be concise, clear, and compelling.

It sounds like a great idea—particularly because it gives the fund-raiser enormous control over the interaction. The problem is that it never really works. People aren't parrots, nor do they appreciate being talked at by one. Squawking an agreed-upon organizational line doesn't touch people. It doesn't establish an emotional bond. It certainly doesn't offer a promise of personal or organizational transformation. (In later chapters of this book, we'll delve into more detail about the shortcomings of the elevator-pitch approach—and we'll provide specific alternatives that are far more effective at creating real human connections.)

When seeking resources for the causes you love, don't be afraid to let go of some control. Bring your true self and the stories that encapsulate it to the table. Yes, this kind of transparency can make you feel vulnerable. But it's also exhilarating—and in the long run, it's the only way you and the organizations you care for are really going to grow.

Obstacle #4: Fear of Rejection It hurts to be turned down. But if you remember that people really do want to make a difference on the planet with their lives and with their money, you realize that *rejection is fundamentally impossible*.

This claim may be hard to believe. It flies in the face of what every fund-raiser "knows." But remember our definition of fund-raising: it's not about the money, it's about transformation.

If your goal is larger than just directing resources to your own cause—if your goal is to guide people to look inside themselves and discover what they truly care about, as part of their personal journey to a transformed, more meaningful existence—then there is no possibility of rejection. What masquerades as "rejection" is really just the flow of resources into a different channel.

Suppose you're raising money for, say, poverty eradication. It may happen that the person you are meeting with will say, "You know what I've recently discovered about myself? That my deepest passion is for art. I think what I want is to find a way to spend the next few years of my life bringing the joy of great painting and sculpture into the lives of people who know nothing about it."

Is this an experience of "rejection" or "failure"? Sure it is—if you choose to take it that way. And if you've entered the dialogue with the attitude "It's all about the money," then you'll surely take it that way. A few months of conversations like that and you'll be well on your way to fundraiser burnout.

Instead, learn to take a different mind-set—to recognize that your acquaintance's self-discovery is a victory for the world, not a rejection of you and your organization. After all, the world needs people mobilizing resources for a wide range of wonderfully important things—including art.

So rather than mumbling a dejected "I understand" and hurrying off to your next appointment, try responding with a heartfelt "How wonderful!" And perhaps offer the names and numbers of a couple of contacts who might be able to help with your friend's quest to become a patron of the arts.

Scarcity, despair, fear of the unknown, fear of rejection—all of these obstacles make fund-raising a painful, exhausting ordeal. What's worse, they impede the flow of resources that are ready to be moved toward all of the things that are needed right now.

Once you stop allowing these obstacles to stand in your way, you may be amazed by the flow of energy that you experience.

THE NO "OTHER" WAY:
Generosity Becomes You

A thin interpretation of the concept of generosity reduces it to a single act of charity: giving time, knowledge, services, or money. The result is a simple, clearly delineated trade-off: the receiver is helped with a scholarship or a house or a badly needed operation, and the giver gets that warm interior glow that comes with renewed or increased self-esteem.

That's all fine. But a donation of this kind often involves a power dynamic that severely limits the potential for true transformation.

Think about the last time you made a charitable contribution. Remember how it made you feel about yourself. If you're like most people, it gave you a sense of goodness, of efficacy, of control . . . and this in turn made you feel like *someone*: the "donor," the "patron," the "philanthropist."

By contrast, the person receiving the gift is (relatively speaking) *no one*: the "grantee," the "recipient," the humble supplicant whose role is to accept the largesse with appropriate gratitude.

We're exaggerating the nature of the relationship—but only slightly. The point is that, in traditional philanthropy, the giver is always "one-up," while the receiver is always "one-down," an unbalanced relationship between two rigidly defined roles that creates an inherently unfair and unhealthy dynamic.

It takes courage to abandon this dynamic. As Jennifer's friend Katya Andresen puts it, "It's impossible to talk about generosity without being vulnerable, impossible to be truly generous without opening yourself up."

True generosity is generosity that sets the stage for personal transformation for everyone involved—the donor or philanthropist as well as the recipient or fund-raiser. And this kind of generosity happens only when there is no "other." When we break through the preordained roles of giver and receiver, generosity moves beyond a single fleeting act to shape how we live our lives. *Generosity becomes you.* This adds a delectable sweetness to the process, creating a free-flowing positive-feedback loop. Everyone is lifted by this tide. Defensiveness and barriers between people melt away, and the flow of resources to the places where those resources are most needed becomes a natural, inevitable phenomenon.

Nick Ehrmann of the education reform group Blue Engine recalls a time when he let ego get in the way of a human connection—and paid the price for it:

Before I had any experience raising money from individual donors, I was fortunate to get an introduction to a well-known philanthropist I'll call Henry—head of one of the best-known foundations out there, a former venture capitalist, and a really brilliant man.

We traded emails, and he invited me to meet him in his apartment on New York's Upper West Side. This was my big break. And what was supposed to be a half-hour meeting turned into a two-hour conversation.

It started out well. I talked about my experiences as a teacher and my ideas for education reform, and he started doing what many smart people do—asking me really interesting, probing questions. The longer we talked, the more he began challenging my thinking, asking things like, "Are you sure that's the right way of approaching this?" and "Have you considered this possibility, or that alternative?" Henry was an engaging conversationalist, in a kind of needling, provocative way.

But here's the thing. Instead of taking Henry's questions as an opportunity to exchange views and learn, I got defensive. I argued back, blocked every point Henry tried to make, and found myself talking 75 percent of the time—which meant I was doing very little listening.

Looking back, I'm embarrassed by the way I behaved. I think it signaled to Henry that I was a very small person, and that I would be hard to work with. I wrote Henry back a couple of times, but he literally hasn't talked to me since. And I don't blame him.

I had it all wrong. Creating a connection isn't about winning an argument. It's about opening your mind, and inviting someone else to do the same thing. It's about listening, learning, and figuring out how to move forward together.

Lots of us have fallen in the trap Nick fell into. It's a trap that's especially easy to fall into if you've been successful in school and at work, where people are rewarded for sounding smart, logical, well-informed, self-assertive, even aggressive. It's certainly a lot easier—intellectually and emotionally—to try to *argue* someone into agreeing with you than to make yourself open and vulnerable in dialogue with them. There's just one problem: It almost never works.

HUMAN-TO-HUMAN CONNECTIONS:
The Fund-raiser's Secret Rules

So how do we allow real generosity to happen? When we are acting as fund-raisers or otherwise seeking support for a cause we believe in, how can we help allow resources to flow in an actual meeting with a potential contributor, partner, or collaborator? Through opening up, sharing, and listening. And that means stepping out of our preordained roles and behaving in ways that violate traditional norms—coloring outside the lines, you might say.

Generosity happens only when we allow ourselves to be open and fearless enough to truly connect with others—not role to role, but human being to human being. It's an attitude we need to cultivate in ourselves and apply not just during our fund-raising activities but whenever we make connections with people.

How can you strive for greater openness in the course of your daily interactions with people? Here are some simple techniques that can help make it happen.

Don't start a conversation by asking, "What do you do?" Although this standard question might seem to help frame the conversation, it creates a barrier between you and the other person. It forces us to put each other in a box whose dimensions are limited by perceived social ranking and occupational status.

Make contact by asking a "connective" question that touches on interests, experiences, and values. For example, suppose you're seated next to a new acquaintance at a conference about education. Instead of reflexively asking, "What do you do?" try to catch him off guard with the question, "What was your favorite subject at school?" This simple query may create a path that the two of you can follow into a deeper, more meaningful conversation. If your new acquaintance's favorite subject was physics, you may suddenly find yourself discussing the origin of the universe—a far cry from the dry exchange of mini-resumes that usually dominates a first meeting.

Ask "why" questions. If you meet someone who mentions having attended Berkeley, use this as an opening to gently probe the interests and values that led to this particular path. "Oh, you went to Berkeley? Why did you choose that university? You studied philosophy there? Why were you drawn to that subject?" "Why" questions invite self-reflection and openness. They're one of the secret weapons of any human-connections specialist—which includes any fund-raiser.

Watch your ego! Jennifer recalls attending a cocktail party in London full of people with the kind of names you see in boldface in newspaper columns. Her ego reacted as it naturally tends to do, poking its head out from time to time in Whac-A-Mole fashion, looking for a morsel of confirmation that she fit in, that she "belonged" in this illustrious group. When the ego takes charge, the need to impress prevails and we usually stop listening to others, instead concentrating on finding opportunities to shine a spotlight on us— by dropping a name or two, "casually" mentioning some recent achievement we're proud of, or spouting an opinion we think will make us appear well-informed and sophisticated.

Unfortunately, fighting the ego directly usually doesn't work. So instead of trying to hammer it down, we suggest simply, quietly, watching your ego, recognizing it for the illusion it is. With simple observation, it dissolves. And in those moments of dissolution, ease and joyfulness flow in. There's no need to impress, no need to be heard and agreed with. Those moments feel especially spacious and alive. When you're not merely swapping business cards or trying to impress other people, encounters with strangers can actually be opportunities for growth and discovery.

Above all, be mindful. That's a word that most people find needs a bit of explanation.

Our friend Sharon Salzberg is a noted teacher of meditation. In 1976, she established, together with Joseph Goldstein and Jack Kornfield, the Insight Meditation Society (IMS) in Barre, Massachusetts, which ranks as one of the most prominent and active meditation centers in the Western world. In her work, Sharon is often asked to explain the elusive yet crucial Buddhist concept of *mindfulness*. She likes to define it in down-to-earth terms by telling this story:

> Imagine if you're on your way to a party, and a friend comes up to you and says, "I met X today, and he's really, really, really boring." Then, when you go to the party, you find yourself in a corner, talking with Mr. X. How do you suppose you'll respond? If you're like most people, you won't really listen to what X has to say. Instead, you'll be thinking about your email. You'll be looking around the room, wondering, "Who else can I find to talk with? How can I escape from X?"
>
> But you could also drop the expectations planted in you by your friend and really be present for the conversation with X. Maybe at the end of the evening you'll decide, "You know what? X is really, really boring!" But it won't be because you've been told that, but because you discovered it yourself. On the other hand, maybe you'll leave the party thinking, "Wow! He's not boring at all."
>
> The practice of mindfulness is all about entering a space of discovery.

So mindfulness is (in part) about freeing yourself from preconceptions so you can actually perceive and connect with the people around you. It's an exciting prospect. When you open yourself up to new experiences, you never know what you may learn—or from whom. But it won't happen unless you allow it to happen—and that starts with getting your unruly ego and your mind full of preconceived notions under control.

◀ ┄┄┄┄┄┄┄┄┄┄┄ ▶

The ideas and attitudes we've begun to explore in this chapter can take you a long way toward taming the fund-raising demon. And taming the demon can have a huge impact on your professional and personal life.

During 2011, our friend Joi Ito was under consideration for a unique position: that of director of the world-famous MIT Media Lab. Joi is a brilliant young entrepreneur and venture capitalist as well as a leading thinker and writer on innovation, global technology policy, and the role of the Internet in transforming society. On the other hand, Joi had never completed a college degree, which might make a prestigious position at one of the world's great universities seem like a stretch.

But Joi nailed the job through his answer to one interview question: "How would you feel about participating in fund-raising on behalf of the lab?"

Ito's response: a heartfelt, smiling "I *love* fund-raising!" And the results he has achieved since accepting the position have proved that he meant every word.

If you're pursuing a career in the nonprofit world, there's no single statement you can make in a job interview that will open more doors than this one. But of course you mustn't say it unless you really mean it! The ideas and insights in the rest of the book will help you transform "I *love* fund-raising!" from an aspiration to your personal reality.

FOOD FOR THOUGHT

Follow-up questions and activities designed to help you get the most out of this chapter:

- Deep-rooted attitudes about money help to shape many of our feelings about fund-raising. Think about the sources of your own attitudes regarding money. How was money talked about—or *not* talked about—when you were growing up? What sorts of emotions were associated with it?
- The chapter mentions four obstacles—scarcity, despair, fear of the unknown, and fear of rejection—that prevent resources from flowing toward organizations that need them. Which of these obstacles has had the greatest impact on your work, and why? Is there some different obstacle, not discussed in the chapter, that has played an even greater role in impeding your efforts?
- Think back over the encounters you've experienced recently. Recall one such experience that was narrow-minded and unproductive. Can you "rewrite it" to make it open-minded and creative? What can you do differently when you encounter people tomorrow?

2

CONNECTING THROUGH NARRATIVE

The Power of Your Story

It is not the answer that enlightens, but the question.

—Eugène Ionesco

As we explained in Chapter 1, learning how to make deep connections with the emotional needs of potential partners is the key to growing the resources available to your favorite cause. In this chapter, we'll describe the single most powerful tool humankind has ever developed for tapping emotional depths—the artfully constructed narrative.

On some level, we all intuitively understand the power of story. Every skilled conversationalist knows that a colorful, vivid narrative—funny or moving, surprising or suspenseful—is the best way to attract and hold the attention of an audience. And every experienced fund-raiser knows that "On my last trip to Kenya, I met a woman named Anindo . . ." is a much more effective way to capture someone's attention than "Let me tell you about my nonprofit organization that works on . . ."

The power of story is no new discovery; it has been well-known to leaders and teachers around the globe for thousands of years. The wisdom of past civilizations, from Greece and India to the Middle East, is embodied in compelling narratives that modern audiences still find engrossing: the epics of Homer, the tragedies of the great Athenian playwrights, the Sanskrit classics *The Mahabharata* and *The Ramayana*, the legends and histories captured in the Hebrew scriptures, and the parables of Jesus. Humans have always instinctively understood that the key to conveying a message powerfully and unforgettably is to couch it in a story.

The emotional, intellectual, and cultural richness of story bridges civilizations and carries a universal appeal. And yet, in our work as fund-raisers, we still tend to neglect this simple but powerful technique for making connections. When given the opportunity to reach out to potential friends and partners, most of us still lead with information about what our organization does, rather than with a story that shows why it matters.

In this chapter, we'll share some practical techniques that can help you become much more comfortable, eloquent, and effective when it comes to telling your personal story and connecting it with the lives of your listeners.

WHY STORY MATTERS

What is it about story that gives it the unique power to forge connections between people and bring ideas to life? There are several answers:

Stories deal with the universal currency of experience. Stories are crafted from the stuff of everyday life—the basic requirements of existence and the struggle for survival; the varying needs, dreams, fears, desires, loves, and aversions of unique individuals as they strive and contend together; and the relationships we build within families, among friends and neighbors, and in communities and nations. These are things we all experience and can identify with when they are reflected in a compelling narrative.

Stories touch our senses. A well-designed story appeals to each of the physical portals through which we perceive the world—the senses of sight, sound, touch, smell, and taste. When a skilled narrator makes a story come alive for us, we share his experiences through the sensory images he evokes: the aroma of pine needles, the crackle of dry branches on the floor of a forest, the chilly glow of a full moon in a cloudless sky. The vividness of sensory details stirs our emotions and helps us empathize with the narrator—a crucial step toward sharing his values, vision, and goals.

Stories involve challenge, choice, and resolution. Every good story depicts one or more humans caught up in challenge, forced to make a choice, and experiencing an ultimate resolution—good or bad, joyful or tragic. We all know from personal experience that life is filled with problems, great and small, from the petty squabbles of family life to the world-changing struggles that confronted—and elevated—historical figures such as Lincoln and Churchill, Rosa Parks and Cesar Chavez. So when we hear about the challenges experienced by characters in stories, we easily identify with them, empathetically wrestle with the choices they must make, and rejoice or mourn the outcomes. And when we're offered the opportunity to help *change* the story—by contributing to a cause, for example—we're more likely to say yes.

Stories teach us about ourselves and about our world. The challenges we experience vicariously through stories broaden our own outlook on life and the world. Stories of resolution and heroism under fire deepen our understanding of the meaning of courage and strengthen our resolve to exhibit such virtue in our own times of trial. Stories of tragic misunderstandings or errors in judgment serve as cautionary tales that can help to sharpen our own moral and practical instincts. Stories of kindness and compassion inspire our own idealism and help us appreciate the goodness that is latent in all human beings—including ourselves.

Sylvia Ferrell-Jones is president and CEO of the YWCA Boston, a historic nonprofit organization with a proud record of "firsts": the first YWCA in the United States, the first organization in Boston to tackle professional and economic empowerment for women, and among the first to fight for racial and gender equality. Today the Y's programs train Boston-area students in leadership, promote community dialogues around issues such as racial justice, teach health and wellness skills to women and girls, and much more.

Since taking Jennifer's Exponential Fundraising course, Ferrell-Jones has encouraged her team members to expand their use of storytelling as a crucial tool for fund-raising and recruiting partners. "We sometimes use the word *testimonials* to describe the stories we share," she explains, "but the key is that they are *stories of impact*—narratives that illustrate the power of our programs to create change, which is what donors are most interested in."

One example: Ferrell-Jones tells about a group of teenagers who were out on the streets the night after a fatal shooting in their Boston neighborhood. Tensions were high. When the youngsters found themselves surrounded by a group of police officers who demanded their names and ordered them to lie flat on the ground, they quickly sensed that a single wrong move or ill-chosen word might lead to panic and perhaps tragedy.

Suddenly one of the officers noticed that a youth spread-eagled on the pavement looked familiar. "Hey, don't I know you?" he asked. It turned out that the teenager and the officer had met at a Youth/Police Dialogue organized by the YWCA. Having worked their way through the program together, they'd gotten to know and trust each other. "He's okay," the officer assured his colleagues as the teenager rose from the ground. The two young men talked through the situation and assumed leadership roles in deescalating the confrontation—perhaps saving a life or two in the process.

Sylvia Ferrell-Jones comments, "When we tell people that 41 percent of the young people who participate in our Youth/Police Dialogues are more likely to report a crime, they say, 'That's nice.' But when we tell them a life-and-death story like the one about the confrontation on the street, then they *really* understand the value of our work."

STORIES WITH POWER:
Marshall Ganz and the Public Narrative

Marshall Ganz is an inspiring exemplar and teacher of the power of narrative in the service of social change. Back in the 1960s, he left college a year before graduation to work as a volunteer civil rights worker in Mississippi. Later he became a union organizer under the legendary Cesar Chavez, founder of the United Farm Workers in California, as well as a leader of voter mobilization campaigns in election races around the country.

Ganz quickly became aware that many of the most important social movements in history have been powerfully energized through personal storytelling. Ganz points to a number of examples, including the sharing of personal testimonies about suffering, redemption, and achievement among civil rights workers in the deep South, and the "consciousness-raising" group conversations from the early days of the feminist movement, in which women shared the pain, the hard decisions, and the hope they'd experienced while struggling in a world where women were devalued.

Ganz pondered these lessons about the power of story during his years as an activist. More recently, in his role as a senior lecturer in public policy at the Kennedy School of Government, Ganz has taught many students how to craft what he calls their "public narrative." This concept of the public narrative describes a story that captures the truth of an individual's life in a way that brings meaning to other people through specific, evocative incidents, images, and events. "The particular is a portal on the transcendent," as Ganz puts it.

As Ganz explains, the public narrative is an important tool for the practice of leadership. By mobilizing the power of story, the public narrative enables a leader to engage both the heads and the hearts of listeners, instructing and inspiring them. Furthermore, because a well-crafted public narrative also motivates hearers to act, it engages their hands as well. Because we consider nonprofit fund-raisers a special class of leaders, we've adapted Ganz's concept for our purposes. And when Ganz visits with the students at Jennifer's Exponential Fundraising course to share his wisdom about the public narrative, his presentation is almost always one of the most popular of the entire program—and one of the most eye-opening.[5]

In Ganz's formulation, the classic public narrative is composed of three crucial elements: *a story of self, a story of us,* and *a story of now.* A leader seeking to engage the commitment of potential followers in support of a worthy cause should be prepared to reach out with a public narrative that includes all three elements, each one building on the one before.

- ***A Story of Self*** Why you were called to what you have been called to. This part of the public narrative recounts the experiences that have shaped you, including one or moments of decision—what Ganz calls *choice points*—in which you faced a challenge, made a choice, experienced a particular outcome, and learned a moral. Such choice points help to construct our identities, define our vision of the world, and reveal the values that motivate us.

- ***A Story of Us*** What your constituency, community, or organization has been called to—its shared values, purposes, goals, vision. This part of the public narrative links your personal experiences with those of others, including the people you hope to serve. It shows how your story connects with a bigger vision

---

5   To learn more about Marshall Ganz's work and the concept of the public narrative, we recommend the following resources: Marshall Ganz, "Leading Change: Leadership, Organization and Social Movements," chapter 19 in *The Handbook of Leadership Theory and Practice*, edited by Nitin Nohria and Rakesh Khurana (Danvers, MA: Harvard Business School Press, 2010), 509–550; Marshall Ganz, "Public Narrative, Collective Action, and Power," chapter 18 in *Accountability Through Public Opinion: From Inertia to Public Action*, edited by Sina Odugbemi and Taeku Lee (Washington, DC: World Bank, 2011), 273–289; and Marshall Ganz, "Why Stories Matter: The Art and Craft of Social Change," *Sojourners*, March 2009.

that is shared by countless others—including potentially those now listening to your narrative.

- *A Story of Now* The urgent challenges—or threats—our shared community now faces, the choices it must make, and the hope to which we can aspire. This part of the public narrative brings the story up to today, showing why *now* is a crucial choice point in the life of our community. It invites the listener to take a crucial step in his or her own personal narrative by joining the cause that the speaker has espoused, becoming an active part of the living "we" embodied in the story.

Think about the most compelling speeches you've ever heard or read. You might recall the addresses of historic figures such as Abraham Lincoln, Winston Churchill, Mohandas K. Gandhi, John F. Kennedy, or Martin Luther King Jr., or the speeches of some of today's most compelling leaders, from the Dalai Lama to Nobel laureate Muhammad Yunus. Many of the greatest messages delivered by these leaders follow Ganz's structure to some degree. The same applies to the most effective messages delivered by skilled fund-raisers and other nonprofit leaders. Each has developed a unique way of crafting a personal "story of self" that links naturally to a broader "story of us" that embraces an entire community and finally leads to the "story of now"—a call to action.

Ganz illustrates the three-part structure of the public narrative by citing the first seven minutes of Senator Barack Obama's address to the Democratic National Convention in July 2004—a speech that electrified and inspired millions of Americans and helped to launch Obama's national political career.[6]

Obama's "story of self" begins when the senator tells the audience in the hall, "Tonight is a particular honor for me because, let's face it, my

---

6   A complete transcript of the address is available online at numerous Internet sites, including www.washingtonpost.com/wp-dyn/articles/A19751-2004Jul27.html.

presence on this stage is pretty unlikely." He then goes on to recount three key choice points from his unique family history: his African grandfather's decision to send his son to America to study; his parents' "improbable" decision to marry; and their decision to name their baby son Barack, meaning "blessing"—an expression of faith in a tolerant and generous America. As Ganz notes, "Each choice communicates courage, hope, and caring."[7]

Obama then moves into his "story of us" when he declares, "My story is part of the American story." He describes the values of America that he shares with his millions of listeners—the people in the convention hall, the audience watching on television, and the people who will read about the speech or see clips on TV news the next day. Obama traces these values back to choices made by our nation's founders, particularly citing the Declaration of Independence, a repository of the value of equality. And he describes a series of moments that evoke those shared values: "a faith in simple dreams, an insistence on small miracles; that we can tuck in our children at night and know that they are fed and clothed and safe from harm; that we can say what we think, write what we think, without hearing a sudden knock on the door," and several others.

Finally, Obama shifts to his "story of now" when he declares, "We have more work to do." Ganz explains:

> After we have shared in the experience of values we identify with America at its best, he confronts us with the fact that they are not realized in practice. He then tells stories of specific people in specific places with specific problems. As we identify with each of them, our empathy reminds us of pain we have felt in our own lives. But, he also reminds us, all this could change. And we know it could change. And it could change because we have a way to make the change, if we choose to take it.

---

7   Marshall Ganz, "What Is Public Narrative?" presentation, 2011. Quoted by permission.

In the context of the 2004 convention, the step Obama urged Americans to take was to vote for Senator John Kerry for president. Of course, Kerry lost that election—but the point is that Obama's public narrative, and in particular his "story of now," concludes with a very specific choice that he called upon his listeners to make. Leadership is about moving people to action, so for Marshall Ganz, the public narrative as leadership tool is not complete without the "story of now" and its presentation to listeners of a potentially world-changing choice.

The "story of now" also offers a clear link between the public narrative and our work as fund-raisers, since our jobs center on inviting listeners to choose to join us—by writing a check, becoming a volunteer, serving as a board member, or in some other way. As Marshall Ganz shows, this invitation is likely to be far more effective when your "story of now" is built on the foundation of your "story of self" and your "story of us."

SHARING THE GIFT OF YOUR STORY:
Overcoming the Excuses

As you can see, the public narrative enables an individual leader to make an emotional and intellectual connection with potential followers through the power of a personal story. Devising your public narrative—complete with your own "story of self," "story of us," and "story of now"—and becoming comfortable telling it is an important challenge for the nonprofit leader. Unfortunately, many people are reluctant to share their personal stories with those they don't know well.

There are many reasons for such hesitancy. They include messages we've absorbed over the years (often from well-meaning parents, teachers, mentors, and advisors) and that we now repeat to ourselves as a way of excusing and justifying our fear of exposing ourselves to others—messages like:

- "No one is interested in hearing about me."
- "Nothing dramatic has ever happened to me."
- "If I talk about myself, I'll come across as egotistical."
- "My story is no different from that of millions of other people."
- "My story is so odd and personal that no one else will really understand it."
- "I haven't accomplished anything significant."

There may be a grain of truth in some of these excuses—but only a grain. There are deeper realities that underscore the fact that sharing your personal philanthropic journey is an important *obligation* that no fund-raiser or nonprofit partner should try to shirk.

"No one is interested in hearing about me." That's true only if you tell your story in a way that doesn't engage the listener—without specific details, incidents, events, and emotions that bring the tale to life. Actually, human beings are deeply, intrinsically interested in one another—as evidenced by the fact that we all eagerly spend countless hours seeking out stories about people in the form of books, movies, television shows, plays, news reports, magazine stories, and even water-cooler gossip. In fact, the very best way to engage the attention of other people is with a personal narrative—because this is what most people really *want* to hear.

"Nothing dramatic has ever happened to me." You may or may not have personally experienced the problems you grapple with as a nonprofit leader. But every life is filled with conflict—that's the nature of human existence. And conflict is inherently dramatic. Think back to any choice point in your life and reflect on the decisions you faced, the barriers in your way, and the emo-

tional or psychological tug-of-war you had to resolve. Whether you realize it or not, that's the stuff of drama.

"*If I talk about myself, I'll come across as egotistical.*" It's certainly possible to tell your story in a way that seems egotistical—but it's far from inevitable. The key is simply to focus on recounting events *honestly*, exposing the reality of your own uncertainties, mistakes, hesitancies, mixed emotions, and failures. When you share the unvarnished truth about yourself and your life, people appreciate it and identify with it—because in hearing about your own imperfections, they recognize their own.

In an effort to avoid seeming self-centered, some fund-raisers prefer to fall back on *someone else's* story—often that of the founder of their organization. A student we'll call Karen had become accustomed to telling the founder's inspiration story in meetings with potential donors and other partners. This approach was sometimes effective—and it excused Karen from the necessity of crafting her own story and sharing it bravely with new acquaintances. But it also had a tendency to sound "canned," especially after a hundred repetitions of the familiar tale.

When Karen finally began telling her own story, rather than that of the founder when called upon to introduce her organization and its work, she was startled to find how much more intensely her listeners reacted. The founder's tale is still a useful part of Karen's communications tool kit, but putting *herself* on the line yielded far richer person-to-person connections than she'd ever experienced previously.

"*My story is no different from that of millions of other people.*" Actually, everybody is unique, as great interviewers such as Charles Kuralt and Studs Terkel have shown with their endlessly fascinating average-person-on-the-street profiles. The challenge is simply to delve deeply into your memories to unearth the details that differentiate your life from the many others that are superficially similar—the personal spin that your mind and emotions puts on events and so makes them special.

"*My story is so odd and personal that no one else will really understand it.*" This excuse is the opposite of the previous one, and equally false. Yes, everyone's story is unique—but they all share common elements of struggle, loss, hope, despair, failure, and success that we all have experienced and can identify with. Tell your story with all its odd, seemingly bizarre quirks and you will probably find your audience nodding in recognition—because no matter how weird your life may have been, we've all been there.

An African American student in Jennifer's Exponential Fundraising class (we'll call him Ron) remarked that he had been reluctant to spotlight himself partly because he didn't want anyone to think he was claiming special privileges by virtue of his race. But when a colleague noticed that a grant proposal filled out by Ron had completely omitted any reference to his own background—including his origins in a tough inner-city neighborhood—he said to Ron, "You *owe it to people* to share your story. It's unusual, compelling, and important—and that's partly because of who you are."

"That advice stuck with me," Ron told us in class. He no longer holds back on sharing his journey with people, and the result has been a much stronger sense of personal connection with friends and partners, and more effective advocacy on behalf of his cause.

"*I haven't accomplished anything significant.*" That may be true (although most people who say this are minimizing their achievements through a misplaced sense of modesty). But sometimes a story of failure that leads to an important choice point can be more compelling than a story of triumph.

Nick Ehrmann, whom you met in Chapter 1, told us about how he uses the narrative of an early disappointment to explain his passion for results-oriented educational research:

I worked as a teacher in Washington, D.C., right out of college, when I was already very concerned about the poor performance of kids from disadvantaged neighborhoods and wondering what we could do to address the problem. My initial hypothesis was that these kids lacked motivation because they had no awareness of higher education, no expectation of going to college, and therefore no sense of the stakes involved in their elementary school and high school work.

I partnered with philanthropists to provide guaranteed college scholarships for my former fourth-grade students and then spent ten years tracking them through their academic careers. At Princeton, I thought I was going to be writing a dissertation about the lessons we learned from running a successful youth development program. But when the results were tallied, I discovered that our intervention had produced no discernible difference in student performance during high school.

My first reaction was dismay. But then I realized I had to rethink my approach. I changed my focus into a much bigger project about the roots of academic underperformance. And the more I delved into that issue, the more I felt driven to study it in a systematic, intellectually rigorous way. It's likely we were making a difference, just not in the ways we'd set out to measure.

That's what drove me to start Blue Engine. Ongoing research suggests—not surprisingly—that focusing on building more rigorous, challenging classrooms is the single best way to boost student achievement. Now when I meet with potential partners, I tell them the story. It's important for them to know for several reasons. One, it shows them that we are empirically based, grounded in the realities of what research teaches us, not driven by ideology or some preconceived theory of student motivation. Second, it underscores the need for long-term study of what really happens in schools. Third, it shows both my lifelong commitment to transparency and my willingness to change my mind, learn, and grow in the process. These messages resonate with people, and our support has been steadily growing as a result.

When Ehrmann's carefully planned education project seemed to yield no positive results, he faced a crucial choice point: should he give up on his dream of making a difference in the lives of kids, or would he have the courage and honesty to rethink his premises and start climbing the hill again? He chose to keep trying. Now he uses this story of (temporary) failure as an effective tool for person-to-person outreach. His "story of self" easily segues into a "story of us" in which Nick speaks about the kids all over America whose potential is dampened by uninspiring school environments. And this, in turn, leads into a "story of now" in which Nick can challenge his listener to help solve the problem by supporting Blue Engine's work on research and reform.

There is one possible drawback to using your public narrative as a tool for making personal connections: it takes energy. Another Exponential Fundraising student spoke about how exhausting she found it to have to dig down deep inside herself to share the history of her personal passion, especially several times a day. "Just telling about our organization's work seems so much more manageable," she said. This is an understandable feeling, especially for the introverts among us, who tend to find interacting with people mentally and psychologically tiring (as opposed to extroverts, who find it exhilarating). However, you must be able to give deeply of yourself if you want to be the most effective fund-raiser you can be; you won't forge the kinds of lasting, important bonds that you need to if you pull your punches. Above all, remember that the purpose of personal storytelling is to establish a connection with your listeners—and that real connection between people is a two-way street. If you are doing all the talking, or even most of the talking, during a typical conversation, then you are probably talking too much. Use your story simply as a door opener—a way to invite the other person to begin to share something of himself or herself. When give and take are balanced, the possibility of exhaustion on either side of the table is greatly diminished.

CRAFTING YOUR PUBLIC NARRATIVE

How, then, do you go about developing a version of your public narrative that you can share with others—particularly a compelling "story of self" that can serve as a foundation for talking about values, hopes, and crucial choice points with potential partners? Here are some suggestions.

- *Start with introspection.* An easy way to begin developing your "story of self" is through "why" questions. Why do you care so much about children (or hunger, or health care, or education, or the arts) that you devote your time and energy to a nonprofit organization? If you work full-time as a fund-raiser or nonprofit manager, why do you care enough about these values to center your career around them? If you serve a nonprofit on a part-time or volunteer basis, why do you feel driven to dedicate your precious free time to this cause? Why did you develop your particular set of personal and moral values—and not the many others you could have adopted? Why not simply give up, surrender to despair, or pursue a life of pure self-interest (as many people do)? In short, why are you the person you are? In almost every case, questions such as these will lead you backward—to the circumstances, events, and experiences that shaped the person you are today. From these, the bones of your narrative will gradually emerge.
- *Build your story around choice points.* Think back to important moments of conflict and decision in your life—the choice points that have helped to define and shape your identity and values. Pick

out the two, three, or four that seem most crucial to you, and try to describe each one in a brief narrative. Ask yourself: What was the conflict? What choice did you face? How did you reach a decision? What action did you take? What was the outcome? How were you changed by the experience? What moral lesson did you learn? Based on the answers to these questions, draft a short "story of self" that you can deliver orally in two or three minutes.

- *Think in terms of images, scenes, and moments.* Remember that much of the power of narrative comes from its use of sensory details that make crucial moments come vividly to life. When describing choice points, try to remember and reimagine them as specifically as possible, and provide listeners with two or three details that will enable them to picture the moment of crisis as if they were there—and to empathize with the way it made you feel.

- *Share your story with others.* It's very hard to craft an effective "story of self" without input from others. Once you've drafted your story, ask a couple of friends or colleagues to listen to it. Then pay close attention to their reactions, spoken and unspoken (including facial expressions and body language). Were they genuinely and consistently interested? Did they get the emotional and psychological experience you were trying to convey? Did they learn something new about what makes you tick? Also listen closely to the questions they ask and the comments they offer. Which parts of your story worked? Which ones didn't? What did they want to know more about? What sorts of details sparked their interest? Use the insights you gain to revise and refine your story until it resonates effectively with listeners.

- *Be real, not showy.* You may be tempted to dress up or exaggerate your story to make it sound more exotic, glamorous, significant, or dramatic than it was. Don't do it. People can usually tell when your story is inauthentic, and they will tend to reject it—while unadorned reality generally carries conviction. As one of Marshall Ganz's students put it, "This is not about applying an outer gloss, but about bringing out the inner glow."

Once you've developed a brief "story of self" that powerfully expresses who you are and how you got to be that way, you'll find that opportunities to share the story arise quite naturally in the course of your fund-raising work. Often the only tool you need to introduce it is a simple linking sentence like, "You're here to learn about the work our organization does. Let me start by telling you how I got involved and why I'm such a committed supporter."

Kenneth Watkins is director of philanthropy at the Australian Ballet, the largest classical ballet company in Australia and one of the world's leading international ballet companies. In his eighteen years with the company, Watkins has been personally responsible for raising the profile and importance of philanthropy as a vital income stream for the Australian Ballet, securing more than $60 million in grants from private donors, trusts, foundations, and sponsorships, as well as helping to spread understanding of the importance of philanthropy throughout the arts community in Australia. He spoke about the importance of storytelling as a tool for attracting the interest and support of new partners for the ballet:

When it comes to bringing new people into the fold, we have many resources that are powerful. One, of course, is my own story—how I fell in love with dance as a small boy of just seven, and how the beauty of this art form has remained with me as a source of joy and meaning throughout my life. Many of the people I meet with have had similar moments of epiphany in their lives, and so they can readily understand and empathize with my story.

That creates an immediate bond that we can often build upon as the foundation for a fruitful partnership.

I also have many other stories that I can draw upon. Naturally, there are some dancers who are more charismatic than others. However, they're all gifted, dedicated young people that have worked extraordinarily hard to get their positions in the company, so each of them has a very special story to tell. And I find that they're always willing to talk about themselves and their lives. Their storytelling is not about money, it's about enabling beauty in our lives. When you hear what a young dancer goes through from the minute they step through the door to attend their first class to becoming a principal dancer with one of the world's great companies, it's very inspiring. Stories like these empower people and turn them into willing, eager partners.

Every fund-raiser can apply similar storytelling techniques. Are you raising money for your local PTA? Tell the story of how your favorite elementary-school teacher taught you the magic of learning and sparked a lifelong desire to share that magic with others. Have you been asked to say a few words on behalf of your neighborhood Boy Scouts or Girl Scouts troop? Talk about the time you met a kid from a broken home from whom Scouting was a lifeline to greater self-esteem and achievement—and the impact that meeting had on you.

SHARING YOUR STORY WITH A GROUP

Many times, you'll find yourself recounting your public narrative in a one-on-one setting—a conversation with a potential partner. The goal is simple: to create an exchange of life experiences that can foster a connection between two human beings, one with the potential to lead to powerful and unpredictable consequences.

At other times, you may find yourself called upon to speak to a group. When that's the case, the challenge of sharing from the heart is multiplied. Most people find public speaking intimidating, especially before a large audience. But whether the group you're addressing numbers five or five hundred, the basic skill set is the same.

The temptation is to flee to the security of the impersonal and to give a conventional speech that is based around facts, data, logic, and statistics.

Don't give in to this temptation. There's a reason people complain about PowerPoint software and the data-heavy presentations it facilitates. All too often, this kind of fact-centered talk is used as a comfortable refuge from the challenge of forging a personal connection.

This is not to say that using visual aids is always ineffective. Former vice president Al Gore's famous PowerPoint presentation about global warming at the Aspen Institute in 2005 was riveting to audiences. (You'll recall that this presentation later became the basis of the Oscar-winning documentary film *An Inconvenient Truth*.) Not only was Gore's content incredibly captivating, but the visual images behind him were an unusual blend of graphs, charts, and satellite pictures of Earth from space illustrating the startling—and disturbing—effects of climate change. In combination, they didn't distract from the emotional impact of Gore's message but rather reinforced it.

Researchers say that most people learn in one of two ways: verbally or visually. This means that when you put words on a screen and then talk over them, you lose both audiences. You lose the verbal learners because they are trying to listen to your words and also read the words on the screen. They don't know where to focus. And you lose the visual learners because you have no images to reinforce your points; thus, your message is lost in a sea of language.

Instead of inundating your listeners with data, tell stories. To bring these stories to life, show pictures—either literally, by projecting images on a screen, or through the power of well-chosen words. Reward your audience for their time and attention by making your talk an unforgettable, engaging journey. If you are going to use PowerPoint or a similar presentation tool, use it only to put up a few simple photos or graphs to reinforce your narrative. Resist the temptation to create slides of bullet points.

Above all, speak from the heart—not just the head. Here's an example of what we mean.

The Quincy Jones Musiq Consortium is an organization that brings together nonprofits, corporations, foundations, philanthropists, and musicians to ensure that all kids have access to music and music education. At the consortium's kickoff meeting, Quincy Jones introduced a young man named Alfredo Rodriguez who would be performing for us on the piano. Quincy told us about the first time he'd met Alfredo and described his remarkable gifts as a pianist. Then Quincy turned to another legendary musician in attendance, Herbie Hancock, and asked, "Tell us what thoughts ran through your head the first time you heard Alfredo play."

Herbie casually took the microphone and said, "Well, I don't know what I was thinking, but I sure know what I was *feeling*."

That simple, pure response had quite an impact. Herbie could have gotten up and said something like, "I remember thinking he's extremely talented and can become one of the great pianists." But if Herbie had said that, his listeners wouldn't have felt the same connection. Instead, he told them not to think about the music, but to *feel* the music—which is how our deepest reactions to music and to any other experience are formed.

In much the same way, we need to reframe the way fund-raising is usually approached. We need to move away from trying to sell people on why our ideas are better or more important to giving others the opportunity to partner with us, to connect with us, to discover their own passionate commitment in the act of giving.

That feeling of connection is what we are after. That is what moves people to feeling and from feeling to action. And that is what sharing your story is all about.

FOOD FOR THOUGHT

Follow-up questions and activities designed to help you get the most out of this chapter:

- What was the last unforgettable story you heard? It may have been an anecdote told over a dinner table or used in a speech, an item on the evening news, a short story or a novel, or the plot of a movie, television show, or play. What made that story so powerful? What was the nature of the conflict it depicted? What kind of choices did the characters have to make? What outcome resulted from those choices? And what, if anything, did you learn about life or the world we live in as a result of experiencing that story?

- Outline your own public narrative using the advice of Marshall Ganz as a guide. Rather than trying to be all-inclusive, focus on a handful of key events in your story. Describe them as specifically and vividly as possible using details that appeal to the five senses (sight, sound, touch, smell, taste) and information that will allow listeners to share the emotions you experienced at the time. After you've outlined your story, try sharing it with a few close friends, colleagues, or associates. Pay attention to their reactions, including the comments they make and the questions they ask. Use these as guideposts in revising and refining your narrative for use whenever you are asked to explain the cause you support and the reasons for your commitment to it.

- For many people, speaking before a group is the single most daunting challenge in life. Recall some of the times you've been called upon to address a group of people. Then narrow your focus to two occasions: one that you considered successful (in that it led to an effective connection with your audience) and one that was less successful. What made the difference? What lessons can you learn that you may be able to use when you are next called upon to speak in public?

3

BUILDING THE BAND

Creating Community
Around a Cause

This is the true joy in life, being used for a purpose recognized by yourself as a mighty one.

—George Bernard Shaw

One way we like to think about community building is through the traditional folk tale sometimes called "The Story of Stone Soup":

> Some travelers came to a village, carrying nothing more than an empty cooking pot. Upon their arrival, the poor villagers were unwilling to share any of their modest food stores with the hungry travelers.
>
> "That's all right," the travelers said, "We'll just make a pot of the best soup in the world—stone soup!"
>
> Then the travelers went to a stream and filled the pot with water, dropped a large stone in it, and placed it over a fire as a

crowd of curious villagers gathered to watch. One of the villagers asked, "What are you doing?"

"Making stone soup!" replied the leader of the travelers. "It tastes wonderful! But it needs a little bit of garnish to improve the flavor."

"I have a couple of carrots in my hut," said the villager. "If I give them to you for the pot, can I share this wonderful soup?"

"Of course!" replied the travelers, and the carrots got added to the soup. Another villager asked about the pot, and the travelers mentioned that a bit of seasoning would really enhance the flavor. The villager handed them a little salt and pepper to help them out. As the pot continued to boil, more and more villagers were drawn by the smell, each adding another ingredient—a handful of onions, a potato or two, a chopped turnip, even a slice of beef. With each contribution, the stone soup smelled and looked more delicious.

Finally, the head traveler declared, "The stone soup is ready!" All the villagers brought dishes and bowls from their homes, and a delicious and nourishing pot of soup was enjoyed by all. "Isn't it amazing," all the villagers said, "what a wonderful meal can be made from nothing more than an ordinary stone!"

The point of the fable is that it doesn't take a lot from any one contributor to make a delicious, soul-satisfying meal of stone soup. You may even start with ingredients that appear very unpromising—like an ordinary stone from the riverbank. But when many people take part, each offering something small but significant from their personal stock, the results can be amazing. Many of the world's greatest social movements grew up in the same way as stone soup—by combining humble ingredients from many people in a single shared pot.

Another metaphor we like to use for the community-growing process is "building the band." The model of the jazz band, where every member has a unique, free-flowing, creative role to play, helps suggest how it works. Our focus is on *the band*—the music and camaraderie that come out of a true collaboration of each member listening to one another rather than focusing only on themselves. The band becomes a group identity that is greater than the sum of its parts and even more meaningful than the results achieved—music files downloaded or concert tickets sold. We've found that the minute you start thinking that something else is more important than the band, the band suffers, and in a little while the music itself begins to die.

The metaphor of the band is one that's rich in meaning for Jeff Walker. From seventh grade until high school graduation, Jeff played in his school's concert band, jazz band, wind ensemble, and marching band. He became a leader and loved working and playing with his fellow band members. That feeling of team, of creating something amazing with others from thin air, continues to draw him to music today. And it ultimately came to inform his work as a team manager both in business and in philanthropy.

"To be a good member of a band," Jeff says, "you need to know your stuff—to have the talent and skill of a practiced musician—but that isn't enough. You also need to have a managed ego, to be a good listener . . . to let the other performers get their chances to solo . . . to know how to let your sound and theirs come together in a wonderful composition. If you do all that, the process will be joyous and the results will be thrilling—not just to the band but to those you serve: your audience."

The same philosophy works for the enlightened nonprofit leader.

FROM EXCHANGE TO RELATIONSHIP

In this chapter, we'll explain what we've learned about building the band. Keeping the process vibrant and healthy isn't always easy. We Americans especially value individualism and freedom, and there's an inherent tension between being an individual and being in community. How can we be creative, thriving individuals in community, allowing both to flourish? That's one of the big challenges facing any leader—particularly in the nonprofit space, where people come together not because of economic necessity but because they *want* to be there. Unlike in business, where "the boss" may be able to get away with simply giving orders and expecting them to be obeyed (at least for a time), leaders in the nonprofit world need to win hearts and minds if they hope to accomplish anything. Which is why building the band is such an essential skill—and a difficult one.

The key to making it work, we've discovered, lies in moving beyond the notion of *exchange* to that of *relationship*.

An exchange is about a defined and limited quid pro quo: "You give me X, I'll give you Z." An exchange can be delineated in a written contract that is legally binding; when its terms aren't carried out precisely as agreed, the usual result is anger, an argument, even a lawsuit. Many of our dealings in the marketplace are simple exchanges of this kind—for example, when you buy a car, eat dinner in a restaurant, purchase a share of stock, or hire a plumber to fix a clogged sink, you're engaging in a quid pro quo exchange.

A relationship is quite different. It's a connection between people based on a mutual commitment of resources to a shared future. And because the future is inherently unknowable and indefinable, the commitment is open-ended and potentially unlimited: "You start by giving A, and I'll start by giving B. Let's put them together and see what we can create." A relationship is not a fixed state; it's an ever-growing and deepening reality based on mu-tual openness and on a shared willingness to follow mutual passions. It's a beginning, not an ending.

Relationships can't be defined by contracts, and they don't take shape in a marketplace. They emerge organically from person-to-person contacts. A friendship, of course, is a relationship. For many people, marriage is the ultimate relationship, a for-better-or-worse commitment to a lifetime of shared adventures that are impossible to predict. But many other meaning-ful human connections also partake of the open-ended mutuality of rela-tionship. Many of us have established deep relationships with our families, the towns we live in, the schools and colleges we attended, and the country whose flag we wave. In some profound sense, these groups and organiza-tions belong to us and we to them, with a shared, mutual connection that no written contract or quid pro quo could ever fully define. It's the kind of con-nection we explain using phrases like "for the long haul," "through thick and thin," and "whatever the future may bring."

When you join a band, you enter this kind of relationship. And that's the way it is when we become partners with a nonprofit organization. For the most engaged donors, giving is not about writing a check and expect-ing some defined benefit in return (a name on a plaque or a program, a tax deduction, a progress report filled with statistics). It's about becoming a member of the band, with a role to play in making the music soar—and with future outcomes that are not strictly defined but that promise to be exciting and fulfilling. And the same applies to all those who contribute in dozens of ways: the volunteers who keep the homeless shelter running, the local merchants who provide canned goods to stock the soup kitchen, the nurse who spends her day off giving flu shots at the nursing home.

This is why, if you hope to build a community of generous partners to energize the flow of resources toward a cause you cherish, you need to stop thinking in terms of exchange. The sooner you start thinking about a relationship-based model—and living it—the sooner you can begin spreading the virus of unlimited generosity to those whose minds and hearts you touch.

How to begin? One way is by thinking about the emotional, psychological, and spiritual needs that move people to enter open-ended relationships in the first place.

WHAT MOTIVATES PEOPLE?
Gunther Weil on Values and Worldviews

As you build your band, understanding a wide array of individual motivations and perspectives is vitally important—because the key to creating rich and vibrant music lies in combining a variety of sounds. Human motivations vary enormously, based on personal circumstances, cultural influences, individual characteristics, and especially values that are held consciously and unconsciously. Recognizing and respecting this range of variations is crucial for anyone who wants to influence the thinking, feeling, and behavior of other people.

Psychologist Gunther Weil is an executive coach, an organizational consultant, and founder of Value Mentors, a Colorado-based firm that has helped many businesspeople and other leaders expand and fulfill their creative potentials.

Weil has spent years studying how our values affect the way we think about life, often on an unconscious level. He and his colleagues have developed a list of the most common values that they see as motivating actions and behaviors (see the sidebar on page 74).

VALUE MENTORS/MINESSENCE* GROUP KEY VALUES

Accountability/ethics • Achievement • Affection • Art/beauty
Being oneself • Care/nurture • Collaboration
Collaborative individualist • Construction/new order
Control/order/discipline • Creative ideation
Education/certification • Education/knowledge • Empathy
Environmental responsibility • Equity/rights
Faith/creed/worship • Faith/risk/vision • Family/belonging
Financial success • Food/warmth/shelter • Global ecology
Global equality • Human rights • Integration/wholeness
Intimacy • Leadership/new order • Loyalty • Management
Meditation/contemplation • Minessence
Organizational mission • Organized play
Personal authority/integrity • Pioneerism/progress
Property/control • Prophet/vision • Rights/respect
Search/meaning • Security • Self-actualization
Self-competence/self-confidence • Self-preservation • Self-worth
Service/vocation • Sharing/listening/trust • Simplicity/play
Social justice • Status/image • Synergy • Tradition
Transcendence • Wisdom • Wonder/awe/fate

* Defined as "To miniaturize and simplify complex ideas or technology into concrete and practical applications for the purpose of
creatively enhancing society."

When you make a new acquaintance whose interest in joining your cause you want to gauge, it's important to understand the kinds of personal values that motivate him or her. Virtually everyone is driven by values, but for every individual the specific combination of values will differ. There are many ways of inviting a mutual exploration of this topic. A simple one is to ask questions like, "What are you doing in life that really interests you?"

"What gets you going in the morning?" or "Do you have a dream that excites you?" The answers will tell you a lot about the individual you're talking with—and about the values that drive his or her actions.

In his work, Gunther Weil goes on to analyze how an individual's values are also strongly influenced by his or her worldview. Your worldview is an overarching structure of assumptions and beliefs about the nature of the world we live in, how people should relate to one another, the role of the environment in shaping human existence, the nature and purpose of work, and so on.

Most people subscribe to a more or less coherent worldview, which in turns shapes their unique set of personal values. Some have worldviews in which the external world is seen as alien or even threatening, which leads them to place values such as security and self-preservation at the top of their priority list. Others have worldviews that emphasize the importance of home, friends, and family, which tends to give extra weight to values such as hospitality and intimacy. Some people have worldviews that are built around the concept of self-actualization; for them, values such as creative ideation and self-confidence may be particularly important. And still others may subscribe to a worldview that emphasizes collaboration, pointing to such values as empathy and sharing/listening/trust.

You're certainly not required to pigeonhole every partner or potential partner by explicitly defining the particular worldview he or she holds. But when you meet new people, one of the things to listen for is the values they express and the kind of worldview those values imply. Sometimes these values will be stated very explicitly; more often, they're implicit in the stories people tell, the emotions they reveal, and even their facial expressions and body language. Get into the habit of paying attention to these subtle cues as to what people care about, rather than focusing exclusively on the literal meaning of their words. (As management guru Peter Drucker has said, in a famous sentence Weil likes to quote, "The most important thing in communication is hearing what isn't said.")

To help in bringing values and worldviews to the surface in your conversations with potential partners—and to link those elements to the possibility of fruitful collaboration around a worthy cause—you might try shaping your discussion around these three values-oriented questions:

- What kind of people do we want to be?
- What kind of world do we want to live in?
- What are we going to do about it?

The first two questions define our values—the life we want to live and the world we want to be part of. It's possible to have a rich and mutually rewarding discussion with almost anyone about your answers to these two questions, uncovering areas of agreement and disagreement as you talk. And if you find, after answering the first two questions, that you and your potential partner have a lot in common, the third question is the natural follow-up: "What are we going to do about it?" This question should lead quite naturally to a discussion of the work of your organization—which may ultimately become your mutual work, a natural outgrowth of the values that connect you and the worldview you share, at least in part.

It's easy to jump to the conclusion that one or another worldview is "the best" worldview (perhaps the one you personally subscribe to!) or to think that it will be hard to collaborate with anybody who has a distinctly different set of values. But a band isn't exciting if it always plays in unison; as the old saying goes, "If two people agree on everything, then one of them is superfluous." A Generosity Network demands a mixture of diverse values and worldviews. Much of the creative fun in building a great band arises from the blending of worldviews that almost inevitably occurs—as well as their occasional clashing. Brilliant innovations frequently emerge in the spaces where wildly different minds interact with one another.

As you work on building your own great team, ask questions that will help you identify and recognize the variety of values and worldviews you need—questions such as:

- What values do most members of our team currently share? What values are underrepresented in our team?
- How would I describe the worldview that most of our current team members espouse? Does this shared worldview lead to blind spots due to perspectives that we are lacking? Does it mean that certain values are ignored or overlooked in our conversations and decision making?
- How much conflict or disagreement among values and worldviews does our current team experience? Is there too much conflict (leading to hostility or mutual incomprehension) or too little (leading to "groupthink" and unquestioned assumptions about the world)? What kinds of people might be useful to add to our team in order to produce a more lively, interesting, and dynamic mix of values and worldviews?

One of the tools Gunther Weil and his colleagues at the International Minessence Group use to help people delve more deeply into their own values is the Brave New World exercise (page 78). Try your hand at this exercise—and consider inviting a couple of colleagues, friends, or partners to join you. Use it to discover what people's different values and worldviews are in order to start figuring out how the team is made up and how everybody's strengths can be highlighted. It can provoke some fascinating and eye-opening conversations.

THE BRAVE NEW WORLD EXERCISE

THE SITUATION

- You have been told our planet is dying.
- You are to be relocated to a new planet.
- You will have all your basic needs met there.
- You can take only three things with you.

YOUR INSTRUCTIONS

- List the three things you are going to take.
- When you're finished, look through the list of key values (page 74).
- Which of these values lies behind the choices you made?

UNDERSTANDING THE EXERCISE

Values lie behind the choices we make. If you had different values, you would have chosen different things to bring with you to the new planet. To get the most from the exercise, ask yourself:

- What do the choices you made tell you about your own key values?
- How do you express these key values in the choices you make in daily life?
- How have these key values helped to shape your most important life decisions (regarding work, family, education, pastimes, and so on)?
- How have your key values evolved over time?
- How do you think they might be changing today?

THE FUND-RAISER AS MENTOR AND GUIDE

Having a mix of donors who represent various worldviews is perhaps the healthiest situation for any nonprofit, since people from each worldview tend to have different gifts that can bring unique value to the cause. A good band needs people who can play many different kinds of instruments. In the same way, even a small organization needs a blend of partners who can fill widely varying roles: the detail-oriented, left-brained logician who formulates plans with rigorous clarity, alongside the free-associating, right-brained creative type who can be counted on to produce dozens of off-the-wall ideas, some of them brilliant; the hard-nosed strategist who pushes everyone to stick to schedules, as well as the warm-and-fuzzy people person who always has time for a long talk about everybody's feelings. The best bands we know make room for them all.

For these reasons, it's important to help the people you meet and work with to understand other worldviews. One of the joys of the philanthropic journey is opening up to new perspectives that can broaden and deepen our relationships with others and with the causes that we cherish.

Philanthropy based on strong, deeply committed personal connections can become a powerful opportunity for people to become more fully aware of their own values, assumptions, and worldviews—and even, in some cases, fundamentally shift them. Among many lifelong givers we've seen worldviews that once centered on possessions, security, social status, and the pursuit of (often rigidly defined) success becoming reframed around altruism, collaboration, risk taking, and self-discovery. (We don't mean to imply that this is a shift from "bad values" to "good values"; rather, it's simply that the practice of generosity can provide the means by which people discover new vistas in themselves and in life, often achieving a greater sense of fulfillment and satisfaction in the process.)

Helping people use the act of giving as a means of self-discovery is the side of our work that we love best. Of course, we love making the world a better place—feeding the hungry, healing the sick, protecting the environment, and so on. But it is incredibly rewarding on a personal level to see the gleam of excitement in the eyes of an individual who is learning amazing new things about himself or herself through the experience of giving.

It may come as a surprise that a fund-raiser (or anyone else connected with a nonprofit organization) can serve as a mentor or guide to a philanthropist. After all, we think of philanthropists as being wealthy, often highly successful in business, and therefore as rich in the kinds of resources—money, power, and prestige—that give people high status in society. How can you serve as a mentor to someone who is supposedly of higher social status than you?

The answer lies in breaking away from the usual status assumptions and taking on a peer-to-peer relationship with everyone you partner with—no matter their level of wealth, success, power, or prestige.

We usually think being a peer to someone means being in the same socioeconomic class or sharing a similar career title. But that's just not true. Real peerhood is about sharing common values, a purpose, and a vision, and agreeing to act together. Being a peer is being a partner—equally passionate about what you're doing together, which isn't finite or measurable. It means being members in the same band, focused not on how fancy someone's instrument may be or how many Grammys he may have won in the past, but on what kind of music you can make together. This is why a twenty-three-year-old nonprofit manager with a sociology degree and an income of $30,000 a year can serve as an effective peer for a fifty-year-old hedge fund manager who owns a private jet—provided the two have learned to truly connect on the basis of shared values and a mutual passion.

One nonprofit leader we know decided to demonstrate his passion for the organization in a direct and powerful way, through a gesture that he knew would be meaningful to the philanthropists he was hoping to attract. Having been named president of the organization, he reached into his own pocket to donate $100,000 for a special project. This was a hugely generous gesture on his part; though the president had enjoyed a successful business career, he was not an extremely wealthy man, and this gift was the largest single charitable contribution he'd ever made.

Soon thereafter, the president was approached by a wealthy donor (previously unknown to him) who said he wanted to fund a new million-dollar program. When asked why, the donor replied, "I heard about your six-figure gift, and it amazed me. That's not the kind of thing that a person of modest means with a family to support normally does. I figured if *he* can step up to make a commitment like that, the least I can do is to match his generosity at a level that reflects my own personal resources." Through his act of giving, the president had become a guide to the art of philanthropy for a donor whose income may have been a hundred times greater—because in terms of generosity, the two were truly peers.

Not every nonprofit leader is in a position to make a dramatic gesture like this one, nor should it be expected. But many have made equally generous commitments of their time and talent—for example, by forgoing careers in business and accepting lower salaries to work in the nonprofit sector. The point is that showing your own personal commitment in a way that makes sense for you can encourage others to make commitments of their own.

MOTIVATING THROUGH VALUES

One of the key insights that grows out of Gunther Weil's work on values and worldviews is that people are motivated to do things that actually match their values. When people are invited to take actions that don't match their worldviews or the assumptions, values, and beliefs that underlie those worldviews, the usual result is resistance or procrastination.

This critical principle hit Jennifer like two dozen Pokémon plushies one weekend as she was encouraging her nine-year-old stepkids to make their beds and clean their rooms. (If you have kids, you've probably had the same movie playing in your house.)

Jennifer: "Okay, kids, go make your beds and tidy up your room."

Kids: "In a minute."

Jennifer: "C'mon, guys, we're a team here."

Kids: "I know, but we're just finishing _____." (*Fill in the blank with whatever activity has captured their fancy now.*)

Jennifer: "Maybe you can just take a minute here and reflect on why we all have to pitch in—it's because we all live together."

Kids: (*Blank stares, as if Mom had just requested a mathematical proof of cosmic string theory before lunch.*)

It finally dawned on Jennifer that the reason she and her kids have had this same discussion with the same results every day is because she has been trying to motivate them using a set of abstract values that she holds—values such as mutual accountability, interdependence, and responsibility. But the fact is that those values simply aren't in their lives yet. At some point, they will be—our values, of course, change and develop as we mature through life. But at present their values are much more focused on *independence* than interdependence.

So Jennifer decided to use the kids' own values as a motivator. As twins, they'd shared a room from conception and had recently begun petitioning for their own spaces. Jennifer and her husband have a small office downstairs, so they decided to let one of the twins move his bed there if both bedrooms were kept neat and clean during a trial period. In effect, they said to the kids, "If you show us your responsibility by making up your beds and keeping your rooms tidy, you'll be rewarded with the independence you value."

Every day since then, the twins' beds have been tightly made and their rooms couldn't be cleaner if Martha Stewart herself had a go at it. Their values have been energized and they are moved to action.

A wise leader knows that the appeal to values has to begin where people really are. It must be grounded in a way that harnesses the values that people are actually living for inspired action and real results.

That's one of the uses to which Weil's insights into worldviews can be put. If you understand the worldview espoused by someone whom you're hoping to motivate and guide, you will understand the values you need to appeal to in order to maximize your chances of connecting with that person. Simply assuming that the other person shares your worldview—and the values that go with it—is likely to leave you both disappointed.

Our friend (and Exponential Fundraising student) John Maeda has been putting some of these ideas into practice.

Maeda is a leader who integrates technology, design, and business into a twenty-first-century synthesis of creativity and innovation. His work as an artist, graphic designer, computer scientist, and educator earned him the distinction of being named one of the seventy-five most influential people of the twenty-first century by *Esquire* magazine.

In June 2008, Maeda became president of Rhode Island School of Design

(RISD), where he has prioritized fund-raising for scholarships to ensure the broadest possible access to a great design education. Under his leadership, RISD has enjoyed a significant increase in annual giving, received its first two-million-dollar gifts for academics, and raised eight million dollars for scholarships, a record in RISD's history. When we asked Maeda about the strategies he has employed, here's what he told us:

> Before RISD, I knew how to raise funds for research contracts. That's very much like selling a product—in that case, "selling" the promise of research results to commercial organizations. Philanthropy is something very different, and it was quite foreign to me. But I jumped into it with enthusiasm and a willingness to learn.
>
> My learning curve started with looking at past history. Studying our track record showed me that there had been many people who had funded RISD in the past but had stopped donating for one reason or another. I talked to many of them and asked what would excite them about becoming contributors in the near future. I learned about what our development team had done well in the past and where we had room for improvement. Little by little I began to get a feel for what philanthropy is all about.
>
> The real epiphany came one day when the real difference between salesmanship and raising money for a great university suddenly hit me. I'm not selling anything, I realized. I'm enabling people to contribute to a dream. When I started presenting my case for RISD in those terms, my fund-raising results began to skyrocket.

Like Jennifer with her kids, Maeda had to shift his thinking in order to reach his target audience. The key was recognizing that the values he needed to appeal to were different from those he'd previously assumed. When he moved from a "salesmanship" model to "enabling people to contribute to a dream," he suddenly became able to connect with donors for whom bringing great design education to a new generation of young people would be a compelling vision.

That's as good a definition of "motivating through values" as we've seen.

THE RELATIONSHIP FORMULA?

As we've seen, the process of launching open-ended, creative, commitment-based relationships begins quite simply with two (or more) people getting to know each other—not in terms of prescribed rituals or roles (fund-raiser and philanthropist, alms seeker and benefactor) but in a more profound way, based on a deep understanding of each other's values, assumptions, dreams, aspirations, and worldview. This process of mutual discovery, if conducted with openness and honesty, may lead to an awareness of areas of shared passion—and that's where the potential for a fruitful philanthropic partnership can be found.

There are specific skills you can use that will make it easier to achieve true relationships. However, we're not offering a formula for building such relationships. There's no way to script real human connections. And that's a good thing. The outcome is so much more interesting—and potentially rewarding—than what we'd get if we followed a formula.

Best of all, this approach is implementable immediately, right now. You don't have to do research, draw up a business plan, create a PowerPoint presentation, or raise funds to get started—you just need to go out and experience it. You can start building the band today and begin making amazing music almost immediately.

Here are some of the skills we've learned over the years that are most crucial to becoming a great band builder.

LEARN TO *REALLY* LISTEN

Jennifer recalls attending a fund-raising seminar where a big part of the curriculum was about developing listening skills. A number of basic tips were imparted that most people have heard: "Lean forward when you are talking to someone," "Make eye contact," and so on. In addition, the class was taught to "reflect"—that is, to repeat back to the other person what he or she just said. The specific line Jennifer was taught to use was, "So, what I hear you saying is . . ." followed by a paraphrase of the other person's words.

Jennifer didn't walk away from the workshop with a set of great new tools for listening. Just the opposite. Everything about the workshop felt manipulative and false. (Maybe you've felt the same way when you've spotted someone practicing that "reflection" technique on you during a conversation!)

Listening is not a technique. It's a *way of being*. It's about attention and awareness and genuinely *wanting* to hear someone else's story.

Make no mistake, listening is absolutely critical in fund-raising. Without it, we will never develop deep and authentic partnerships. And if you think about it, there's nothing terribly mysterious about it.

Take a moment to remember what it felt like the last time someone *really* listened to you. What happened? What was the experience like? When Jennifer asks her students to describe it, the answers are usually pretty similar: *They listened without interrupting. . . . They didn't try to fix anything. . . . They didn't offer answers. . . . They just seemed to be really interested.*

Sometimes when we are trying to forge a connection, we might interrupt people when they are telling us their story so that we can tell them something similar that has happened to us. It's usually a well-meaning attempt to make a human connection with the other person: *I know what you mean because I've been through the same experience.* The reality, though, is that when we interrupt someone's story to tell ours, we are subtly turning the attention back on ourselves, demonstrating unmistakably that we are not really listening but rather thinking about ourselves.

The next time someone is telling you a story, try not interrupting at all. Just listen to the other person. To the very end. There is incredible power in that simple act of being fully present. (For a valuable perspective on how we listen and on what makes true listening so unique, see the sidebar "Four Levels of Listening" below.)

FOUR LEVELS OF LISTENING

C. Otto Scharmer is a senior lecturer at MIT and co-founder of the Presencing Institute. In his book *Theory U: Leading from the Future as It Emerges: The Social Technology of Presencing* (Berrett-Koehler, 2009), Scharmer presents his model of listening. Here's a summary of the four levels of listening as described in that model.

1. *Downloading* "Yeah, I know that already": listening to reconfirm what I already know. Listening from the assumption that you already know what is being said; therefore you listen only to confirm habitual judgments.
2. *Factual* "Oh, I didn't know that": listening to pick up new information. Factual listening is when you pay attention to what is different, novel, or disquieting when contrasted with what you already know.
3. *Empathic* "I know exactly how you feel": listening to see something through another person's eyes, forget one's own agenda.

Empathic listening is when the listener pays attention to the feelings of the speaker. It opens the listener and allows an experience of "standing in the other's shoes." Attention shifts from the listener to the speaker, allowing for deep connection on multiple levels.

4. **Generative** *"I can't explain what I just experienced." Listening from the field of possibility.* Generative listening is difficult to express in linear language. It is a state of being in which everything slows down and inner wisdom is accessed. In group dynamics, it is called synergy. In interpersonal communication, it is described as oneness and flow.

Which levels of listening do you habitually employ? When was the last time you managed to get below levels 1 and 2 to the deeper connections possible at levels 3 and 4? In the words of the old limbo tune, "How *low* can you go?"

TRADE DEPENDENCY FOR PARTNERSHIP

We've already explained why "salesmanship" is not the right model for non-profit fund-raising. For too many people, "selling" smacks of manipulation, trickery, coercion. That's not the mind-set to employ when striving to create true partnerships with people.

In a more subtle way, the term *client* is equally problematic. The word *client* happens to be derived from the Latin word *clinere*, which means "to lean against." Hence the suggestion of dependency that it carries to this day, as you can hear in phrases such as *client state* (referring to tiny countries supported by superpowers). We prefer a word such as *partner*, which implies two individuals of equal strength who choose to work together—a peer-to-peer relationship model that is far more fruitful in the long term than the client-patron model.

Several years ago, when Jennifer and Jeff began working with the legendary music producer Quincy Jones on his varied philanthropic enterprises, the team sought a name for the growing organization they were building. Jennifer and Jeff proposed calling it the Quincy Jones Musiq Consortium. The word *consortium* comes from the Latin *consors*, which refers to a partnership or a "shared fortune." Members of a consortium don't lean on one another as clients do; they share everything they are and everything they have, and so gain greater strength from one another.

TURN ATTACHMENT INTO COMMITMENT

Just as we prefer to have *partners* rather than *clients*, we prefer the word *commitment* to the word *attachment* when describing our relationships around a cause. In our minds, the concept of attachment is about *What can you do for me?* By contrast, the concept of commitment is about *What can we do together?* Attachment limits possibility, while commitment opens it up. Attachment leads to confinement and dependence, while commitment leads to mutual discovery and flourishing.

One way to tell whether you are attached or committed is to ask yourself whether a particular relationship is becoming more constricted over time or ever more open. Are you able to talk about more things, share more ideas, experiment more freely, push each other more positively, and evoke each other's strengths more fruitfully than in the past? Or are the possibilities shrinking and dwindling over time? The latter is a sign of a dying relationship; the former, of one that is flourishing and nourishing two people (and often many more).

When you climb to the highest levels of fund-raising, you grow from a salesman into a mentor, a team builder, and a leader—someone who helps the band produce music that is far more beautiful than what any individual could create alone.

LESSONS FROM RAY CHAMBERS, MASTER BAND BUILDER

Ray Chambers is one of those people with enough accomplishments to fill several lifetimes—and he's not done yet. By the age of forty-six, he had helped to create the leveraged buyout industry, retired, and become a philanthropist focusing on giving back, anonymously, to the city of Newark, Boys and Girls Clubs of America, and many other causes.

Over time, Ray saw that he could have an even bigger impact if he used his network and contacts to create new ways to help others. So he founded and co-founded a number of successful nonprofits, including the National Mentoring Partnership (collaborating with Geoff Boisi), the America's Promise Alliance (with Colin Powell), Millennium Promise (with Jeff Sachs), and several others. Ray has been a central inspiration and guiding light behind the growth of our own Generosity Network—just one of the many networks of giving, creative people that Ray supports with his wisdom, energy, and abundant spirit.

One of Ray's philanthropic creations is a global project dubbed Malaria No More. The goal of Malaria No More is to neutralize the threat of that disease, an insect-carried scourge that kills one million people a year in Africa, half of them under five years of age, despite twenty years of efforts by hundreds of organizations and the investment of hundreds of millions of dollars.

Thanks in large part to the success of this project, malaria deaths worldwide have fallen by more than 50 percent, and by more than one-third in Africa. More than half a million lives are being saved every year. Now Malaria No More is working to virtually eliminate malaria deaths around the planet by 2015.

Maybe the most impressive thing about Chambers and his philanthropic efforts is not the impact of the work—powerful and important as that is—but rather the ever-expanding circles of community that Chambers manages to create around the causes he espouses. Take the malaria initiatives that he has helped create. Chambers pulled together resources from a host of organizations, including his own Malaria No More, the Gates Foundation, the International Red Cross, the Global Fund, the World Bank, the MDG Health Alliance, the U.S. government, and the United Nations. Talk about a collection of powerful groups run by leaders with strong perspectives, varying agendas, and (often) giant egos! Yet Ray Chambers is gifted with the passion, tact, persuasive skill, self-discipline, and managed ego needed to pull together this "team of teams" (a phrase suggested by Bill Drayton of Ashoka) and help it coalesce around a transcendent goal.

There's much more to the story—so much more that we don't have room to recount it all. But here are a few illustrative elements that may help to strengthen your sense of what makes Ray Chambers such an effective band builder.

First, Chambers was able to convince major players from the world of government to throw their support behind the malaria initiative. Agencies such as the U.S. Agency for International Development, the World Bank, the government of the United Kingdom, and the World Health Organization lined up in support. President George W. Bush created the President's Malaria Initiative, and his successor, Barack Obama, eagerly embraced the same cause. But Chambers also sensed that support from average citizens, in the United States and around the world, would also be important. Why? Because in democratic countries, elected officials take their cue from the voters. If citizens cared about malaria, members of the U.S. Congress and the British Parliament would vote to support malaria programs; if not, they wouldn't. To be sustainable, the malaria campaign needed to be backed by the public will.

So Chambers set out to make partners of a series of key people and organizations who could help mobilize public opinion around the issue of malaria. He invited Peter Chernin, then president of News Corp., to become co-chairman of Malaria No More. Soon, News Corp.'s Fox television network presented a special version of *American Idol*, "*Idol* Gives Back," which raised $80 million in donations in a single night—and, more important, educated 50 million people about the importance of the cause. Chambers also enlisted the support of the NBA, Major League Soccer, and other media powerhouses. The result: awareness among Americans about the global malaria crisis rose from 21 percent to over 55 percent.

Here's a second example of Ray Chambers in action. In Africa, as in much of the world, religion and politics are closely intertwined. This meant that the effort to bring malaria prevention to the peoples of Africa would need to walk a tightrope across religious/political conflicts of long-standing and extraordinary virulence.

Chambers quickly discovered that ground zero for these conflicts was Nigeria—the largest country in Africa, the one with the greatest malaria problem, and a nation deeply divided by religious and political rifts. The northern half of the country is largely Muslim, while the southern half is mostly Christian—and getting leaders from these two regions to cooperate on anything has long been difficult.

Chambers didn't hesitate. He approached the board of an organization called the Center for Interfaith Action (CIFA) and asked for their help in tackling the Nigeria problem. CIFA's leaders responded by creating a subsidiary called the Nigerian Inter-Faith Action Association (NIFAA) and convening a meeting between the sultan of Sokoto, from the north, and the Catholic archbishop of Abuja, from the south. Ray Chambers—and the malaria epidemic—made it possible for these two leaders to find common ground. They agreed to put aside their differences so as to launch a joint effort to train 300,000 leaders from both faiths to distribute the nets and educate Nigerian communities, north and south, about the disease.

Today there's hope that this joint malaria campaign may foreshadow further cooperation between the two religions. Hostilities between Muslims and Christians in the border states appear to have lessened; leaders of the two faiths are talking about possible areas for future collaboration. Once people see that it's possible for them to work together, there's no telling what more they may dare to achieve.

And now a third example. Major countries such as Nigeria—which has rich oil reserves—have the money and other resources needed to help support a nationwide antimalaria campaign. But smaller, poorer African countries do not. In 2008, Ray Chambers visited one of these countries—the West African nation of Benin—while on a business trip to the region. The president of Benin made a personal appeal: "Can you help us launch a malaria program?" But without money, personnel, and other resources, the idea seemed hopeless—especially since even simple supplies, such as lifesaving bed nets, cost twice as much when purchased in smaller quantities.

But Ray Chambers is a band builder. "It struck me that there are forty-three sub-Saharan countries that are malarious," he later recalled. "Why not do what the Florida orange growers did, and form a cooperative?"

Under Chambers's guidance, those forty-three African countries created the African Leaders Malaria Alliance (ALMA)—a one-stop shop that allows poorer nations to pool their resources as needed for the fight against disease. "Now the price of bed nets is down to less than $3 apiece," Chambers says. "And thanks to ALMA, everybody in Africa has access to them at the same price."

Of course, Ray Chambers minimizes his own role in these stories of team building. He says it this way:

> Working in partnership, thanking people, giving them credit— it's easy for me, because I believe in the cause. It's so obvious that we can't be happy with our comfortable lives in the United States when we know that, elsewhere in the world, three thousand babies are dying from malaria every day. Communicating that has brought everybody on board. It's no different than putting a complex business deal together. You listen to all sides. You construct something that is appealing to everybody. If necessary, you cobble together different sources of funding to make it happen. Above all, you keep trying. I'm not waiting another minute, because every minute we wait, another couple of kids will have died.

There are a host of other problems around the world that demand the efforts of a coalition of organizations, each contributing a unique set of skills and resources to the solution. Those who hope to solve these global problems should look to Ray Chambers's work on malaria as a model of effective coalition-building.

What's more, the same approach—seeking out key partners, reaching out across lines of distrust or antagonism, minimizing one's own ego, and having the courage to simply *ask* for partnership—can work with projects of every scope. It's the same model to use when assembling a neighborhood team to get that trash-strewn lot cleaned up and transformed into a community garden; when convincing leaders from the local Catholic, Protestant, Jewish, and Muslim houses of worship to join forces in an effort to reduce interfaith tensions; or when working with town officials, business leaders, and the nearest hospital to organize and fund a free Saturday clinic where the uninsured can get the immunizations they need.

Want to build a great band? The example of Ray Chambers shows how it's done.

FOOD FOR THOUGHT

Follow-up questions and activities designed to help you get the most out of this chapter:

- Early in the chapter, we discuss the difference between an exchange (a limited quid pro quo) and a relationship (an open-ended mutual commitment). Think about how this distinction applies to your philanthropic work. Consider, for example, how you connect with the single most important partner of your cause. Is your connection exchange-based or is it a true relationship? If the former, what can you do to begin transforming it? Now ask the same questions about others you have worked with, including your longest-term partner, your newest partner, a partner for whom you have high hopes, and a potential partner whom you have not yet won over to the cause. In each case, try to formulate a plan for creating a true relationship as the basis for future collaboration.
- Revisit Gunther Weil's list of key values (page 74). Think of a friend, acquaintance, or partner. Which key values are important to him or her? Try to imagine how you could discuss the work you do and the cause you support in terms that might appeal to those key values. The more "multidextrous" you can become in

conveying your passion to individuals of many persuasions, the better your chances of attracting a diverse array of partners.

- List the ten most important relationships you have on behalf of your organization. For each one, ask: *On a scale of 1 to 10, how deeply engaged is this relationship?* (A score of 1 describes a connection based on simple, limited exchanges; a score of 10 describes a profound relationship that is rich, multifaceted, open-ended, and growing.) Then ask: *How often have I touched this individual in the past thirty days?* (If the answer is "not at all," you've missed an opportunity.) Now consider: *What can I do to encourage the development of a stronger bond between my organization and this individual? And what would success look like? That is, what specific actions and behaviors would I see once this stronger bond has been established?* The answers to these questions may amount to a potent to-do list for your work in the coming weeks and months.

4

THE CARE AND FEEDING OF THE BAND

*Enriching Your Relationships
with Your Team Members*

I want to be thoroughly used up when I die, for the harder I work the more I love. I rejoice in life for its own sake. Life is no brief candle to me; it is a sort of splendid torch which I've got a hold of for the moment and I want to make it burn as brightly as possible before handing it on to future generations.

—George Bernard Shaw

"We need new donors!" That's the mantra we hear in almost every meeting with leaders of a nonprofit organization. There's a belief, so widespread it passes for common sense, that if an organization seems to have hit a fund-raising ceiling, a growth plateau, or an energy limit, the logical solution is to quickly fill the pipeline with fresh, new, energetic donors.

Of course, it's good to continually introduce new partners to your organization. The passage of time and the realities of life mean that turnover among your partners is inevitable, which in turn means that replacing them with new blood is a vital process in any healthy organization. But when you have short-term needs that are going unmet, your most powerful recourse—and the most effective way to climb beyond the plateau where you feel stuck—is to do a better job of deepening your connection with your *current* donors.

In this chapter, we'll examine the ongoing challenge of how to build on the foundation of mutual commitment you've already created. We'll consider some proven techniques for maximizing collaboration while going deeper into the creative realms to which true partnership provides access. And we'll also discuss ways to bring donors and other partners along with you even as the mission, needs, abilities, and work of the nonprofit evolve, melding your partners' philanthropic journey with yours in a mutually beneficial way.

KEEPING THE COMMUNICATION CHANNELS OPEN

One obvious yet often neglected principle for nurturing healthy, growing relationships with your team members is simply to *stay in touch*. Many organizations fall into the trap of focusing on fancy quarterly stewardship reports—or, even worse, the lone annual report, accompanied by a solicitation for a donation. They allow these impersonal, generic communiqués to become the only time their donors hear from them. Don't make this mistake. Talk to your donors often—by phone, mail, email newsletter, website, Facebook, YouTube, or any other communications medium. The message doesn't have to be highly personalized every time, but it should always include something of substance: a story from the field, details of a new initiative, the latest data measuring your results, or a quick quiz to just take your partners' pulse and discover what's on their minds.

Keeping people informed about your work is very important, of course. Sharing facts and statistics about your performance is one aspect of the transparency that nonprofit managers need to practice in pursuit of the kind of boundaryless connections they aspire to enjoy with their partners. You never know which data point may turn out to be the one that triggers a powerful reaction on the part of a partner, so it's important to share many different kinds of stories and metrics (and of course this will also make your communications more interesting for the people you're reaching out to). But just as important as information is connecting on a human level, beyond just facts and data.

We're all very busy, and in the press of daily activities it's easy to neglect the necessity for personal outreach. But we must find time to treat one another as human beings. This may be something that comes naturally to you. If not, it's an instinct you need to cultivate.

One nonprofit fund-raiser we know tells this story about her CEO:

The wife of one of our board members died recently. She was just fifty years old, so it was a sudden and unexpected loss for the family. When I heard the news, I asked my boss, "Did you call Ben to express your condolences?"

Our CEO, John, shook his head and said, "No. He's got to be very busy. I probably wouldn't get him on the phone."

I said, "John, you *need* to call Ben on the phone. He is on your board. You've known him and worked with him for ten years. He has given a lot of time, energy, and money to our work. He is a friend, and this is a time when friends connect with friends. You need to call him, and he needs to hear your voice—even if that means leaving a message on his answering machine."

We don't mean to criticize this CEO too harshly. John is like a lot of successful organizational leaders: goal-oriented, efficiency-minded, hard-headed, and practical. A personal message of condolence to an old friend and partner is not *directly* related to the goals of John's nonprofit organization, and so he tends to dismiss its importance. But human connections are actually *more important* than organizational goals—and treating people as the living, breathing, emotional (and sometimes irrational) beings they are is an essential element in establishing and nurturing those connections.

Here's one way to start the process of improving your links to people who make your work possible. Sit down with a sheet of paper and list the ten most important people or groups whose philanthropic activities are focused on your organization. (Depending on the size of the organization and your specific role, the number may be larger or smaller, but ten is a reasonable target for many nonprofit advocates.) The ten people on this list should be your number-one advocates. They may be significant donors (though this will vary based on their individual resources and the needs of your organization), but it's likely they are also contributing in other ways—through their volunteer efforts, board membership, communications work, in-kind contributions, networking activities, and so on.

Now ask what it would look like if these ten people were giving you everything they could. What if your relationship with them was such that you could pick up the phone to call them at (almost) any hour of the day or night—to seek advice, share wonderful news, brainstorm an idea, enlist help, or just reaffirm your personal bond? What if they felt equally ready to communicate with you—to pass along a valuable contact, offer a helpful suggestion, warn you about an unforeseen danger, propose a great initiative, or just provide encouragement and support?

Having fantasized for a few moments about enjoying that level of close-ness, transparency, and commitment from your chief partners, next ask: *What more could I be doing to achieve it?* There may be many answers, from reaching out via phone, text message, email, or handwritten letter to planning a breakfast, hosting a dinner party, organizing a conference, or traveling to a work site together. (We've already discussed some of these possibilities in this book, and we'll be talking about many more in later chapters.)

Whatever your heart tells you, start doing it. Today.

Here are some other steps you can take to make sure that person-to-person communication doesn't suffer amid the press of daily responsi-bilities:

- *Set aside part of each day for personal communication, and keep it sacred.* Choose an hour or two at a time that suits your schedule and personality, and don't allow anyone to usurp that time for staff meetings, report reading, or other routine activities. During this time, shut the office door, pick up your phone, and reach out to some people you haven't recently been in touch with. You'll be amazed to realize how much the sound of your voice on the other end of the line means to them.
- *Never eat lunch alone.* Break the habit of wolfing a sandwich at your desk. Instead, use lunch hour as a time to renew acquaintances with someone important to you, either from inside or outside your organization. Even if it's something as simple as inviting someone from outside to join you for a brown bag lunch in your office's conference room, make lunchtime an opportunity to deepen and expand your human connections in the context of your work.
- *Make time for regular contact.* This step is about eliminating those awkward, embarrassing moments when you find yourself calling someone to ask for a favor—and having to start the call by

apologizing for having allowed many months or even years to pass since your last conversation.

- *Over time, expand your list of key contacts.* Create a more extensive written list of important donors, partners, allies, and friends of your organization, and then make certain you talk with each one according to a regular schedule. The length of the list and the frequency of your conversations will vary according to the size and complexity of your organization. You might decide, for example, that it's important to speak to each person on your two-hundred-person list of key contacts at least once per quarter. Maybe that sounds daunting—but if you do the math, it works out to just two or three phone calls per day. The payoff in terms of stronger, more meaningful human connections is incalculable.

- *Use downtime to maintain your personal connections.* When you're riding in a taxi, train, or bus to a meeting; when you're at the airport preparing for a flight; when you're waiting at the doctor, the dentist, or the hairdresser; or while you're in line at the supermarket or the Department of Motor Vehicles, pull out your cell phone and catch up on a call or two. Or carry a stash of notecards or stationery with you (as many effective leaders in the business and nonprofit worlds do) and seize spare moments to jot down a personal note to be dropped in the mail at the next opportunity. You may believe you're "too busy" to stay in touch with people, but if you start using the time you're currently wasting, you may find that the problem largely solves itself.

Creating great relationships isn't only about feeding the spirits of other people. It's also about paying attention to your own needs, values, and motivations—and making sure they are tended as well. Remember that you too are a member of the band. You need outlets for your creativity, energy, and passion just as your partners do. So get into the habit of taking your own psychic temperature from time to time, and being sure to provide yourself with the emotional and psychological refreshments you need.

One student in Jennifer's Exponential Fundraising course—a very successful nonprofit executive and fund-raiser—spoke in class about the challenge of being an extreme introvert in a field where "celebrities" attract the lion's share of attention. "Personally, I find it very exciting to spend time with movie stars, world-famous experts, and prize-winning activists who are partners of our organization. But it's also mentally exhausting. Sometimes I wish I could just sit in my office with the door closed and the telephone unplugged and spend a day working on our strategic plans instead of having to interact with people constantly!"

Many people in the nonprofit world share this student's problem. Having a deep personal commitment to a worthy cause doesn't necessarily make you an extrovert or even a "people person." Luckily, there are many things you can do if you are in this camp. In fact, our student went on to explain the techniques she'd developed to nurture herself psychologically during a hectic week of social engagements. "I make sure to exercise several times a week, I take a quiet walk in the park every day, I listen to my favorite music whenever I can, and I get plenty of sleep. It's a simple regimen, but it enables me to keep my sanity."

Self-nurturing is important for leaders in any field, but perhaps especially in the nonprofit space, where we're socialized to think continually about doing things for other people rather than for ourselves. Don't lose sight of the importance of solitude—the quiet place we go to be replenished and revitalized for the demanding work we've chosen.

ORGANIZING FOR CONNECTION

One of the skills that makes Kenneth Watkins of the Australian Ballet so successful is the care with which he nurtures personal relationships—including organizing a team of staff members to ensure that both routine communications and more personalized outreach are handled with efficiency and energy:

> The biggest challenge for me has always been continuing to keep our volunteer board members up to speed, sharing stories with them, and helping them reach out to the community with their own stories and with the stories of what the Australian Ballet means. So that's about time management for myself.
>
> We have thirteen members on our main board and seven on our foundation board, so that's twenty people I need to stay in close contact with. It's always easy to get sucked into things that are going on around the office—this or that meeting or presentation or debate—as opposed to pulling yourself out.
>
> Fortunately, I've been able to organize a team of staff members to help keep the communications vibrant. We've got eleven staff members, so the group is relatively small, but it's robust. We have a philanthropy-services area as well as an annual donor program and a major-gift program. Each of these is run by different people.
>
> Then there are three people on the philanthropy services side, which handles the banking, manages the budgets, and all that sort of thing. They also open the mail, do all the data entry, research prospective donors, prepare tax receipts and thank-you letters, and create reports for the team. You might call them our back-end of-

fice, and they really run like a well-oiled machine—very efficient and tremendously helpful.

The other eight are the front end of our philanthropy group. They include the bequest manager, two patrons managers, a senior manager in annual giving, a senior manager in major gifts, myself, and my assistant. And there's a trust and foundations person writing grants proposals and other documents. In sum, this team acts as an extension of me, making it much easier for our organization to stay in close contact with our partners and supporters, not just once or twice a year but continually.

Depending on the size of your organization and the resources available, you may not have a staff as large as Watkins's. But the task of different kinds of outreach must be specifically and clearly assigned to someone on your staff, even if it's one of many jobs they are responsible for. No matter how big the organization, this is a task that will fall through the cracks unless somebody knows that they have to take responsibility for it!

BRINGING PARTNERS TOGETHER IN NEW COMBINATIONS

The job of maintaining strong relationships with your team members and others in your network may seem particularly daunting if you think of it solely in spoke-and-hub terms—with you at the center and a collection of outside nodes that are connected only through you.

In fact, you should work to make sure that your network is a true network, with plenty of connections among the nodes that are not reliant on your personal involvement. Like open communication, this requires a bit of transparency and courage. Some leaders feel nervous about letting their contacts develop personal links with one another, because it means ceding control of the relationships. ("Oh my gosh," you may think, "they'll be getting together without me! What will they be doing and saying when I'm not around?!") But that's all right—you'll lose control over what your friends and acquaintances say and do when you're not in the room, but in exchange they will be free to generate all kinds of interesting new energies, ideas, and activities, some of which are likely to rebound to your benefit and that of your organization. So don't be shy about introducing your contacts to one another, either through one-on-one events (such as breakfast, lunch, or dinner meetings) or through larger gatherings (such as cocktail or dinner parties, press events, receptions, presentations, and seminars).

At times when your organization's energy level seems to be flagging—when donations are down, new ideas are scanty, growth is anemic, and people are losing interest in your mission—it may be time to make a conscious, deliberate effort to encourage new connections among your partner base. Mix things up! Introduce current donors who don't know each other but have something in common—for example, they may live close to each other, work in the same industry, or share an alma mater. If they hit it off, try asking them to tackle a project together. Many dynamic new teams have been launched through this simple but effective device.

As always, the specific language you use is surprisingly important. When inviting people to take part in a new activity, asking them to "take responsibility for" something is much more effective than asking them to "help you" or "do you a favor." Thus, a simple shift in wording from "Would you help me call five other donors to ask them to renew their annual gift?" to "Will you take responsibility for calling five other donors to ask them renew their annual gift?" is a powerful one. The latter phrasing gives *ownership* to the partner who accepts the invitation, in itself a profound step toward deeper involvement.

It's also helpful to explore offering people new assignments within your partnership network. Board committee roles tend to become ossified over time; particular partners develop so much expertise in a particular area that others refer all activity in their area to them. Sue becomes the site-visit expert, Ralph the go-to guy on organizing cocktail parties, Pat the chief liaison with local banks and financial firms. Division of labor that takes advantage of individual interests and talents can be a great strength for an organization, but it can also mean that new ideas have no opportunity to be explored or adopted. What happens if Steve, who has headed the board's development committee since time immemorial, is laid up by illness for a year? What if Nora, who has twenty years' worth of knowledge about how to organize the annual gala locked up in her brain, suddenly moves to Australia?

So sometimes the fact that "We've always done it this way" is the best reason to introduce a change. If Debbie has been in charge of rounding up donations for the annual charity auction since time immemorial, call her two months early this year and have an open-ended conversation about whether there's some exciting new project she might like to take on instead. (Such a conversation is far better, of course, than simply informing Debbie of a change without consultation—it's possible she might take it as punishment or an attack of some kind.) If you discover there's an intriguing new task Debbie will enjoy, you may benefit the organization in at least four ways—by refreshing Debbie's involvement and perhaps reenergizing her; by giving someone else (Joanne, let's say) a new way to enhance her connection when she takes over the donations canvass; by triggering a new link between Debbie and Joanne as the former passes along her wisdom to her successor; and by creating opportunities for new and creative approaches to the donations process thanks to the new blood you've brought on board.

It's also helpful to build the collective narrative through small-group interactions. Bring your partners together to get to know one another, learn from one another, and energize one another. Treat your tried-and-true friends as if the future of your organization depends on them. To a large extent, it does!

COMMUNICATION BEYOND WORDS

Connecting to your partners verbally, through phone calls, person-to-person chats, emails, letters, and other written missives is very important. But different people respond naturally to different forms of communication. For some, words have little emotional impact. Look for opportunities to convey messages using multiple forms of expression.

In 2004, Alexander McLean, an eighteen-year-old UK citizen volunteering in a hospital in Kampala, Uganda, visited and treated a group of prisoners in Luzira Upper Prison. Struck by the living conditions of the prisoners, he bought materials and supervised the renovation of the prison infirmary.

Alexander returned to the United Kingdom but continued to work for the cause of prison reform both there and in Uganda. Initially, Alexander collected books and money to return to the prison and founded a library. Over time. Alexander's effort grew into the African Prisons Project (APP).

As of 2012, APP has touched the lives of more than 25,000 prison inmates and staff in Uganda, Kenya, Sierra Leone, and Nigeria. This includes sending more than 120,000 books to create libraries in prison, building and refurbishing prison clinics and hospitals with a total inpatient bed capacity exceeding 200, and providing literacy classes and other educational assistance to more than 500 inmates every week. APP has also provided legal assistance to several hundred inmates, arranged for dozens of children in prison to receive medical treatment in government hospitals, and helped dozens of terminally ill prisoners to receive care that allowed them to die with dignity and without pain, including getting some of them released from prison before they died.

McLean was trained as a barrister, so he is highly knowledgeable about the art of logical argumentation, which he deploys with skill in support of APP's fund-raising efforts. But he has also come to appreciate the unmatched power of using personal stories to connect with potential partners—and has discovered some unique ways of communicating such stories for which words are sometimes unnecessary:

One way we connect with our donors is through a unique form of thank-you note—hand-painted wooden trays made by the prisoners whom we serve. I got the idea when I first refurbished the maximum-security prison in Uganda in 2004. To thank me for my help, the prisoners made two trays—one for me and one for my grandmother, because she'd given me much of the money that enabled me to do that initial work in prisons. The tray they made for her was painted with a picture of a setting sun, mountains, and a river, symbolizing both how she was getting older and the support and generosity that she was giving through me.

Now we ask prisoners who want to thank our donors to craft wooden trays of the same sort, sometimes painted with the donor's name, sometimes with a picture of something that the prisoner has on their heart to share at that moment. It means a lot to our supporters to be able to hold in their hands an object that was actually painstakingly created just for them by an individual whose life they have touched through their generosity.

At the moment we're exploring opportunities with several filmmakers who are interested in producing a documentary about our work. We're also in the process of establishing a choir of ex-death-row inmates from Uganda to perform in concerts throughout the country and around the world. Handwritten letters, painted trays, voices raised in song—these are three different ways of bringing the story of APP and the prisoners we serve to the people of the world.

Look for similar opportunities to communicate through nonverbal means with your organization's partners. In today's world of social networking and other forms of electronic communication, these include audio, photo, and video files, which are easy to create and upload to your website, Facebook page, YouTube account, or email newsletter. But don't underestimate the impact of physical artifacts, which can be even more powerful in today's Internet-dominated world. Does your organization serve the needs of children? A crayoned thank-you drawing from one of your clients may become a keepsake that a partner will treasure forever.

USING SOCIAL NETWORKING TOOLS TO TURN CASUAL DONORS INTO PARTNERS

We've talked about the importance of creating true partnerships with those who support your organization's work. But the notion of partnership doesn't apply only to major donors—the wealthy philanthropists, corporations, or foundations that are the financial backbone of many large organizations. It also applies to individuals who make modest contributions—small monetary donations, a few hours of volunteer work—to local nonprofits.

It can be difficult to provide such casual donors with the personalized attention that nurtures the spirit of partnership. Even a small organization—a church or synagogue, a community or senior center, a local library, a Boys or Girls Club—may receive support from several hundred or a few thousand contributors, many of them donating just $5, $10, or $20 at a time. If you're a fund-raiser for a group like this, how can you create meaningful connections with such a large number of individuals?

This is where the enormous power of social-networking media can play a part. Very few people in the nonprofit world understand how to effectively use new media such as Facebook, Twitter, YouTube, and Pinterest to achieve specific marketing, communication, and community-building goals. The result is often ill-conceived social media advertising or publicity campaigns that sap time, energy, and other resources but produce disappointing results. A better way to deploy the power of social networking is as a tool for creating intimate, person-to-person connections between your organization and its partners as well as among the partners themselves.

Katya Andresen, chief strategy officer of Network for Good, is an authority on nonprofit marketing. Andresen emphases that the value of social media—no matter which platforms you use—lies in their ability to help change your relationship with donors from a transactional one to a transformational one. Social media make it possible to reach the "long tail" of relatively small donors in a more intimate, interactive way than was formerly possible, creating a close connection that rivals your link with major donors and other key partners.

Remember that people are most motivated to give when they feel that giving makes them part of a broader community. One form of this community is the electronic one found on every social networking site.

This truth has a number of practical applications. For example, research shows that the power of peer-to-peer connection means that social media users respond more favorably to *personal* messages rather than *organizational* ones. Suggestion: rather than relying on your organization's "official" page on Facebook, Twitter, YouTube, or other sites, encourage individual members of your team as well as outside partners to create personal pages where they share their own messages about your work. The impact is likely to be far greater.

In a similar way, don't simply use social media to recount your organization's "official" story or even a handful of personal accounts selected by your marketing team. Instead, invite individual staffers, donors, and other friends to post their personal stories about your work.

Other research studies have shown that peer-to-peer solicitation of a gift is the most acceptable form of solicitation, and this is true whether we're talking about young people in their twenties and thirties or about older folks who didn't grow up in the era of computers, the Internet, and Facebook. It's easy to take advantage of this reality on your social media pages. For example, if you are a regular contributor of posts, comments, photos, or links to your organization's Facebook page—and you should be—try inviting your friends to make a donation to your cause when your birthday rolls around every year. Not only will your request generate a number of welcome checks, you'll be modeling the concept of peer-to-peer solicitation for everyone who sees your post. You may find other supporters making the same suggestion to friends on their special days—not just birthdays but anniversaries, graduations, bar and bat mitzvahs, holidays, and so on.

The interactive nature of social media also makes it possible to "automate" communications among outside supporters, members of your organization, and your recipients or beneficiaries. Thanks to the power of instantaneous messaging, you can now make individualized contact with hundreds of even thousands of casual donors—not just the relative handful you've personally gotten to know.

The innovative organization DonorsChoose.org, which raises money for worthy educational efforts in schools, makes excellent use of this technological tool. Visit their website and you'll be presented with hundreds of specific school projects in need of funding—a request for art supplies from a teacher in Harlem, a program to provide iPads for a math class in Chicago, the opportunity to support a trip to a dance studio for kids in Los Angeles. The projects are sortable by field of study, geographic location, financial urgency, and other characteristics. You get to pick the project you'd like to support and decide whether to donate enough to cover the entire project or just a portion of it. (The average project costs $500; the average gift is around $60.) But whether you give $500 or just a buck, you're rewarded with a personalized thank-you note from the teacher and one or more photos of the project in action. And if you give a minimum of $50, you also receive a physical thank-you letter from the students, often including hand-drawn pictures illustrating the impact of your gift on their classroom studies.

Charles Best, founder and CEO of DonorsChoose.org (and an Exponential Fundraising student), explains the power of the model this way:

> The classic giving experience for someone who has $20 to spare has usually been getting hit with a heartrending solicitation—a photograph of someone in dire need, or a message or slogan that's designed to make you feel terrible if you don't respond. But if you write a $20 check, you don't really know what happens with your $20. You're not invited to participate in the allocation of that $20. You can't follow it into the field. You don't get to meet the people you've chosen to help. You are, in effect, just a passive writer of a check.
>
> DonorsChoose.org is endeavoring to create a new giving experience, one that enables somebody with $20 to be an active philanthropist. They can search for projects that match a personal passion, like the town where they grew up or their favorite book or their favorite subject in high school or the sport they played.

They can pick the very project that most inspires them, see exactly how their money's being spent, hear back from the students and the teacher they chose to help, and even have the ability to correspond with them and forge an actual relationship.

Best reports that many of the donor-classroom relationships launched through the site grow into ongoing partnerships. Many make multiple donations to the same school or teacher. Others become long-term pen pals or make in-person visits to classrooms they've supported. Best reports with a laugh, "We hear from teachers who tell us, 'Oh, one of our donors was just here with a batch of brownies he baked for the whole class!'" A husband-and-wife pair of donors from Michigan with a special interest in music education has given dozens of donations to classroom projects in New York City. They've also become friends with many of the teachers and students; some classes have even written songs for the couple as a music project and performed the songs when the donors made an in-person visit.

In the days before the Internet, it would have been difficult, if not impossible, for a nonprofit organization to facilitate so many interpersonal connections among once-anonymous, far-flung donors and recipients. DonorsChoose.org has used today's interactive technology to make the experience of partnership, once reserved mainly for "big donors," accessible to anyone who cares enough to share some of their time, talent, or treasure.

Furthermore, they use the same interactive media tools to continually attract new partners. When you make an online gift to one of their classroom projects, you're asked, upon checkout, to answer this question: "Why did you give to this project?" The "why" question, of course, is designed to invite a story. So, for example, if you just funded a classroom science project, you might answer: "When I was a kid, my father bought me my first microscope and the whole world opened up to me. I want that same experience for the kids in your classroom." With the donors' permission, some of these stories get posted on the DonorsChoose.org website or its Facebook page.

They then become part of the organization's collective story and a powerful form of peer-to-peer outreach.

DonorsChoose.org has used technology impressively to scale up its operations: in 2013 it expects to attract some 200,000 donors, and eventually it hopes to reach millions. But there's no reason a similar system of personalized, peer-to-peer partnerships couldn't be employed by a much smaller nonprofit. For example, think about a local branch of the United Way, the United Jewish Communities, Catholic Charities, or a church or synagogue that contributes outreach funds to support local charities (the neighborhood soup kitchen, homeless shelter, day care center, or tutoring organization). The umbrella fund-raiser could create a simple website or Facebook page that would allow donors to pick which organization they want to support. Photos and written descriptions could detail specific projects in need of support: a new freezer for the soup kitchen, bookshelves for the day care center. Personal communication between donors and recipients could also be facilitated. There's no doubt that a system like this would encourage many supporters to develop their relationships with gift recipients into full-fledged partnerships, with big benefits both for the givers and for the causes they favor.

PARTNERSHIPS ARE ABOUT YOU AND ME —NOT CELEBRITIES

Our innate preference for peer-to-peer connections helps explain one counterintuitive truth about social media—the relative ineffectiveness of appeals that rely on celebrity endorsements. One Exponential Fundraising student told about devoting a lot of time, energy, and resources in creating a powerful video about his organization's work that included narration by two well-known and widely admired movie stars. The stars followed up by posting about the organization on Twitter two to three times per day for a period of five days, each tweet requesting an instant donation of $5. The grand total raised by this effort: $135. On the other hand, one celebrity-based fund-raising campaign that achieved notable success was actor Kevin Bacon's SixDegrees.org—and that campaign worked because of its unique, noncelebrity spin. Bacon arranged for several of his Hollywood friends to post stories about their favorite charitable causes—and then invited ordinary people to add their own stories, together with invitations to donate, using the slogan "Be a celebrity for your cause." Bacon topped off the whole program by offering to donate $10,000 of his own to the most popular charities—which turned out to be the causes espoused by unknown participants, not celebrities.

The lesson is clear: philanthropic partnerships aren't about celebrities— they're about you and me. That's why you and your individual teammates out in the "real world" are the most powerful and effective social media advocates you'll ever find.

The world of social media is still relatively young and ever-changing. New tools for using it are continually being developed. Spend time on the Internet and pay attention to the latest community-building techniques being used by both for-profit and nonprofit organizations. We recently heard from Sylvia Ferrell-Jones of the YWCA Boston that her group attached a QR code to the pledge sheet at the organization's annual breakfast. Attendees who scanned the code with their smart phones immediately jumped to the Y's "Donate" page, making it easy for them to make an instant gift. Other nonprofits are sure to adopt the same technique.

But no matter how the technology changes, the underlying psychology of giving remains the same: *people want to be members of your team.* Treat them that way and they will respond in kind.

DEMOCRATIZING THE BRAND:

Involving Your Partners in Shaping and Executing Your Brand Strategy

We live in a world of brands—names, logos, images, and personalities that define companies, products, and organizations of every kind. We're inundated by brand presentations. They saturate the thousands of commercial messages to which we're exposed on a daily basis. The names and meanings of major global brands, from McDonald's and Disney to Apple and Nike, are as familiar to billions of people around the world as national flags or the symbols of the great religions.

Brands rule our world. And yet, in the nonprofit world, brand thinking has not reached the same level of sophistication as it has in the for-profit arena. Those of us who lead and help to build nonprofit organizations haven't yet learned to think about, analyze, and shape our brands and our brand messages with the same creativity and insight as the best marketers in the business world.

This is a gap that we need to close in the years to come. The nonprofit brand, which Harvard branding expert Nathalie Kylander aptly summarizes as "who you are, what you do, and why it's important," is the face your organization presents to its partners as well as to the broader world. Ensuring and maintaining the accuracy, clarity, consistency, vividness, and broad appeal of that brand is a crucially important element in your communications efforts.

Many nonprofit leaders make the mistake of assuming that "the brand problem" can be solved simply by defining, honing, and perfecting a capsule message that captures in words the mission of the organization: "who you are, what you do, and why it's important." This capsule message is often described as "the elevator pitch," since the idea is that it should be memorable yet brief enough to be recited during an elevator ride.

There's nothing wrong with working to clarify and articulate a brief, effective mission statement for your organization. If you can't explain in a sentence or two what you are trying to do and why, you may well have a problem with focus. But don't fall for the fallacy of thinking that having a great elevator pitch is synonymous with having a powerful brand.

By forcing people to recite a single, unvarying message, you're actually creating an obstacle to genuine communication. It means you waste all the rich experiences and talents of your supporters by limiting and packaging their individual passions inside a prepackaged marketing box. The resulting homogenized pitch is often so lacking in distinctiveness that it could be applied to any one of a thousand different organizations.

By all means, create your strategy statement. Make it clear and convincing. But before your team sallies forth to trumpet your brand to the world, they should first hold up a mirror. When your elevator pitch reflects your personal story and passion, the telling—and the results—will be far more compelling.

Nathalie Kylander is a forceful advocate for what she calls the democratizing of brand strategy. Rather than turning the process of defining your brand over to a handful of organizational leaders (such as the members of the board or your executive committee) or, worse yet, simply outsourcing it to a consulting firm, she urges nonprofits to engage their own staffers, donors, and outside partners in the task:

> The important thing is to make sure that people can express your brand identity. The best way to make that happen is to allow them to participate in the development and the articulation of that brand. If they really know what the organization is, what it does, and why it's important, then they get wrapped up in that emotionally, and

they can communicate the brand in a way that's very personal and authentic.

And that's why the notion of brand democracy is really important. It is no longer very useful to say to employees and volunteers, "This is our brand identity, and this is what you need to say about the organization." That kind of top-down communication strategy is often practically useless. It's much more important to say, "Who do *you* feel we are? Why is the work we do important to *you*?" And then use the information you gather to help inform and shape the overall branding message.

Collecting input from hundreds of internal and external supporters and then really incorporating that input into a powerful brand message takes time, and it's hard to do. But when you follow this process, you get much greater cohesion about the brand identity and a team of people who are able to express that identity with much more enthusiasm and genuineness. And you also end up with a much stronger organization, because everyone on your team will be pulling in the same direction, having shared in the process of defining and articulating that direction.

A democratic approach to branding involves dialogue with several groups of stakeholders: your employees, your board members, your clients or beneficiaries, your donors, your corporate and organizational partners, your social-networking "friends," and perhaps others who know about your work and your reputation, such as members of the media who have covered you and colleagues in organizations that operate in the same space. You may discover that the meaning of your brand is quite different from what you intend or believe, and that it may vary widely from one stakeholder group to another. Listening to these inputs with an open mind can be challenging, but it's important if your branding decisions are to be based on reality rather than flawed assumptions.

Yes, democratizing the brand process means allowing your partners to talk about you in ways that you do not directly control. Of course, they will do this anyway, particularly in today's era of instantaneous communication and social networks—but it's important to accept the legitimacy of these varying voices and stories rather than trying (usually unsuccessfully) to impose your own elevator speech on every supporter. There is risk involved in this "open mike" policy. It's possible that a staffer, board member, donor, corporate partner, or Facebook friend may present your organization in an inaccurate or embarrassing way. But seeking to clamp down on communication about your organization is likely to be futile.

In the long run, transparency that encourages partners to embrace what your organization truly stands for will enhance your brand in a way that far outbalances the risks.

FOOD FOR THOUGHT

Follow-up questions and activities designed to help you get the most out of this chapter:

- Create your own list of key partners—donors, supporters, board members, volunteers, advisors, colleagues, allies, and others who are important to your success and that of your organization. Specifically assign responsibility for communication with each group to a specific staffer, and develop a schedule for keeping in touch with these people, including a plan for the kinds of communications you'll use. (For example, you might send a personal email newsletter once a month and make an individual phone call at least once every three months.)

- Think of your most important partners—donors, board members, volunteers, and so on. How many of them appear to be participating at a less-than-optimal level? Develop a plan for energizing these semidisengaged partners. It may include connecting them with one another in new ways, proposing new activities or assignments for them, or creating opportunities for them to engage with you and one another in small-group settings where their connection with your organization can be revivified.

- How are you using social media to promote your cause? Analyze your social-media sites in the light of the four principles listed in Chapter 1: *giving is emotional, giving is personal, giving makes people happy,* and *giving is social.* Are your sites designed to maximize each of these four effects?

- Consider democratizing your approach to your organization's brand. Ask the people you work with, "What does our organization mean to you? Why is its work important?" The answers can help you begin to define what your brand *should* look like. Then extend the process to outside supporters. If you have a website, Facebook page, or other interactive presence, invite donors, friends, and others to answer the same two questions. Study the results and use them to shape your future brand communications.

5

IT'S NOT ABOUT THE MONEY

From Transaction to Transformation

Taking a new step,

uttering a new word is

what people fear most.

—Fyodor Dostoevsky

In the preceding chapters, we've provided you with a lot of ideas, some of which may have been unfamiliar to you from your past experiences as a fund-raiser, nonprofit executive, or simply a supporter of a worthy cause.

We've talked about converting the narrow, financially centered concept of fund-raising into a broader quest for personal transformation—because that, after all, is what our work in the nonprofit space is ultimately about. We've suggested that you begin thinking about fund-raising not simply as "getting them to write a check" but in a more all-embracing fashion as "overcoming the obstacles that prevent the natural flow of resources." These resources include not just money but time, talent, networks, creativity, expertise, ideas, and all the other tools that can help energize a cause and give it the power to move mountains.

We've explored the kinds of personal connections that grow organically out of this new conception of fund-raising. These connections are based not on prescribed roles, a sense of social hierarchy, or the manipulative game playing that goes by the name of "salesmanship," but rather on openness, transparency, and a mutual sense of discovery. The more you practice creating such connections, the closer you approach the state we call the no "other" way—where the links between people are so powerful the borders so open that energy flows naturally, making generosity effortless.

We've also identified personal story as one of the most important paths to creating such deep peer-to-peer connections. Your own thoughtfully crafted narrative, which begins with a "story of self," expands into a "story of us," and then hits home with the urgency of a "story of now," can be a powerful way of reaching into the hearts and minds of people and offering them an opportunity to share your passion.

Finally, we've spoken about the importance of transitioning from thinking about your connections with partners in terms of exchange to thinking in terms of relationship. As we've seen, exchange is about limited, strictly defined, quid pro quo transactions; relationship is about unlimited, open-ended, creative partnership that leads to an unknown, mutually shaped destination. Such relationships are built on understanding, respecting, and appealing to the values and worldview of the other person.

All of these concepts, taken together, offer a road map to a revolutionary approach to fund-raising—one that allows you to connect with people in a deeper way than traditional methods of fund-raising, salesmanship, or persuasion. It begins with listening to them, getting to know them, and exploring ways to partner with them based on mutual, shared passions. In this new approach, you see yourself not as a supplicant or salesperson, but as one node in a network of individuals whose potential connections are unlimited. When you offer yourself as a connection point to many other individuals, you become a natural focus of energy for them to link to in turn. The resulting natural connections often lead to results that are amazing in their explosive power.

Perhaps the single most important concept underlying this new approach to fund-raising is the importance of removing money from the center of your relationships.

One of the most insidious traps into which you can fall as a nonprofit leader or partner is focusing on money. Money is required to keep your organization running, of course. But the mere transfer of money doesn't constitute a real relationship between a donor and an organization. In fact, the sense on both sides that the writing of the check constitutes the sum total of the connection between the two parties is often fatal to the hope of creating a deeper, richer, more creative link.

More powerful connections—including, paradoxically, much richer financial connections—happen when the relationship is based on far more than money. For example, consider the work of Jeff and his fellow team members at the MDG Health Alliance, the global organization working to achieve the Millennium Development Goals in the area of health, particularly in regard to women and children.

When soliciting support, Jeff and his colleagues don't just ask people to write checks. Instead, they bring smart, gifted, creative individuals together around questions such as: *Can you help us figure out how to finance the hiring and training of one million community health workers for the global South? Do you have some ideas for a strategy to improve local sanitation services in the countries of the developing world? Can you help us with a marketing campaign focused on reducing maternal mortality in sub-Saharan Africa? What can we be doing to foster greater empowerment around women's health issues in the nations of South Asia?*

Of course, it's clear that money is needed to support the effort, and when the right band members are gathered around the table, the money flows naturally. But so do other resources that are even more valuable: ideas, talents, connections.

To begin practicing this new style of fund-raising, move money away from the center of the conversation. Put the work you are doing and the band you want to build there instead. The result is *transformational giving*—a connection between donor and recipient that produces learning, change, and psychological, emotional, and spiritual growth on both sides. Transformational giving helps donors travel a path of self-discovery, finding out more about their values, goals, and ultimate sources of satisfaction in life. At the same time, it opens up nonprofit organizations to unpredictable insights, including new ideas about how to achieve their goals, new ways to deploy their resources, and new missions they can undertake.

When nonprofits shift from transactional to transformational philanthropy, there's no limit to what they and their partners can accomplish together.

WANTED:
Much More than an Encounter

We have all had wonderful encounters with people—meetings over lunch or a cup of coffee where we exchange our stories and (if we're lucky) even share some moments of pure connection. Some of the ideas we've discussed in these pages, concerning openness, transparency, and the willingness to share your philanthropic journey, can help make such encounters meaningful. But unless we agree to take our connection to the next level through a shared commitment to do so, the encounter does not lead to a relationship. We had a nice exchange, which in itself isn't the basis for anything but a one-time, nice exchange.

So one of the biggest challenges we face is getting beyond nice encounters to the real acts of commitment that make up a relationship.

Consider the situation from your prospective partner's point of view. If I am going to give you my most precious resource—my time—I have to expect that you are going to give me something even more valuable in return. There's risk in that, and uncertainty. If I am using my time in a known way, there is certainty and comfort. So my decision to commit time to you, and to continue to commit it to you after the first meeting, must have inherent in it at least a promise of something deeper.

This commitment to building a relationship won't be achieved through a casual meeting with a lot of small talk, or even through a nice encounter with a meaningful conversation at its heart. There must be intentionality put into learning something real about each other beyond bios, something real and rich enough that we not only want but *need* to know more.

We will give each other that most precious resource of time only when we believe that without this relationship being taken to the next level, something very important might never be discovered. So if you want to initiate that kind of relationship, you need to take the responsibility for creating the circumstances of openness, transparency, and sharing that will make such commitment both possible and attractive.

TRANSPARENCY = VULNERABILITY

On the donor's side, transparency means talking candidly about the values, goals, dreams, anxieties, and desires that underlie giving. It means being willing to open up about topics such as:

- How important it is for the donor to get personal, public recognition for his acts of generosity. For some donors, recognition is all-important; for others, it's something to be avoided at all costs.
- Whose approval is necessary before a sizeable contribution can be made. A spouse is often crucial—but in some cases, a parent, child, business partner, or other significant individual may play an important behind-the-scenes role.
- The deeply personal motivation behind a gift—which is different for virtually everyone. One person may give to the local dance company to honor a parent who loved The Nutcracker; another to cling to her own childhood dream of becoming a great ballerina; still another simply to get access to the best seats at the season-opening performance.
- The kind of connection the donor wants to have with the organization. Some donors love to receive an occasional call from a staff member, some cherish having their opinion asked about a topic of personal or professional expertise, and still others find such calls annoying.
- The larger role played by charity in the donor's life. Many people become philanthropists because of a life-changing experience—a death in a family, a serious illness, a career change, a spiritual awakening. Others are driven by religious values, political or social convictions, family tradition, or other forces.
- The doubts and worries the donor may have about giving. "If I make a donation, will my money be wisely spent? Do the organization's officers really know what they're doing? Is the problem they're trying to solve really curable—or are they simply sticking Band-Aids on an inoperable cancer?" Many donors have thoughts like these, but few are honest enough to express them in so many words.

Not every donor is ready to talk about such topics with a fund-raiser or other nonprofit representative. But many are—and when the door is open to this kind of conversation, a deeply rewarding relationship often develops as a result.

But transparency isn't a one-way street. Fund-raisers, too, need to practice openness when communicating with their philanthropic partners. They must learn to be candid about such topics as:

- *The organization's mistakes and missteps.* All nonprofits proudly trumpet their successes, as well they should. Fewer go public about their failures and, more important, what they've learned from those failures.
- *How the organization's strategy has changed over time.* Some organizations behave as if having changed their minds is embarrassing—a confession of past error. But great corporations evolve their strategies based on changing circumstances, and great nonprofits do, too.
- *Areas of weakness, ignorance, or uncertainty surrounding the organization's work.* The truth is that there are huge knowledge gaps even among leading experts about most of the biggest problems our world faces—global poverty, health care, education reform, international peace. The solutions nonprofit organizations pursue may be unproven or imperfect, yet they still deserve support. Effective advocates aren't afraid to say so.

Of course, learning to communicate transparently with the partners who support your organization is a tough personal challenge. Sometimes it can be embarrassing or painful. But there's really no alternative, as those who try to avoid transparency eventually discover. In fact, the more you try to fend off challenges or criticism from your partners, implicitly promoting an image of near-infallibility, the greater the level of mistrust you are likely to encounter. By contrast, when you are honest and forthcoming about your mistakes, uncertainties, and areas of ignorance, you'll probably find that partners will offer more appreciation, cooperation, and help. Transparency—including openness about your past failures—helps to transform "I" into "we," strengthening the bonds that connect team members and paving the way to future successes.

Today's best nonprofits recognize this truth. They welcome two-way transparency, even when it's difficult or stressful—and that includes being willing to entertain tough questions and challenges from well-intentioned supporters. Painful conversations, they've found, can be a path to discovery, learning, and growth.

Tracey Durning is an impact entrepreneur and the founder of 49 prince street, a platform from which she co-creates and supports innovative projects aimed at large-scale impact around social issues. Tracey's key focus areas are oceans, conservation, climate change, and putting an end to animal overpopulation and euthanasia. Under the 49 prince street umbrella, she drives and manages the philanthropic activities for Planet Heritage Foundation (PHF) and works in partnership with an array of philanthropists. "For me," she says, "there are no boundaries between friendship and work. Life is short and precious, and I want to spend it around open people—people I want to work with, play with, and be on a long journey with. That's why Jeff and Jennifer are part of my team—and I'm part of theirs."

Tracey is also one of the most insightful thinkers we know about the relationship between nonprofit leaders and the partners who enable their work. She has examined the challenges of transparent communication between donors and recipients from both sides of the equation, and she is an ardent advocate of more honest, open sharing—even when (*especially* when) that sharing takes the form of tough, challenging questions and conversations:

> I know pretty quickly whether I'm talking to a potential partner or not. A partner is as comfortable talking about uncertainties and question marks as they are about strategies for success. I absolutely

love people who can comfortably lean into tough questions and go deeper in a dialogue, including ones that reveal that they don't have all the answers. That's authentic and real to me, because, after all, no one has all the answers!

It's the folks who get irritable or defensive or just keep smiling and telling me what they think I want to hear that I steer clear of. Those behaviors tell me they're not comfortable with being vulnerable or revealing. That's definitely *not* the kind of person I want to be in business with.

Durning is right. When partners and would-be partners ask nonprofit leaders tough questions about their plans, programs, and vision, they are doing them a favor. Part of a deep, creative relationship is confronting challenges, resolving them together, and growing and learning in the process.

So if you are a donor to a nonprofit cause, don't hold back when you have tough questions to ask. And if you are a nonprofit leader or fund-raiser, resolve to outgrow your fears and embrace vulnerability. As many leaders before you have discovered, vulnerability is not a form of weakness, but strength.

PARTNERSHIP:
What It Is and What It Isn't

Open communication with donors can lead to other challenges—for example, having to deal with donors who seem to want to take over your organization or drive it in directions you just don't want to go.

When Jennifer uses the word *partnership* to describe the ideal donor relationship in her classes, some nonprofit veterans get nervous. A student in her class once remarked, "The word *partnership* is problematic for us. When we teach our partners about our work with people in the developing world, they get to thinking they know how to do it. Pretty soon, they start pushing us to redesign our programs based on things they read in a magazine article or on a website somewhere. The truth is that you really need to be a professional in the field to understand fully what works and what doesn't, and all the parameters that have to be considered in designing an initiative. So we're not really eager to encourage our donors to feel as though they are equal partners with us in shaping our efforts."

Another student, who works on economic development programs in the countries of the global South, nodded. "One of my potential donors is a big hedge fund guy," she commented. "I'd love to get a financial contribution from him, but he is already telling me that he will want me to shift my focus to microcredit, even though I know it's not what the specific people we serve really need or want."

Stories such as these underscore the reality that a relationship can't be controlled or limited in advance. If you commit to a true partnership with your partners, you must expect open communication in both directions—which may sometimes mean listening to things you don't find particularly helpful or pleasant to hear.

Being open to feedback and new ideas is crucial for any organization that truly wants to learn and grow. It should be clear to everyone who participates in the organization that this is how things work. Let people know that there is a forum for discussing new ideas and that the group takes all feedback seriously and enthusiastically.

Which raises a question: how do you gently guide your partners so that they can truly be active participants in your mission—and feel that way—but without sidetracking the program into unproductive byways?

Fortunately, there are a number of good answers to this question.

One is to realize that a true relationship is a two-way street. Yes, you need to be prepared to listen to and learn from what your partners say—but they need to listen to and learn from you as well. Healthy, informed debate about the best approaches to problems from poverty alleviation to health care reform to improving education is often necessary and beneficial, provided all parties to the debate are truly listening to one another with open minds. Partnership does *not* mean rolling over or accepting without question whatever a donor says.

If you find it intimidating to consider the prospect of arguing back when a donor is making a forceful demand that you change your program, you may be suffering from the vestiges of the power imbalance that is one of the worst effects of the traditional approach to fund-raising. Perhaps you feel, deep down inside, like a humble supplicant dependent on the capricious generosity of the all-powerful donor, who may abandon you if you dare to challenge his wisdom. You won't have a real relationship until you manage to eliminate the last remnant of that thinking from your mind.

In many cases, if you have a well-reasoned, evidence-backed explanation as to how your strategic policy was developed, partners will quickly come to recognize its value and accept your position—their commitment to your organization reinforced by the fact that you were willing and able to defend your choices in a frank conversation with them. As our friend Joi Ito of the MIT Media Lab puts it, "If you have a very good strategy and plan, most people are not interested in imposing their plan on you. That usually happens only when people have reason to doubt whether you've really thought through your strategy."

In other cases, a partner's apparent desire to take control of your program may really reflect a particular set of values that is being reflected indirectly and expressed ineffectively. If you can engage the partner in honest conversation about his deepest goals and aspirations, you may be able to suggest an alternative plan that will work to benefit both the individual partner and the organization. As Kenneth Watkins of the Australian Ballet remarks, "The key is to figure out the specific thing a particular donor is interested in and channel them toward it."

For example, a deeper conversation with the potential donor who is a strong advocate of microcredit might lead to the revelation that he is really passionate about harnessing free-market forces to help the poor, with microcredit being simply the most famous example that he is familiar with. Based on that discovery, it might be possible for you to suggest one or more specific initiatives that your organization is already undertaking—or that could fit naturally into your portfolio of programs—that reflect the free-market values that mean so much to this donor.

One simple but effective communication tool you might try when striving to create healthy two-way relationships with donors is to verbally prioritize the ideas they propose (see the sidebar "Prioritizing New Ideas," below).

In the most extreme case, it may simply be that a particular donor and a particular organization are not a good fit for partnership. That's fine. It's not possible for every passion to be shared equally by all people. If a frank conversation leads you to that conclusion, then be honest about it with the potential partner, and, if you can, suggest the name of another organization that might be a more natural home for his or her resources.

That's not a bad outcome—in fact, it's a wonderful way of living out the reality that all of us are nodes on a network of connections, and the more freely we allow energies to flow from point to point, the more brightly the entire web will glow.

PRIORITIZING NEW IDEAS

It's great to have a partner, such as an important donor, who is full of ideas for your organization. Sometimes great innovations get started through conversations with people like that. But harnessing the enthusiasm and creativity of partners who may lack the knowledge one can gain only from years of work in the field—without making them feel disrespected or ignored—can sometimes be challenging.

Here's one effective way to meet the challenge. Verbally assign one of three priority levels to any new idea from the partner:

- **A** designates a high-priority idea that deserves prompt and energetic exploration.
- **B** designates an idea with some potential that is worthy of further consideration and thought.
- **C** designates a low-priority idea that doesn't justify any significant investment of time or other resources.

This three-level priority system is a relatively nonjudgmental way of offering feedback. Responding quickly to proposed ideas with an A, B, or C designation provides honest, useful guidance to the partners as to which ideas are genuinely promising and which are not. This can and should be done tactfully and with good humor: "Gee, Tom, that's an interesting idea. It might work well for some other organization. But for us I'd have to label that a C—something we'd put on the back burner by comparison with the other projects we're working on."

Of course, a partner is likely to be disappointed to learn that an idea of his is viewed as a B- or C-level idea. But most partners prefer honest feedback to insincere praise or promises to follow up on an idea that leads only to silence and inaction. They're likely to say, "At least I know where I stand"—and they'll appreciate not having their time wasted in efforts to pursue an idea that was never likely to succeed.

TRANSFORMATIONAL GIVING WITH A CORPORATE DONOR

Transformational giving doesn't apply only to individual givers. A nonprofit organization can also create transparent, open-ended relationships with other kinds of donors—for example, corporations and foundations—that can lead to growth, discovery, and transformational change on both sides.

Here's a story that illustrates how a deep partnership between a nonprofit and a corporation can produce transformational changes for both.

Earlier in this book, we described the African Prisons Project (APP), created by Alexander McLean. One of APP's major donors is a British law firm, Clifford Chance. The relationship started with just a single partner at the firm, but over time it has grown into a transformational partnership between the two organizations:

> We could see from the beginning that Clifford Chance was open to creating what I call a multistranded relationship with us, because they immediately began talking about providing both financial support and pro bono staff hours. They've now committed to giving us five hundred hours of their staff time, and you can imagine how very valuable that is.
>
> What's remarkable is how deeply engaged we've become with a wide array of people within Clifford Chance. We're in constant touch with their senior partner, who runs their office in London, and we have contacts with their offices in other parts of the world as well. I've met with their staff in New York and had correspondence with their staffs in Amsterdam and Washington. About

eight people from Clifford Chance are involved in mentoring prisoners and prison staff who are studying for law diplomas and degrees with the University of London by correspondence. Others are involved in our Web development, our public relations, our marketing, and our branding. All told, we have relationships with about twenty of their staff members. This makes the connection between our organizations unusually deep and rich.

We consciously nurture this relationship through a variety of means. We send regular emails, keep them abreast of our activities, invite them to our events, and supply them with our newsletters. They also receive regular requests for support and advice from our staff members. These kinds of regular contacts produce enormous concrete benefits for us, since the people at Clifford Chance are very smart, knowledgeable, and talented. But they also ensure that our work and our organization are always at the forefront of their minds. There's no mistaking the fact that the commitment from both sides is very strong and real.

Later this summer, Clifford Chance and APP will co-host an evening reception aimed at our existing partners, prospects we've identified, and prospects suggested by Clifford Chance. So Clifford Chance is not only committed to us themselves; they also have a desire to create a much stronger relationship by bringing their clients into our shared network as well.

We're constantly finding new ways to strengthen and deepen our connection to one another. For instance, I was at Clifford Chance's offices this week to help judge awards that they give to university students who are interested in working for the company. They seem very keen to give us opportunities like this, and my feeling is we're both committed to investing in the relationship, updating one another, informing one another, constantly helping us both to be aware of how the relationship is benefiting us, and sharing and celebrating the relationship with others.

The story of Clifford Chance's ever-deepening partnership with APP illustrates how a philanthropic connection can lead to transformation not just for an individual but for an organization. Originating with a single caring individual at Clifford Chance, the relationship with APP has grown and spread to encompass numerous members of the law firm. These talented individuals provide not just financial assistance but a wide variety of professional and business services as well as access to their broader network of clients and other contacts. This extraordinary level of involvement is changing the way the people of Clifford Chance think about themselves—as well as the way the world sees them. No longer "just another law firm," Clifford Chance is becoming a powerful participant in a world-changing humanitarian effort.

Another nonprofit that is crafting transformational relationships with donor organizations is KaBOOM! Its founder and CEO, Darell Hammond, grew up with seven brothers and sisters at Mooseheart, a group home outside of Chicago that is completely supported by charity through the Loyal Order of Moose fraternity. It was an experience that deeply shaped Hammond's life. Instilled by the community with a sense of the power of volunteerism, the need for people to care for one another, and the importance of playtime as a tool for growth and discovery, Hammond discovered even as a child that he had a special instinct for reaching out to serve those in need. "My nickname at Mooseheart," he recalls, "was 'the Lawyer,' because I became an advocate for other kids who were getting the short end of the stick. I was a mediocre student, but I was persuasive."

The vision for KaBOOM! came when he noticed a story in the *Washington Post* describing how two small children in the southeastern part of the District of Columbia had suffocated while playing in an abandoned car. Struck by the contrast between his own impoverished yet socially rich childhood and the deprivation suffered by so many American kids, Hammond decided to do whatever he could to prevent such tragedies from ever happening again. In 1995, he launched KaBOOM! with Dawn Hutchison. More than six hundred community-built playgrounds later, Hammond has become a widely recognized spokesperson for the child's right to play and a leader in the battle to transform "play deserts" into oases of fun.

Most interestingly, KaBOOM! has made transformational relationships with corporate and other organizational partners into the cornerstone of its strategy. KaBOOM! doesn't just move into a neighborhood with tools and supplies and leave behind a few sets of swings and slides. Instead, it organizes a cooperative effort involving one or more corporate sponsors, small businesses, community groups such as churches or YMCAs, local government agencies such as parks departments, and volunteers to help with the actual construction work.

The result is a project that produces immediate benefits in the form of a new playground, but even greater benefits in the form of a strengthened sense of community empowerment. In fact, Hammond likes to say that the playground itself is simply a "Trojan horse—a means to get the community to fight for something instead of fighting *against* something." He explains:

> From the beginning, the playground was always a by-product of the process. The process was that people could self-organize from within, have an amazing experience, build confidence and trust, and out of that get an enormous confidence boost. The goal is to get the local people at the end of the adventure to look at one another and say, "We built a playground—now what else is possible?"

This notion of transformational giving also applies to KaBOOM!'s corporate partners. Hammond consciously rejects the notion of raising money by soliciting one check at a time—"That's not a strategy," he says. Instead, he has prodded KaBOOM!'s staffers to seek long-term corporate partners that are interested in funding playgrounds by the dozen around the country as part of a multipronged effort to build local communities, solve the social problem of "play deserts" that deprive kids of healthful opportunities for exercise, and even address such broader issues as childhood obesity and lagging educational performance. "It's a partnership that's about much more than having them write us a check," Hammond says.

Corporations, community groups, and other organizations can be generous sources of money. But as the stories of APP and KaBOOM! illustrate, you needn't be satisfied with a merely transactional relationship. Organizations are made up of people who want more out of their work than just the chance to write a check to a worthy cause. Like all of us, they are hungry for opportunities to explore the deeper meaning of life. You can offer them that gift.

THE EVOLUTION OF A PHILANTHROPIST:
The John Megrue Story

John Megrue Jr. is an extraordinarily successful businessman—chief executive officer of Apax Partners, U.S., an independent global private equity advisory firm managing more than $37 billion in private equity funds. But what makes Megrue even more extraordinary is his record of achievement as a philanthropist.

An active champion for extreme poverty eradication and the development of global health systems, Megrue currently leads the Business Leadership Council (BLC), a private-sector initiative to support the UN's Global Plan Towards the Elimination of New HIV Infections Among Children by 2015 and Helping Mothers Stay Healthy. He is also on the board of the Millennium Development Goals Health Alliance and is a board member of Grameen America, a microfinance nonprofit that provides loans, savings programs, credit establishment, and other financial services to entrepreneurs living below the poverty line in the United States.

Megrue's journey vividly illustrates how the worldview of a philanthropist can change over time, evolving from a transactional view of giving to a transformational one. Here is how he shares his "story of self":

I've found my philanthropic activity evolving through three stages. The first stage—where I think many people remain all their lives—is the transactional level of giving. An organization asks for a donation, and you write a check.

There's nothing wrong with that. But some of us discover we want to go deeper. Maybe it's a result of maturity and the self-examination that goes with it. You want to learn more about the meaning of life, and this desire leads you into an extended connection with one or more philanthropic causes. That's the second stage—the stage where you find yourself helping to build organizations, involving others in giving, and recruiting supporters from business and government.

Now I've moved into what I think of as the third stage in my philanthropic evolution. It began when I was introduced to Millennium Promise through a longtime friendship with Jeff Walker. Now I've spent the better part of four or five years on that project, getting more and more deeply involved from a transformational standpoint—giving time, energy, creativity, and ideas—as opposed to a transactional standpoint, which is just about writing a check.

It's the stage in which I'm working to create true partnerships around humanitarian efforts. And *partnering*, of course, is easy to talk about but hard to do. True partnership demands so much of you as an individual. It means constantly giving of your time, your energy, and relationships. It means lowering your ego, learning to really listen, ignoring hierarchy, and holding yourself and others responsible for the outcomes of the work.

This third stage of my personal evolution is a fascinating time of challenge and growth for me. Fortunately, I can learn from the examples of others who have led the way—people like Ray Chambers, George Soros, and Bill Gates—who have developed a worldview and a value system that enables them to maximize the impact of their passion. These are philanthropists who've truly transcended the transactional and elevated giving to the transformation level. I hope that's where I'm heading.

LEARNING FROM YOUR PARTNERS:
Metrics as a Tool for Discovery and Growth

For the fund-raiser, it's deeply gratifying to work with a partner such as John Megrue and to share in his adventure of self-discovery. But it isn't only your partners who may be transformed through an intimate and open relationship. You and your organization may be transformed as well. One example is the increasing importance of "impact investing"—a new model of philanthropy that emphasizes mutual learning and growth for both nonprofit leaders and the partners who support them.

In this model of philanthropy, a gift to a nonprofit is viewed as analogous to an investment in a for-profit business: a specific "return on investment" in the form of measurable, positive outcomes is expected in exchange for the commitment of funds. These outcomes are quantified in the form of metrics—statistical or financial data, generally based on predetermined targets, that track the nonprofit's progress toward its goals. As more philanthropists, foundations, and other donors request such metrics, nonprofits are having to devote time and energy to defining, collecting, and reporting them.

The nonprofit world can certainly learn a lot about smart management from the for-profit world, and it makes sense for nonprofit leaders to want to track their results, learn from their mistakes, and improve their practices over time through the use of hard data, just as effective leaders in business do. The existence of well-designed metrics that are tracked over time provides nonprofit leaders with useful tools that can help them gauge their own performance and find ways to enhance it. And the existence of metrics creates an opportunity for philanthropists—many of them successful business leaders in their own right—to analyze the performance of the nonprofits they support, identify inefficiencies and opportunities for improvement, and offer valuable insights, ideas, and advice. It's a great example of letting powerful resources flow naturally to where they are needed—with the resources, in this case, being information and expertise.

Metrics can also play an important supportive role in your efforts to communicate and work with partners. Donors and would-be donors find it reassuring to receive numerical data about the impact of their gifts—after all, no one wants to think that the money they are giving to an important cause is being wasted. Figures that chart the tangible good being done by a nonprofit—lives saved, needless economic losses reduced, families lifted above the poverty line, students' test scores elevated, and so on—can form a compelling part of the story you share with partners and potential partners.

One example is the Centering Healthcare Institute, a nonprofit based in Boston and Silver Spring, Maryland, that promulgates an innovative, group-based model of health care through "Centering sites" around the country. Currently focused on prenatal care, well-woman and well-baby care, and diabetes treatment, the Centering model is designed to create systemic health care change that improves outcomes, lowers costs, and enhances patient satisfaction.

The Centering Healthcare Institute has an important and compelling story to share about its innovations in an area of enormous current importance. But one key to the power of its story is the impressive, well-documented metrics that demonstrate the effectiveness of the Centering model, including such data points as:

- The Centering Pregnancy model reduces the rate of preterm births between 33 and 47 percent across various clinical studies.
- The model saves health care systems around $2,094 for each mother who receives prenatal care through the model.
- A study of pregnant adolescents using the model showed a 52 percent reduction in sexually transmitted infections.[8]

Eye-popping numbers such as these make the value of the Centering model real and vivid, especially for potential partners who have been seeking tools with this kind of impact to help improve America's troubled and costly health care system.

Another example: In May 2011, the African Leaders Malaria Alliance created a new scorecard for measuring progress in the battle against the

---

8   See www.centeringhealthcare.org/pages/about/history.php.

disease. Updated quarterly, this graphic tool tracks key indicators including government malaria policy, financing, intervention coverage, and specific maternal and child health metrics in the forty-six different countries covered by ALMA programs. The cells in the scorecard are color-coded (red for "not on track," yellow for "good progress, but more effort required," and green for "target achieved"), so it's easy to spot areas of concern and compare progress in different regions at a glance.[9] The transparency and currency of this data help donors and other partners feel confident that they are up to date on key malaria trends in the region and enable them to target their questions, challenges, suggestions, and future gifts even more effectively.

Metrics are a way of speaking a familiar language to potential donors. But they should also help nonprofit leaders learn how to run their organizations more effectively. That requires metrics that are carefully designed and wisely used. See the sidebar "Making Metrics Meaningful" (below) for a number of specific suggestions about how to achieve that.

MAKING METRICS MEANINGFUL

Most nonprofits today feel a sense of pressure to generate metrics that measure their progress toward their goals. Here are some recommendations that can help you ensure that the process of tracking your own metrics will be a useful, rewarding one rather than a rote or superficial exercise.

- *Design your metrics thoughtfully.* The performance numbers you choose to track and share with the public will inevitably be used as shorthand indicators of success or failure. Therefore, you need

---

9 See www.malariapolicycenter.org/news/africa's-leaders-are-committed-winning-fight-against-malaria?page=3.

to design them wisely so that they accurately define the heart of your mission. Make sure the metrics you choose reflect what you are really trying to accomplish, that the numbers are reasonably easy to collect, that they are objective rather than subjective, and that their relevance to your mission is immediately obvious to anyone who considers them.

- *Measure outcomes, not inputs.* The most meaningful metrics track results that affect the lives of human beings rather than merely the effort expended by the nonprofit or the resources deployed. As an example, counting the dollars spent on building wells in sub-Saharan Africa is an input metric, while the number of wells built and the number of villagers who now have easy access to potable drinking water are outcome metrics. The latter two are more meaningful as gauges of success.

- *Enlist the help of partners in designing your metrics.* Some of your organization's leading partners can provide valuable expertise in designing useful metrics. Foundations, corporations, professional service firms, and other NGOs may all employ experts who have studied organizations similar to yours and can offer unique insights into the kinds of metrics that work and the management or IT systems needed to implement them. When donors participate in designing your metrics, the results you obtain will be doubly meaningful to them.

- *Live with the numbers and learn from them.* If your metrics are well-designed, you should find them valuable tools for managing your organization. Many nonprofit leaders assemble "dashboards" of three to five key metrics that they study on a weekly, monthly, or quarterly basis, searching for clues as to which programs and initiatives are proving to be effective and which ones need to be modified.

- *Use your metrics honestly.* Don't fall into the trap of thinking about your metrics purely as selling tools—"red meat" to attract donors and satisfy their demands. This attitude creates several temptations: to fudge the numbers, to alter your processes or procedures in order to hype your metrics (without producing any real-world benefits), and to continually redefine the metrics in order to make them look better (and to disguise the fact that your program may be foundering). Play fair! If your metrics look bad for a season, be transparent about the problems and about your plans for improvement. In the long run, your partners will respect you more for being honest with them—and with yourself.

METRICS MATTER —BUT NUMBERS AREN'T EVERYTHING

For many people, it's important to know that scientific logic demonstrates the value of a program they support. But you need to remember how factual information actually influences the decisions people make.

The great twentieth-century poet T. S. Eliot was often asked by readers to explain the meaning of his (rather abstruse) poems. Tiring of the question, he finally took to explaining that "meaning" in poetry is only of secondary importance, like the piece of juicy meat that a burglar brings to distract the watchdog while he goes about his *real* business—which is connecting with the emotions of readers through imagery, music, symbolism, and so on. In the same way, rational arguments on behalf of your mission can help by engaging and satisfying the needs of your audience's "left brain," while the emotional power of your story connects with their "right brain." And both experience and scientific research into human decision-making show that, when it comes to shaping action, it's the right brain that ultimately rules.

So, by all means, provide donors with the most pertinent data about your organization and its work, and be prepared to answer questions about that information. (Our left brains insist on getting a bit of red meat to satisfy our sense of logic and rationality.) But *don't build your partnership around the metrics. The metrics support the story—not vice versa.*

Our friend Sharon Salzberg, the gifted meditation teacher and talented nonprofit leader, offers this perspective on the role of metrics:

> We know, of course, that it's easy for philanthropy to be ill-advised or misspent. So one wants a certain kind of metric—a set of results that we're looking for.
>
> At the same time, beneficial things may happen in our work that may not have been in the direct line of our intention. Suppose we create a program to improve classroom teaching. It may be that we don't achieve the graduation rate we set out to achieve, yet for some of the kids whose lives we touch, maybe something really positive will happen along the way—for example, they may meet a teacher who, two years later, inspires them to try something that they wouldn't have dared to attempt.
>
> So we live in a world of unintended consequences, and it's important to recognize and understand that. But is there a spiritual discipline we can apply to try to ensure that our work produces the best possible consequences?
>
> I think the discipline is twofold. First, always take a look at your intention, and make it as broad and clear and truthful as possible. Are you trying to help people? Are you trying to achieve fame? Are you trying to be better at your work than someone else? The goal is not to wait until you achieve a perfect intention—that

would be a long wait for most of us! But differing motivations may lead to very different feelings about the results. So understanding these differences is important in defining success or failure.

Second, be mindful and aware all along the way. Otherwise there will be unintended consequences, good and bad, that you will miss. And this is tricky, but there's a difference between resolve and attachment. It's good to have resolve—to work hard to achieve what you think should happen. But sometimes we cling so hard to what we want when reality has moved or morphed and needs our energy to be sent in a different direction. That is attachment—when there's a very narrow set of possibilities that will bring you satisfaction. Attachment leads us to reject new possibilities, and that can be a very unfortunate outcome.

Salzberg's distinction between resolve and attachment can be helpful in defining how and when metrics are useful. Metrics that help us maintain our resolve in pursuit of worthwhile goals can be valuable; metrics that feed our sense of attachment and prevent us from recognizing when it's time to change can be destructive.

In our world of more and faster data, it's best to let metrics and analytics push the cart, not pull it. Gather data about nonprofit performance, analyze it carefully, and learn from it—but don't allow it to mindlessly control the choices you make, either as a nonprofit leader or as a philanthropist. And remember, always, that metrics are not a substitute for real-life stories when communicating with partners and would-be partners. As Jeff likes to say, "We honor the story and we honor the numbers—and we need both."

FOOD FOR THOUGHT

Follow-up questions and activities designed to help you get the most out of this chapter:

- Although many fruitful relationships begin with a "nice encounter" (as described on page 127), not all nice encounters lead to true relationships. Think of two recent positive encounters you experienced, one that proved to be the start of an expanding relationship and one that did not. Can you identify the reasons for these differing outcomes? Can you list some things you might do differently the next time you have a first encounter with someone in order to increase the odds that it will lead to a long-term relationship?

- As discussed on pages 132–136, interacting with partners who want to push your organization in directions you'd prefer not to follow can be challenging. Have you faced this problem recently? If so, how did you manage it? Were you able to channel the partner's interest and passion toward a positive contribution for the organization? If not, can you develop a plan now for working positively with this partner to find a suitable outlet for his or her desires?

- If you work with a nonprofit that receives funds from businesses or other organizations, take a close look at the nature of your relationships with those organizations. Does the connection involve merely receiving periodic financial donations, or are there other opportunities to interact, share resources, swap ideas, and otherwise grow together? Choose one of these relationships and map out a plan for deepening and enriching the connection, so that more individuals are involved, more kinds of shared activities are encouraged, and a greater sense of mutual commitment is created.

PART TWO

FUND-RAISING AS THE ART OF CONNECTION

6

THE ALL-IMPORTANT
FIRST MEETING

Veritas simplex oratio est—

the language of truth is simple.

—Seneca

There's an old adage that circulates widely in fund-raising circles: "It's harder to get the first meeting than the first gift." Actually, we've never found this to be true! Most people who are likely candidates to donate money, time, or other resources to a cause are fairly open to the idea of a brief, informal meeting. Many are experienced philanthropists who are accustomed to being "pitched" on a regular basis. Some are successful businesspeople or entrepreneurs who attend presentations about new concepts all the time. Still others are simply caring, charitable individuals who enjoy learning about the efforts that people and organizations are making to improve the world we share. Even people who are very busy (and successful people are almost all very busy) are generally willing to share twenty or thirty minutes of their time with a visitor who comes with a referral from a respected source. The *real* challenge is getting a *second* meeting—converting the initial face-to-face into the start of a true relationship with potential for growth, discovery, and mutual benefit. That's why handling the first meeting is tremendously important.

CASE STUDY: PETER STONE AND THE FIRST MEETING

Here's an exercise to test your first-meeting IQ. Read the following case study, which describes a fairly typical fund-raising scenario. It concludes with a few simple questions that will help you focus on what the case can tell you about what you should do—and not do—to make the first meeting more effective.

You are a fund-raiser for a nonprofit organization that is currently raising funds for a very important and potentially groundbreaking new project— we'll call it Project X. Naturally you're always eager to hear about possible new donors. So you're excited when board member John Brown calls.

"I had dinner with a close friend of mine last night," John explains. "His name is Peter Stone, and he's interested in hearing more about your organization." Like John, Peter is a partner in a private equity firm. The two men live near each other in suburban Connecticut; their families are close and often get together at dinner parties and on weekends.

John introduces you and Peter via email. Peter responds almost immediately and asks his assistant to find a time for the two of you to meet some time in the next few weeks. His assistant contacts you within a few hours, suggesting that you meet the following Monday at 11:00 a.m. in Peter's office.

You prep for the meeting by putting together a collection of materials to share with Peter, including a short video that you'll show him on your computer and a copy of your printed case for support—a document with details about Project X, data on the underlying problem, and evidence indicating that your strategy for tackling it is likely to be highly effective. You also chat with John Brown, asking him for any suggestions. John tells you a little about Peter's company, including some of its current investment strategies. "He's a great guy," John emphasizes, "a really warm, wonderful person. I'm sure he'll be very receptive to getting involved."

On the appointed day, you and Peter meet in his spacious, handsomely decorated office. You spend the first few minutes asking him questions and developing rapport. You find out that Peter has three kids, two in college and one in a private high school. You also discover that he shares your interest in fly fishing (there's a photo book on the subject on his coffee table), and the two of you compare notes on your favorite fishing spots. Peter is very friendly and outgoing.

When Peter asks you to tell him more about your organization, you share the six-minute video you've brought, which includes several great stories from the field as well as some compelling data. You also tell him about some other people he may know, in addition to John Brown, who are major supporters of and donors to your organization.

Finally, you tell Peter about Project X. You discuss straightforwardly the amount the project is expected to cost, and you suggest a dollar range for the gift you would like him to consider. (You've thought about this range in advance, talked about it with John Brown, and feel very comfortable about this approach.) Peter responds warmly. "I really appreciate your visiting me today," he says. "I think I need to talk this over with John, and with my wife, of course. But I'm definitely going to consider your request."

He asks you to leave the materials for him to review and invites you to call his office in a week or so. You return to your office, feeling optimistic about the new connection you have forged. You make a note in your calendar to call Peter's office early the following week, and settle back into your other duties.

Question: Upon review, how would you analyze the strategy you employed for your first meeting with Peter Stone? Considering each of the choices you made, what do you think you did right? What do you think you did wrong? What do you think is the likely outcome of this story?

You'll read our analysis on page 167 of this chapter.

SETTING THE TONE

In planning for the first meeting with a potential partner, as in so many areas of life, having a clear sense of purpose is crucial. Always remember that your purpose is not to enjoy some pleasant chitchat. Instead, you are making a very intentional effort to induce your prospective partner—and yourself—to take some real risks: the risk of being transparent, the risk of revealing something about oneself without knowing what the reaction will be, the risk of exposing one's frailties, disappointments, aspirations, and needs. The ultimate purpose: to find an area of common ground where you and your potential partner can work together on a project or cause in a way you'll both find meaningful, rewarding, and even transformational.

Launching a conversation with this goal is an art form that requires clarity of purpose, self-confidence, self-knowledge, and a genuine sense of concern about the well-being of the other. It also requires practice; as with any art form, you'll get better at it over time.

You can help ensure that the right tone and attitude are created and maintained throughout the conversation by paying close attention to certain important details.

Don't meet in his office. The office is the most commonly proposed place for a conversation between fund-raiser and potential donor—yet in many ways it is the *least* appropriate setting. The office is where people are thinking about business. They are surrounded by files, papers, computer screens, and other reminders of how busy they are. Their phones are ringing, and periodically the door will open for "just a quick question" from a colleague or associate. The distractions are simply too numerous and too persistent.

What's more, the psychological, social, and spiritual atmosphere of the office is rarely conducive to a truly open exchange. The office is a place where egos do battle—where power plays, turf battles, and jockeying for prestige are the daily fare. It's a place where we generally wear masks, and often armor. This is precisely the kind of mind-set you're hoping to break down and replace with an attitude of self-reflection, sharing, transparency, exploration, and growth. Achieving this in a wildly dissonant environment is incredibly difficult, no matter how gifted a communicator you may be.

So avoid the office. A visit to the potential partner's home is much better. As an alternative, invite him to a nearby restaurant for breakfast or a snack.

One of Jennifer's students likes to meet potential donors in a local coffee shop that happens to be frequented by clients of his organization. When they say hello, he introduces them to the donor—"This is Miguel, a student from Ecuador that we found an apartment for." This kind of unplanned, spontaneous encounter provides a more powerful endorsement for the work of the nonprofit than you'll find in any printed brochure.

Stick to a one-on-one meeting. When you've been given the name of a potential donor who is interested in learning more about your organization, arrange a one-on-one meeting. If the participation of another team member seems crucial—for example, if the person who has provided the referral feels it's important to attend the discussion—make it a two-on-one meeting at the very most. Avoid the temptation to bring along one, two, or more colleagues for support. It's harder to authentically connect with someone in a group of three (or more). The smaller the group, the greater the likelihood that the conversation will be informal, relaxed, spontaneous, and open—with the possibility of real human connection as the result.

Don't go in blind, but don't overprepare. Although you are meeting the potential donor for the first time, you know at least a few facts about him. The mutual acquaintance who provided the introduction probably offered a bit of background information; you may have been given a brief bio or resume, or perhaps located one on the Internet. (Jennifer prefers *not* to use resources such as Google to research people before a first meeting, feeling it reduces spontaneity and openness; many other fund-raisers swear by the practice, believing the information it yields can help stimulate conversation. You may want to experiment with both systems and decide which one works better for you.)

Use *"why" questions to cut through the noise of competing interests and create the possibility of open dialogue.* Whatever you may know about your new acquaintance—or whatever you may learn during the first few minutes of your conversation—your goal should be to get past the mere data points on a resume or fact sheet and transform those facts into springboards for exploring the inner human reality behind the facts, and for sharing a bit of what makes you tick as well. Questions that ask for more information can be a powerful tool for this kind of transformation. And "why" questions are crucial to understanding the nature of your new acquaintance's personal philanthropic journey:

> **"Why did you first get involved in supporting arts-education programs?"**
> **"Why do you have such a passion for children's rights?"**
> **"Why did you choose cancer research as the focus of most of your giving?"**

The more you know about the "why" behind a person's life choices, the easier it will be for you to really understand what shapes their thinking and behavior—and the closer the connection you may be able to forge between him, yourself, and a worthy cause that's appropriate for you both.

Describe your cause in positive terms. We have a friend who works for a non-profit that is focused on the environment. Recently, we asked her why she was so passionate about her work. Her answer surprised and thrilled us. She said, quite simply, "I am for a healthy and sustainable planet."

You may wonder, what's so thrilling about that answer? It seems logical enough, perhaps even predictable. But many people frame their personal passions in "against" terms: "I work on the environment because I'm against the degradation of the planet," or "I'm against unaccountable corporations," or "I'm against oil dependence." When we set up our conversation in terms of separate, opposing forces, we're tapping fear as our chief motivating factor. We stimulate anxiety that the "wrong side" will be victorious and the "right side" will lose.

This can be intensely motivating—for a while. But over time, humans tend to weary of endless struggle. Eventually we succumb to battle fatigue—or, in the case of our nonprofit work, what many experts refer to as "compassion fatigue." People lose interest and drift away toward different activities that promise more positive benefits.

A subtle shift from "against" to "for" is enormously powerful. Gandhi famously spoke of this in his talks and writings: "It's not that I'm against British rule. It's that I am for Indian independence." When we are clear that our goal is for something, we stop moving away from something negative and start moving toward something positive. This kind of movement has a whole different quality to it—a quality of gentleness, generosity, and light.

So when you meet with a potential partner for the first time, don't lead with a case for support that shows why your idea is better than someone else's or why the world will fall apart if your organization doesn't receive a donation today. Your goal should be to stir something inside them that is for something.

Don't rely on props. When we're nervous about a conversation, it's easy to use documents, slide shows, videos, and other presentation tools as crutches. Avoid this tendency. Sending a video link, PowerPoint deck, or report *as a follow-up* to your conversation can be effective, especially if the potential partner requests additional data. But sitting across a computer screen kills the flow of the conversation and stifles your attempt to create a real human connection. Instead, rely on your most powerful and effective presentation tool: your physical, mental, and emotional presence.

Most of us find it quite rare to experience a conversation with someone who is simply *there* with us, in every sense of the word. Give that gift in your first meeting, and you may find that it's received by your new acquaintance with a surprisingly profound sense of gratitude.

Name-drop only with a purpose. If your organization is lucky enough to have some prominent or highly regarded partners, you may wonder whether and how to drop their names into the conversation. Our advice is: Don't name-drop simply with the goal of impressing someone with the fame, power, or wealth of your partners. That's all too likely to turn off your new acquaintance; it smacks of boasting, self-aggrandizement, posturing, and manipulation, all of which are sure to reduce the possibility for a really open person-to-person encounter. It may even prompt a reaction opposite of what you intend. Rather than stimulating a desire to give on the part of the prospective donor, it may spur the thought, "These people are so well-connected they surely don't need my little contribution!"

Instead, use the names and stories of other partners to *model behavior and experiences for the potential partner*—to vividly illustrate how giving and participating has been rewarding and enriching for others, and to suggest that the potential partner is likely to find it equally meaningful.

It's hard to overstress the importance of setting a positive tone for your first meeting. Point the relationship in the right direction by following the suggestions we've offered, and you'll be amazed at how far you can travel together.

BANNING THE ELEPHANT:
A Path to Real Conversation

Perhaps the biggest obstacle we face in trying to build relationships is our failure to *really* listen to one another. If you're like most people, you've experienced the problem frequently. Even with friends and family members, conversation has a way of becoming rote.

One of the biggest reasons for the difficulty of true listening is the existence of "elephants in the room"—circumstances, issues, and ideas that loom large in the minds of one or both participants in the conversation but which, for one reason or another, are not generally acknowledged or openly discussed. (For an example or two, just think back to your last family gathering and consider the bits of shared history or conflict that everyone knew were not to be mentioned around the dinner table!)

In the case of a first meeting with a potential partner, both of you may be distracted by one of the most common fund-raising elephants. It's the question hanging in the air over both heads during most first meetings: "Is this conversation about fund-raising? Is everything we're going to talk about today just a courtly dance leading up to a request for money?"

The fact that money is such an emotionally fraught subject for most people helps to explain why this elephant is a particularly troublesome one. Many potential donors spend the entire meeting half-listening to whatever the fund-raiser says, using the rest of their mind to wonder, "When is she going to ask me for money? How much will she ask for? What should I say?" The longer the conversation lasts, the bigger and more distracting the elephant becomes in the donor's mind, which means that a large portion of your eloquent, moving, and fact-filled case for support goes unheard and uncomprehended. And if the first meeting ends without a request for a check, the elephant generally breaks loose from its seat in the corner of the room and takes over the entire conversation. The donor's memory of the meeting is dominated by the unanswered question, "Why didn't she ask me for some money? What was the point of the meeting?!"

Similarly, as fund-raisers, we are often distracted and anxious during a first meeting. The same elephant is to blame. Because we're uncertain and nervous about when to ask for a gift, how much to ask for, and what the likely response will be, we are also not listening to the potential donor with our whole selves. We aren't completely present. No wonder so many first meetings lead to disappointing results.

For this reason, we recommend you not ask for a financial commitment during a first meeting. And we suggest you open the conversation by clearing the elephant out of the room. The best way to achieve this is to say, right up front, "I'm not going to ask you for a gift today."

Once you get the question of a donation off the table, you can make some space at the beginning of the relationship to really listen, and for you and your potential partner to get to know each other.

BUT DO ASK FOR SOMETHING—INCLUDING A SECOND MEETING

Clearing the elephant from the room doesn't mean you shouldn't ask for anything at the first meeting. In fact, our recommendation is: *ask for something, either financial or nonfinancial, in every meeting with a partner or prospective partner.* The things you ask for may include:

- Networking contacts ("Who else do you know who would like to hear about our organization?")
- Ideas and insights ("What suggestions about our work do you have that we need to consider?")
- Technical skills ("We've been trying to solve problem X—do you have any advice for us, or can you connect us with someone who will?")
- In-kind gifts ("Can you or your company provide us with some of the goods and services we need to continue and expand our work?")

- Organizational resources ("Are there people or departments in your company who should get involved with our cause?")
- Time and talent ("Can I sign you up to participate in our next volunteer-training session?")
- Leadership ("Would you like to consider a role on our board, our advisory council, or another part of our team?")

The possibilities are limited only by your imagination and by the tastes, talents, and resources of your partner. Maybe you'll ask him or her to host a dinner or to introduce you to someone whom you've been wanting to meet. Maybe you'll request an endorsement message to appear on your organization's website or an interesting donation for a charity auction. Maybe you'll invite some ideas about how to improve the organization's communication efforts or a bit of advice about a lobbying effort you are planning.

It almost doesn't matter what you ask for—but get in the habit of asking for something. It strengthens your confidence when the time comes to ask for a financial donation (as we'll discuss in the next chapter), it creates a built-in opportunity to follow up with your new partner a few weeks later, and it helps establish a bond between the two of you that makes each additional commitment feel easier and more natural.

In addition, of course, as your first meeting comes to a close, you should ask for a second meeting. In most cases, the initial meeting will have been scheduled for a brief time. But if it has gone well, your new partner will be willing to offer a greater amount of time for a second meeting. We suggest wording your request for a second meeting approximately like this: "I'm so grateful for the time we've had together today. It seems there's a lot more for us to explore. Can we schedule another visit to go deeper into some of the topics we touched on this morning?"

A yes to one or more of these requests means that a new partnership has been launched—its future unknown, its potential unlimited.

CASE STUDY ANALYSIS:
PETER STONE AND THE FIRST MEETING

Many of the choices made in the Peter Stone case study (see pages 157–158) are ones typically employed by nonprofit fund-raisers in planning and conducting a first meeting. Unfortunately, they combine to produce a strategy that is likely to lead only to a superficial relationship rather than a true partnership. This, in turn, is likely to stimulate a merely transactional gift (or no gift at all) rather than a transformational one, as well as a smaller financial commitment.

Here are the mistakes made by the fund-raiser that are likely to create obstacles to a fully successful relationship:

- *Inadequate Preparatory Research* The fund-raiser in the case study had only a brief conversation with John Brown, the source of the referral. Instead, he should have asked John, "Tell me what you know about Peter," seeking clues about Peter's background, interests, personality, values, goals, and philanthropic mind-set. Advance research can significantly improve the odds of success of your first meeting.

- *Inappropriate Venue* As we've noted, the potential partner's office is a poor choice of location for a mission-oriented conversation. Rather than meeting with Peter in his office, the fund-raiser should have suggested a home visit or some neutral third site without distractions.

- *Overreliance on Supporting Materials* Showing a video and presenting written materials is generally an ineffective way to introduce the story of an organization. Instead, the fund-raiser should have used the power of a personal narrative to bring the mission to life and connect it to Peter's own story.

- *Failure to Establish a Personal Connection* In the case study, the fund-raiser exchanges a little small talk with Peter, then presents a sales pitch for the organization. Instead, he should have launched an open-ended conversation with a question like "Why are you interested in us?" The purpose is to invite an in-depth discussion of Peter's life experiences, goals, values, and aspirations. If the mission of the organization fits naturally into that context, the conversation will make that connection obvious.

- *Rushing to Ask for a Donation* Asking for a gift in a first meeting is almost always premature. Put yourself in the shoes of a prospective donor, who may have received a dozen requests for philanthropic funding this week. What makes *your* organization special enough to stand out from the pack? That question can only be answered on the basis of a deeper personal connection—which is why jumping straight to a request for a donation is just as big a mistake as delaying it needlessly.

- *Inadequate Follow-Up* In addition to calling the prospective donor in a week's time, the fund-raising should have capitalized on the meeting by sending an email or personal note to the other members of the board—prominently mentioning John Brown's role in making the introduction. This simple step is likely to inspire other board members to make referrals of their own.

FINDING MEANING IN EVERY CONVERSATION:
The SIM Challenge

When meeting with prospective partners, we urge you to leave behind the selling strategies, presentation techniques, and marketing methods you may have learned. Try to forget the tricks you may have developed in past experiences as a fund-raiser. In fact, we propose that you even shed the very role of "fund-raiser" and try instead to think of yourself as simply a human being sharing a bit of yourself with another human being. The goal is not to convince him, impress him, or manipulate him in any way, but merely to connect with him on some genuine emotional and psychological level.

Here is a simple strategy that will help you make the transition.[10] It's an exercise called the SIM challenge, which we believe can add to the value of every meeting you participate in. As you leave any meeting, ask yourself:

- S: What surprised you?
- I: What inspired you?
- M: What moved you?

If you can't answer at least one of these questions, you probably weren't listening. Instead, perhaps you were selling—yourself, your organization, or the worthy cause you represent. Or perhaps you were worrying, distracted, or trying too hard to guide the conversation in a particular, preordained direction. Whatever the underlying cause, you were not truly present in the encounter, and, as a result, you may have missed something very important—both for you and for your partner in the conversation.

Getting into the habit of thinking about the SIM questions before every meeting is a great way of sensitizing yourself to the hidden meanings just below the surface of every conversation.

---

10 The SIM challenge presented here is adapted from the teachings of Dr. Rachel Naomi Remen, Clinical Professor of Family and Community Medicine at the University of California, San Francisco, School of Medicine and director of the innovative UCSF course "The Healer's Art."

FOOD FOR THOUGHT

Follow-up questions and activities designed to help you get the most out of this chapter:

- Think about the last conversation you had with a prospective donor or partner. Try to recall the conversation in as much detail as possible. Then apply the SIM challenge to the experience: What surprised you? What inspired you? What moved you? In each case, try to explain why you were surprised, inspired, or moved. If none of these three responses applies, try to consider why. What was your focus during the conversation? Do you see what you can do differently the next time you participate in a similar discussion to help facilitate a more open, deeper connection between you and your conversational partner?

- Make a list of potential donors or partners whom you have not yet met. Depending on the number of recent referrals or contacts you've received, the list may be short (just two or three names) or more extensive (between five and ten names, perhaps). For each name on the list, make a basic plan for an effective first meeting using the techniques from this chapter. Decide on an appropriate location and a time that will permit for uninterrupted, informal conversation. If you wish, conduct some simple research to identify a few key pieces of background information about the potential partner. Think about the kinds of "why" questions you may want to use to learn more about the thinking and behavior of the potential partner, as well as the kinds of information about yourself and your organization that you may want to discuss during the conversation. When you're ready, make a call to the potential partner to arrange a first conversation. Then enjoy it!

7

THE ASK

*Wrong and Right Ways
to Say "Join Us"*

If you want to build a ship,

don't drum up people together

to collect wood and don't assign

them tasks and work, but rather

teach them to long for the

endless immensity of the sea.

—Antoine de Saint-Exupéry

The innovative tools we've been describing for establishing strong connections between partners and causes can go a long way toward making the job of fund-raising easier and more effective than ever before. But one traditional element of fund-raising remains unchanged: the necessity of asking for the gift, whether it takes the form of a financial donation or a contribution of time, talent, connections, or any other resource.

The Ask is the moment of truth that many nonprofit professionals and partners find most difficult to face.

There are several psychological and emotional reasons for the reluctance of so many people to confront the challenge of The Ask (see the sidebar below). But overcoming this natural reluctance is crucially important. Failure to elicit the first gift is one of the biggest obstacles to creating a meaningful, lasting partnership.

This chapter will present some very concrete, specific advice that every fund-raiser can benefit from when asking for support. Who knows—you may even find yourself saying, as some of our students now do, "I *love* fund-raising—including The Ask!"

THE TERRORS OF "THE ASK"

Here are five of the most common psychological and emotional reasons for dreading The Ask. Which of these haunts *your* dreams the night before the big meeting?

- *Societal Taboos Associated with Discussing Money* We live in an era of unprecedented frankness about many topics, but money and personal finances continue to be loaded topics. Many people were raised to avoid public conversations about money. No wonder so many are uncomfortable asking relative strangers for money.
- *Fear of Rejection* Asking someone for something is about putting yourself on the line—exposing yourself to the psychological pain of a no. It's easy to tell yourself not to take rejection per-

sonally, but actually responding with such dispassionate logic is tremendously difficult.

- ***Myths about "Salesmanship"*** Many nonprofit leaders think of fund-raising as a form of salesmanship, with all the negative connotations that word implies. The common image of the salesperson (cynical rather than idealistic, manipulative rather than cooperative) clashes harshly with their self-image.

- ***Power Imbalance*** Especially in our egalitarian society, most people dread the idea of being in the role of supplicant, begging for help from another who is wealthier, in control, and more powerful. Unfortunately, many nonprofit leaders feel this way when requesting support—especially when the person at the other end of the dialogue is a well-to-do individual.

- ***Embarrassment about "Being in Need"*** We admire people and organizations that "pay their own way," that have "lifted themselves by their bootstraps," that "stand on their own two feet." The implication is that there is something embarrassing or shameful about asking for help. This can be especially troubling for nonprofit professionals who are effectively raising resources to cover operating expenses, which can feel uncomfortably like begging for one's own salary.

MENTAL SHIFT:

Overcoming the Psychological Barriers to Asking

Let's consider each of the five psychological and emotional stumbling blocks listed in the sidebar, and how each can be overcome through a shift in perspective.

Societal Taboos Associated with Discussing Money Yes, it can be uncomfortable to talk with a relative stranger about money. This is one of the many reasons it's important that conversations about philanthropy not center on money. The focus should be on the mission and on how carrying out that mission can bring satisfaction to everyone involved.

This implies (among other things) that money should never be the only thing you ask for. Remember that other resources are equally important, and in some cases even more challenging to obtain. Broaden the terms of the conversation—as you should already be doing in focusing on the mission at large, and the many ways of supporting it, rather than the single act of writing a check. Ask about the many other steps your new supporter can take to launch a creative partnership with your organization: hosting a dinner, providing introductions to friends, or offering pro bono services from his or her business, for example.

Fear of Rejection No one likes to hear a no. Luckily, there are many ways to mitigate the psychological pain associated with the experience. One is to deploy a set of proven tools for converting a no into a maybe and ultimately into a yes. We'll be providing you with these tools a little later in this chapter.

It's important to jar your own mind free from its habitual attachment to the yes/no, win/lose, success/failure dichotomies. The key question after a meeting with a potential partner should be not "Did I get a check?" but rather "Have we made a fruitful connection?" Both work and life get richer and more rewarding when we stop slotting every experience into a box labeled "success" or "failure."

Myths about "Salesmanship" Always remember: as a nonprofit professional or partner, you are not "selling" anything. You are helping your partners meet their philanthropic objectives in an open and collaborative way. Asking for the gift is not about "selling" something but about establishing an open-ended, mutually rewarding relationship that will benefit everyone involved and, ideally, deepen over time.

When you walk into the meeting with prospective donor, you are, of course, hoping for something—and that "something" may well include financial support. But the prospective donor, too, is hoping for something—most often for an encounter with a new corner of the world that offers new possibilities for self-discovery, growth, satisfaction, and fulfillment. So both sides have something valuable to offer—and if the resulting partnership is a successful one, both will obtain what they're hoping for, and much more besides.

Power Imbalance It's easy to fall into the trap of feeling like a supplicant when you speak to a potential donor. The sense of a power imbalance may be exacerbated by particular circumstances—for example, when a relatively junior staff member from a nonprofit organization calls on a prosperous individual as a potential donor. In such a case, all the markers of power in our society—age, status, experience, wealth, power—tilt lopsidedly in one direction.

For the nonprofit representative, the key to escaping this kind of power dynamic is remembering that your job is connecting people to activities, organizations, and opportunities that are fascinating, mind-expanding, and transformative. And that means that the agenda for your conversation is not, "Can I convince Ms. Successful to give us a little money from her huge stockpile?" but rather, "How can the two of us find ways of being together that will be creative, positive, and mutually rewarding?" That agenda places the two of you where you both belong—on an equal footing, rather than one up and one down.

Nick Ehrmann of Blue Engine talked with us about the crucial importance of this mind-set of equality:

I used to think that the most important thing was fund-raising tactics. But over time I've learned something unexpected—that the way I was asking the world for help was actually counterproductive.

I was always conscious that other people could help make Blue Engine successful by giving things like money and time and energy. What I didn't think about was the incredibly valuable assets that Blue Engine and I had to give back. I'm talking about assets like proximity to the cause of education reform, a deep knowledge of the problem, a community of dedicated team members, and an opportunity for meaningful engagement—extraordinary resources that people who care about education reform desperately want to access.

So the donors I approach have tremendous assets, and Blue Engine has other amazing assets—and the point is to get them together. *The relationship is one of equals, of peers*—not of a supplicant with a tin cup begging for help. It's a relationship based on equality of mutual exchange and learning that sets the stage for meaningful, sustained information sharing and the growth of healthy partnerships.

Recognizing this has been tremendously liberating and empowering for me. And it has also helped me recognize how dysfunctional the traditional supplicant posture is. You see, if someone feels that you're approaching them with a tin cup in your hand, it makes you seem small while they are big. And that's a very confusing situation—because after all, no one wants to follow someone who is small into battle. They want to follow a leader who is big—a passionate, engaged peer.

If you find yourself feeling small when approaching potential partners, you need to make the same mental shift Nick Ehrmann did. Recognize the value of what you have to offer, and escape the unhealthy power imbalance that is holding you back.

Embarrassment about "Being in Need" Don't be ashamed of needing resources for your cause. Remember the biblical adage "The workman deserves his wage." It applies even to workers in the nonprofit world! It's important to talk about the resources needed to fulfill the mission—resources that include ideas, time, energy, talent, connections, networks, and, naturally, money. When The Ask is put into this broader context—as just one of the many tools we employ in the quest for personal and social growth—it loses much of its power to intimidate, embarrass, and stifle conversation.

YOU ARE NOT "WASTEFUL OVERHEAD"

There is a false but very common assumption that, in a nonprofit organization, overhead (which includes employee salaries) is always bad. It's a belief that is unfortunately fostered by various "charity rating" systems that are based on the notion that the mark of an effective nonprofit is the smallest possible overhead percentage. The implication is that, in the nonprofit world, overhead is *by definition* wasteful—which relegates everyone who makes a living working for a nonprofit organization to the status of "wasteful overhead"! How's that for a kick in the ego?

This assumption leads to the starvation for resources from which most nonprofits suffer, as experts Thomas J. Tierney and Joel Fleishman note:

> Suppose we all decided to fly on the airline that reported the lowest maintenance costs? Or went to the hospitals with the oldest, most depreciated equipment? In many circumstances, consumers gladly pay for more overhead if it delivers value to them. Nonprofits, too, have good overhead and bad overhead . . . and yet we consistently fall into the trap of believing that nonprofits can deliver A-level results with a malnourished team.[11]

Don't buy in to this misconception. As Dan Pallotta, author of the 2010 book *Uncharitable*, points out, the "overhead = bad" fallacy deprives nonprofits of necessary resources in several distinct ways:

- Employee compensation is far lower in most nonprofit organizations than in comparable for-profit businesses.
- Funds for advertising and marketing are much less in the nonprofit world (averaging just around 2 percent of revenues) than in the for-profit world.
- Funders are far more willing to underwrite worthwhile risks on the part of for-profit business than with most nonprofits.
- Funders have longer time horizons when investing in for-profit companies than when donating to nonprofit organizations, which means that nonprofits are expected to show impressive results more quickly than their for-profit counterparts.

If you are a nonprofit leader, employee, or partner, you need to internalize the lessons offered by these nonprofit experts. You need money (as well

---

11 Thomas J. Tierney and Joel Fleishman, *Give Smart: Philanthropy That Gets Results* (2011).

as other resources) to pursue your goals, just as you would if you were an entrepreneur or manager of a for-profit company. That's nothing to be embarrassed or apologetic about—especially since, in exchange for your paycheck, you are providing people with something priceless: the opportunity to live lives that are deeper and more rewarding through their connection with your cause. (And, of course, if you are a part-time or volunteer supporter of a nonprofit cause, you should recognize the importance of providing financial security to the professionals you work with, and refuse to feel embarrassed about soliciting funds for that purpose.)

If an organization in the nonprofit sector is going to grow in size, reach, and effectiveness the way for-profit companies do, there needs to be an investment in leadership. It's time for a fearless conversation about this issue—which has to start with a fresh, more realistic attitude on the part of nonprofit leaders themselves.

WHEN TO MAKE "THE ASK"

Rethinking your mind-set about asking for support will carry you a long way toward making The Ask a much less formidable obstacle than it might otherwise appear. But it also helps a lot to have a number of specific, proven techniques to employ when tackling The Ask itself. In the next several pages, we'll share some approaches that have worked well for us and for our students.

Let's start with the issue of timing. It's one that Jennifer had to wrestle with from an early stage in her career. When she was a new fund-raiser, one of the first things her boss told her was that the average cultivation period for a gift was twelve to eighteen months. "Take your time," he said. "Get to know people. Get them fully convinced about what we do. Then make The Ask."

This sounded reasonable to Jennifer's very green ears. So she planned her strategy accordingly. In those early years, she would visit with people a half dozen times or more before ever making an Ask. Over the years, though, she discovered that waiting this long to ask is not only unnecessary, it's counterproductive.

The fact is that nonprofit fund-raisers generally wait too long to invite people to join with them. Often they wait so long that asking feels awkward and may even, in extreme cases, become impossible. When you ask someone to partner with you in a concrete way—whether by donating funds or through some other kind of contribution—you raise the quality of the dialogue and elevate both the relationship and the work you will do together. The sooner you can make this happen, the better it is for both parties.

Here is a good rule of thumb to follow: *If you don't know what to ask for— either a specific sum of money or some other contribution—it's a good indication that you don't really know the prospective partner, which means it's too soon for The Ask.*

In most cases, two or three conversations are enough to establish a solid foundation of rapport, to switch on the light of urgency inside someone, and to make The Ask.

This philosophy runs counter to the conventional wisdom in the world of nonprofit management. But here's why we're convinced that a relatively quick move toward The Ask makes sense for everybody.

First, it's not the case that people get committed to a cause and then make a financial contribution. That cause-and-effect sequence sounds logical. But experience shows that the cause-and-effect sequence really works in the opposite direction: *people give first, and then develop their commitment.* It's *after* they write the first check that they start to get involved in a meaningful way.

Therefore, it only makes sense to go for The Ask relatively early in your relationship. A financial contribution establishes a kind of foundation upon which a larger structure of commitment and involvement can be built. The sooner you put the foundation in place, the sooner both of you can get started on envisioning and erecting your dream house.

Second, *prospective partners want to be asked*. They wouldn't be talking with you otherwise. People don't need to understand every last nuance of your organization to make a first commitment. Delaying the inevitable request simply sows seeds of doubt, frustration, and annoyance.

Jennifer explains, "I've talked with lots of philanthropists over the years who describe their encounters with fund-raisers this way: 'I've met with Jim from my kid's school five times already, and he still hasn't asked me for anything. I'm confused! The fact that I continue meeting with him clearly implies that I'm interested in being supportive, but I'm getting tired of taking meetings where we don't get down to what's really needed.'"

Nice as it may be to imagine prospective donors asking you first, they're not going to do that. They want to be asked—especially when their energy and enthusiasm are at their highest, which is usually fairly early in the relationship. (Think back to your last big love affair—wasn't the sense of romance and excitement near its peak on the second or third date rather than a few months later?) People want to commit. So set aside your anxieties and make The Ask when the time is ripe. Dawdling serves no purpose.

THE HEART OF "THE ASK":
Your Story of Self, Us, and Now

We've talked about *when* to make The Ask. Now, *how* do you go about doing it? Are there more and less effective ways to pop the question?

Many fund-raisers assume that The Ask should be centered on the "case for support"—the logical, data-based argument for the unique value of your work and the social benefits it provides. The case for support is important—but it should *not* be at the core of The Ask. Remember, there are more than one and a half million nonprofit organizations in the United States.[12] Each and every one is convinced it has a clear and compelling case for support—a serious problem that demands solution, a plausible approach developed by experts, and a collection of convincing data to support the argument. And if your prospective donor is like most philanthropically minded people, he has probably heard a pitch for support from every one of those millions of U.S. nonprofits—or at least feels as if he has.

So trying to persuade people based on facts alone is not going to be enough to motivate them. What sets your organization apart from all the others is the one thing you have that's unique: your story.

We've already spoken (in Chapter 2) about the special power of narrative to bring ideas to life, to connect people heart to heart, and to light the fire of possibility within the minds of an audience. In making your request, narrative is the single most important weapon in your arsenal. *Lead with story and use facts, information, logic, and data to support the story.*

When your prospective partners see themselves as a vital part of a compelling story, The Ask feels effortless—not because you've sold them on an idea, but because they can envision an exciting, enriching future where they are partners with your organization. With your guidance, they will write themselves into your narrative. They'll be on fire to give their money, time, talents, and energy so that they can play a supporting role in your powerful and ever-unfolding story.

If you're having difficulty keeping your story focused, consider adopting the structure designed by Marshall Ganz, as we outlined it in Chapter 2:

---

12   See http://grantspace.org/Tools/Knowledge-Base/Funding-Research/Statistics/Number-of-nonprof its-in-the-U.S.

- *A Story of Self* This portion of your narrative describes how and why you became involved in the mission of your organization. Be clear, specific, and as vivid as possible in painting a word picture of the experiences that opened your eyes to the importance of the cause and ignited the passion that drives your work. It's paradoxical but true: The more deeply personal, heartfelt, and uniquely individual your story, the greater the chance that it will conjure a powerful connection with the hearts of your listeners.

- *A Story of Us* This is the part of the conversation when it will be natural and appropriate to talk about the unique strengths and capabilities of your organization. You need to be able to explain these in a way that will make clear why your team is especially suited to tackling the mission you've chosen—and why you need and want partners to continue and extend the work. Explore what everyone in this special circle has in common and the individual gifts they bring to the project. Ideally, you'd like to leave a prospective donor with the feeling, "I have a unique role to play in making this vision come true."

- *A Story of Now* Explain how the world will be different—and better—when you succeed. Once again, use specific examples of how individual lives will be transformed by the work you are doing. It's not very logical, but most people find the story of a single person far more compelling than a collection of statistics demonstrating how thousands or even millions of people will benefit from a particular program. Then, having excited your listeners with a vision of the kind of change you hope to create, you can clinch the deal by simply inviting them to join you through some concrete, specific behavior (whether a financial gift or some other contribution)—and to do it today.

One important caveat about your "story of now": many nonprofits try to encourage prompt action by pointing to horrific emergencies that demand an immediate response: a devastating tsunami, a raging epidemic, a war that has created hundreds of thousands of refugees. This kind of "now" appeal can work well, as demonstrated by the millions of gifts generated in cases of such emergences. But relying on a sense of external urgency usually doesn't work as a *long-term* motivator. In a world of instantaneous global communication, we're all aware that there is *always* some disaster under way, or in the making, somewhere in the world. The result is that compassion fatigue quickly sets in: We become inured to the images of suffering on our TV sets and eventually tune them out. Furthermore, if you infuse your "story of now" with a feeling of despair—"The world is coming to an end if we don't act immediately!"—it will often discourage people from wanting to participate; after all, we are all naturally drawn to hope and possibility rather than gloom and defeatism.

Instead, strive to focus on the *positive potential* latent in a timely response. If the problem you're addressing is at a tipping point, where action now can produce cascading long-term benefits, say so! If you're pioneering an exciting new approach that may lead to a much-needed breakthrough, explain it! Narratives like these have the potential to create a hopeful sense of urgency *inside* the listener, which is far more effective than one that is imposed from without and driven by anxiety.

THE LANGUAGE YOU CHOOSE

Even the exact words you use when making The Ask can dramatically impact your effectiveness and the results you'll achieve.

As a young fund-raiser, Jennifer was taught that the most effective way to ask for a financial contribution was to use these words: "Would you like to consider a gift of $X?" Over the years, as her approach has shifted from sales-focused to partnership-focused, she discovered that this line was off the mark. She now says instead: "We would like you to consider a gift of $X."

The change from "Would you consider" to "We would like you to consider" may seem insignificant. But the subtle alteration in language gives my invitation a confidence and authority that it didn't have before. Rather than *asking* the potential partner a question (to which he can answer yes or no, whichever he prefers), Jennifer is *asserting* what she wants (and tacitly challenging the potential partner to respond appropriately).

For similar reasons, we recommend against using the word *help* to define what you are asking for, as in a sentence like, "I hope you will be able to help us with this project." This formula subtly defines you and your organization as needy, weak, insecure—in a one-down position in relation to the donor, who is perceived as one-up on you. One of Jennifer's students uses an alternative formula that sends a much better message: "I hope this project is something you and I can work on together." The language here conveys that the organization and the donor are partners, sharing their efforts on behalf of a common cause—which is both a more emotionally appealing depiction of the relationship and a more accurate one.

When requesting money, we also recommend asking for a specific amount, not a range. Obviously the donor is free to give whatever amount she chooses, so my request for a specific sum has no element of compulsion in it. But requesting a definite amount is more assertive and less hesitant than suggesting a range, and in our experience it generally yields a larger commitment.

Finally—and this may be one of the most difficult recommendations we'll offer—after making The Ask, *be silent*. Let the prospective donor absorb your invitation, think about its meaning, and seriously consider its potential impact on him. You may feel an almost irresistible impulse to obliterate the silence with needless chatter or, worse yet, a quasi-apologetic retraction ("Of course, if you don't feel comfortable with a gift of that kind, I understand").

Don't yield to that impulse. Instead, just let the silence be.

You've made an important request that deserves to be taken seriously. So listen generously, and give the concept some space in which to flower.

If you've laid the groundwork thoughtfully, you may be pleasantly surprised by the response.

WHEN THE ANSWER IS NO

Of course, even if you've engaged thoughtfully and effectively at every stage of The Ask, you aren't in ultimate control of the outcome. There are times when the answer is no. It's disappointing, of course. But what really matters is how you react to the no.

One way of reacting—a very common one—is to withdraw, turtlelike, into your shell. It's understandable. Rejection hurts, and even if you know that the decision isn't a personal matter, it's hard not to take it personally. You may wonder whether you did something wrong—whether you said something inappropriate or even offensive to turn off the prospective donor.

You may feel embarrassed or humiliated about having "wasted" your time and energy on a hopeless cause. You may start to doubt whether you can ever succeed as a nonprofit fund-raiser or manager; you may even entertain broader doubts about your self-worth in general.

These reactions are natural—and highly counterproductive. Now is not the time to waste energy on hurt feelings. You want to find out the reasons for the no and discover what, if anything, you can do to reverse it.

FOUR POWERFUL FOLLOW-UP QUESTIONS

As a general rule, there are four reasons why potential partners may say no (or "I have to think more about this," which is really just a slightly obscured variation on no).[13] To determine which reason applies in a particular case, there are four probing follow-up questions you can use. The goal of these four questions is to never leave the meeting without understanding the *real* issue behind the no—which, in turn, will enable you to respond to that answer in a way that is genuine, meaningful, and helpful to your would-be partner.

Follow-Up Question #1 "It seems as if you like our organization and appreciate the work we are doing. Is that true?" Most prospective donors will answer yes to this question. Use your instincts to gauge the depth and sincerity of that answer. If you sense it is a lukewarm, halfhearted, or insincere yes, you may want to follow up with a tactfully probing question

---

13 This four-part analysis of reasons for saying no is based in part on the work of Jerold Panas, author of many books on fund-raising, including *Mega Gifts* (2003) and *Asking* (2009).

designed to test that feeling; for example, you might ask, "Are you thinking that our organization may not be a good fit for your needs and interests at this time?" If, on reflection, your prospective partner has decided he simply doesn't see a fulfilling role for himself in your organization, it may be best to shift the conversation to other topics—such as whether there are different ways that the two of you can connect that will be more mutually beneficial.

Follow-Up Question #2 "We've been talking about our Project X and the kind of support we need to make it a reality. Do you need to know more about the project?" If the potential partner seems to have a sincere interest in and appreciation for your organization, then the problem may be a lack of clarity about the specific project or program you've sought to connect him to. It's possible the prospective donor doesn't have enough information on the potential impact of his gift and the urgency of it. If you sense this may be the case, ask straightforwardly what is unclear or not compelling. Remember, philanthropy is learned behavior, and your job is to play the role of teacher, mentor, and guide. It's okay if a donor needs more time and information to consider the gift decision—you want thoughtful partners rather than impulsive ones. But don't let an information gap become a permanent obstacle. Listen thoughtfully to any questions and objections that your prospective donor may have, and work together on moving the gift toward closure.

Follow-Up Question #3 "Is the donation amount I've suggested right for you?" If this is the problem, resolving it may be relatively simple. People are often flattered if you ask for an excessive sum, unless they feel you've presumed upon a scanty relationship in a way they find offensive. In that case, back off tactfully—apologize if necessary—and ask the donor straightforwardly to propose a more appropriate figure. Of course, if you are told (or if you sense) that a financial gift of any kind may be problematic for this donor, you can easily shift the conversation to the equally important nonfinancial contributions that may be more appropriate. (We listed many of them on pages 165–166.)

Follow-Up Question #4 "Is the timing of a financial donation an issue for you? If so, what if we spread it out over X years, or defer your first payment until X? I'd like to come up with a scheduling strategy that will make it work for you." When the reason for hesitation is timing, it may tie into the amount you've suggested. Very often, a donor actually wants to make the monetary gift you've asked for but feels unable to finance it all in cash. This is where planned giving can play a role. It's a useful tool to help your partners reach their philanthropic goals. For example, you may want to ask, "Do you know that your gift can be financed over several years? Or that you can make a gift of securities as well as cash? Did you know that you can make a gift to fund the operating cost of Project X for a number of years and endow the gift permanently as a bequest in your will?" There are many options available, each with specific financial, legal, and tax implications. You'll want to educate yourself about them so you can teach your donors whatever they need to know.

The key is not to overreact to a no. In most cases, a no is not the end of a relationship but rather the beginning of a new phase of the conversation.

FOOD FOR THOUGHT

Follow-up questions and activities designed to help you get the most out of this chapter:

- Is The Ask a source of anxiety for you? If so, why? Spend half an hour free-writing about your thoughts and feelings regarding The Ask—the memories, associations, emotions, assumptions, thoughts, reactions, and beliefs it evokes. The next time you have a significant conversation scheduled with a prospective donor, you may be able to say to yourself, "Oh, there are those thoughts and feelings again," and then simply *observe* them and *let them pass* rather than allowing them to control you.

- What kinds of things have you asked potential partners for *other than* money? Possibilities include contacts, ideas, technical skills, in-kind gifts, and so on. Have you tailored The Ask so that it is designed to lead to a deep, long-term relationship rather than a one-time financial transaction?

- Try writing a narrative recounting an unsuccessful or unsatisfying experience with The Ask from your own life. Wait one day. Then write a second narrative recounting a successful, rewarding such experience from your life. Put both documents aside for a few days to allow any emotional reactions to subside. Then read and compare the two narratives. What similarities and differences do you notice? Can you define how the choices you made led to such varying outcomes? Are there any lessons you can take away from this comparative analysis that may be useful the next time you are preparing for The Ask?

- Recall the last time you made a request that resulted in a no. Can you identify the obstacles that stood in the way of a yes? Depending on the answer to this question, you may want to consider reopening the dialogue with that prospective partner, in search of a more rewarding result for both parties.

8

THE JEFFERSONIAN DINNER AND OTHER COMMUNITY-BUILDING TOOLS

Surely only boring people went
in for conversations consisting
of questions and answers.
The art of true conversation
consisted in the play of minds.

—*Ved Mehta,* All for Love

We've discussed how to make your first connection with an individual prospective partner, as well as how to navigate the sometimes choppy waters of The Ask—the request for an initial commitment from a person who is ready to become your partner. Now we'll move on to describe some of the tools we've developed for connecting groups of people with important shared causes. Perhaps the most powerful and universally relevant of these tools is something we call the Jeffersonian Dinner.[14]

14　Those interested in a quick oral introduction to the concept of the Jeffersonian Dinner might enjoy Jeff Walker's TED talk on the topic, available at www.youtube.com/watch?v=HuAT0YHQz94.

The Jeffersonian Dinner can be a great way to launch the creation of a new cause-centered community. It can also help you to expand the network of individuals connected with an existing community. And although money is not the central focus of the evening, it's likely that, in the end, a Jeffersonian Dinner can activate far more resources than such traditional fundraising events as the annual gala.

So what is a Jeffersonian Dinner? To introduce the concept, we invite you step into a time machine. . . .

Imagine being invited to a dinner in 1819 at Monticello, the elegant Virginia home of Thomas Jefferson—president, scientist, farmer, connoisseur, scholar, and author of the Declaration of Independence. Around his table, you'd encounter some of the leading spirits of the age, men and women steeped in politics, literature, the arts, the sciences, theology, history, mores, and manners. Mr. Jefferson invited these people because he found them intriguing and delightful to spend a stimulating evening with. And an evening such as this was also a prime source of education both for Mr. Jefferson himself and for the guests around the table, all of whom were engaged citizens, eager to share and debate the varied ideas that would shape the fortunes and spur the development of their rapidly growing young nation.

This was the original Jeffersonian Dinner. Starting with dinners held for years in Monticello itself during the time when Jeff served as chairman of the Thomas Jefferson Foundation, we've turned Jeffersonian Dinners into opportunities to connect people and foment discussions about many different topics. As a result, vibrant networks and a host of passionate connections have been created around a host of important causes.

A DINNER PARTY
WITH A TWIST

For a Jeffersonian Dinner, approximately twelve individuals, some of whom may already know one another but others who do not, gather in a home, a private dining room, or another quiet location for an evening of food and shared conversation with a purpose. The dinner is often organized under the auspices of a particular nonprofit organization, and the attendees may include one or more individuals who are somehow associated with that organization—as staffers, board members, donors, or partners. However, the dinner is usually hosted by someone not directly affiliated with the nonprofit group—for example, a friend of a friend who may have access to a suitable dining room and is willing to provide the appropriate hospitality.

The attendees generally include people with no past link to the group, chosen because they are likely to be interested in the group's mission, have supported other related causes, or have background knowledge and connections that will enable them to contribute to an interesting dialogue about the work. Thus, the guests at a dinner organized by a nonprofit dedicated to education reform might include a professor of education from a local college, a veteran high school teacher, a producer of educational videos, a parent who is an active member of her local school board, the education reporter from the local newspaper, and the founder of a nearby charter school. There should be no dominant individual who will serve as the focal point or "star" of the evening. The dinner invitation includes a request for a brief written biography of the attendee. These bios are emailed to the participants a day or two before the dinner, so those who've never met before will have at least a general sense of the identities and interests of their dinner companions.

Unlike a fund-raising event, there's no formal presentation about a cause, an organization, or a social problem, nor is there a pitch for contributions or memberships. The purpose of the Jeffersonian Dinner is to build a sense of community and partnership around a shared interest or theme. (As you might imagine, the theme is generally related to the work of the non-profit organization on whose behalf the gathering is being held.)

Most important, the dinner should be held in a setting where everyone in attendance can easily participate in a single conversation. Unlike the typical dinner party, guests are not encouraged to engage in one-on-one dialogues with their partners on either side. Instead, everything that is said should be directed to the entire group, just as Thomas Jefferson himself ordained. The following description of dinner at Jefferson's White House is from *The First Forty Years of Washington Society* (1806) by author Margaret Bayard Smith:

> At his usual dinner parties the company seldom or ever exceeded fourteen, including himself and his secretary. The invitations were not given promiscuously, or as has been done of late years, alphabetically, but his guests were generally selected in reference to their tastes, habits and suitability in all respects, which attention had a wonderful effect in making his parties more agreeable, than dinner parties usually are; this limited number prevented the company's forming little knots and carrying on in undertones separate conversations, a custom so common and almost unavoidable in a large party. At Mr. Jefferson's table the conversation was general; every guest was entertained and interested in whatever topic was discussed.

To launch the conversation at a Jeffersonian Dinner, a preannounced question is used to elicit personal feelings, stories, and experiences relevant to the evening's theme. Some samples:

- For a dinner focused on the life-changing potential of philanthropy: "Describe a gift you made that produced a real difference."
- For a dinner about education reform: "Who is your favorite teacher of all time?"
- For a dinner related to plans for a new film center: "What movie is your favorite guilty pleasure, and why?"
- For a dinner related to technology: "What technology innovation in the last ten years has most changed your life?"
- For dinner about bringing music to schoolkids in New Orleans: "What's the first record you ever owned?"
- For a dinner about collaborative philanthropy: "Give an example of a time when you worked collaboratively with others successfully to have an impact."
- For a dinner about nonprofit leadership: "Who do you know who is a good role model for nonprofit leaders, and why is that person a good choice?"

Crafting the right initial question for a Jeffersonian Dinner is important. It must be designed to bring forth stories (rather than, for example, canned opinions, theoretical discussions, or examples drawn from the media). Avoid a question that can be answered with a yes or no, but choose one that can be answered in around two minutes. The goal is to enhance the potential for personal connections among the guests, as well as a personal connection with the evening's theme.

For example, here is an initial question that proved to be too cerebral when it was used to kick off a Jeffersonian Dinner hosted by supporters of a university dedicated to the arts: "What's a design idea that made a difference in your life?" For the average person (not someone engaged professionally in the world of art), the notion of a "design idea" is a bit too abstract and too difficult to connect in a visceral way to everyday life. A more effective alternative might have been a question such as, "Describe a work of art that changed your mind or opened up your perspective about something." Almost everyone has experienced at least one painting, sculpture, building, or other artwork that has altered his or her perceptions in some way, and this question invites personal stories about such encounters.

After each attendee has had a chance to answer the thematic question, open conversation ensues, gently guided by a moderator whose purpose is to channel the energies of the participants and challenge them to consider how they might begin to work together in some way that is connected to the issue of the evening. When the moment is right, the moderator introduces a follow-up question. This is the first time in the evening when a direct connection between the gathering and the nonprofit organization behind the dinner is likely to be broached. For example, when Jeff hosts Jeffersonian Dinners related to the work of Millennium Promise, he often uses a follow-up question like, "Do you think we can end poverty in our time? Why or why not?" or "What do you think might happen if we had a million community health care workers on the planet?"

Moderating a Jeffersonian Dinner is an art in itself. The exact nature of the follow-up questions you ask may vary depending on the specific goal of the dinner (as discussed in the next section of this chapter). One effective approach is for the moderator to gently guide participants along the pathway of the public narrative, as described by Marshall Ganz. That is, after each attendee has had a chance to describe one or more personal experiences related to the theme of the evening (a "story of self"), the moderator can ask how these experiences are connected with the interests of the entire group (a "story of us") and then with the work of the nonprofit organization that has sponsored the dinner (a "story of now"). It's an effective structure because it works!

Finally, as the time for concluding the dinner approaches, everyone in attendance is asked how he or she plans to follow up on the evening's discussion. There's no pressure to respond in a particular way. (And there's certainly no intention to elicit donations or pledges in support of the non-profit organization.) One participant may offer a response as simple as "I intend to learn and think more about the topics we've discussed." Another may make a specific commitment growing out of the evening's conversation: "I'll be calling Susan, whom I met for the first time this evening, to find out more about her work and to learn whether my company might be able to support her in some way." And occasionally the follow-up promises include the birth of a major new philanthropic commitment. Every response, from the most modest to the most ambitious, is entirely acceptable.

In any case, virtually every Jeffersonian Dinner we've hosted or heard about has generated a host of informal connections, networking opportunities, and follow-up conversations among dinner attendees, with long-term benefits that may take months or years to explore and develop.

WHY HOLD A JEFFERSONIAN DINNER?

As we've seen, a Jeffersonian Dinner is not a fund-raising event. No pitch or presentation is made, no brochures are distributed, no checks or pledges are solicited or accepted. So why are more and more nonprofit organizations choosing to use Jeffersonian Dinners as part of their community-building programs? What purposes do they serve?

Jeffersonian Dinners can help you achieve a number of important goals:

- *A Jeffersonian Dinner enlists new allies.* The list of attendees at the dinner should include a number of people who are new to you and your organization. The unusual nature of the evening will make your organization stand out as a place that is focused on collaboration, feedback, and community building.

- *A Jeffersonian Dinner helps to create and disseminate ideas.* Conversations around the table at Jeffersonian Dinners often help to spark fresh thinking about important topics. The interesting, partly random assortment of attendees is likely to generate insights that may provoke worthwhile new initiatives: "The story you just told reminds me of something we did in my community. What if the two ideas were combined somehow?"
- *A Jeffersonian Dinner expands attendees' networks.* Almost every Jeffersonian Dinner we've attended has led to valuable new connections among people. We wish we had a dollar for every time we've heard an attendee say, "It was so great to have a chance to speak with so-and-so! We have so many interests in common, I can't imagine how it is that we never met before!"
- *A Jeffersonian Dinner spreads knowledge about and interest in your organization.* Organizing a Jeffersonian Dinner around the topic of your work helps to position your organization as a thought leader in the community. It will also greatly increase the visibility of your organization on matters pertaining to that topic, perhaps even making you the go-to group whenever related issues are mentioned.

Fledgling organizations have used Jeffersonian Dinners to recruit partners, brainstorm solutions to policy problems, and spread the word about their team among those doing parallel work. Established organizations have used Jeffersonian Dinners to stay in touch with old friends, meet new ones, and get feedback and advice about potential new programs or changes in direction. Organizations that are about to embark on major fund-raising initiatives or expansion programs have used Jeffersonian dinners to energize the community and get the word out about their exciting new plans.

Most important, Jeffersonian Dinners are fun. Participants almost invariably find them far more stimulating, thought-provoking, and engaging than either the typical purposeless dinner party (dominated by small talk and chitchat) or the traditional fund-raising event (in which speakers talk *at* the audience rather than engaging in true, open-ended dialogue). For nonprofit partners who have become weary of the ritual—and the expense—of the annual gala, the informality, openness, and intimacy of the Jeffersonian Dinner can be a breath of fresh air. And the simplicity of organizing a Jefferson Dinner—or even a series of dinners held throughout the year—is in stark contrast to the complexity of planning, funding, publicizing, preparing, and pulling off a star-studded gala. Most people, including nonprofit leaders themselves, regard the usual social activities in the nonprofit space as boring and enervating; they're a major cause of burnout among nonprofit managers and fund-raisers. By contrast, people who've attended a Jeffersonian Dinner love to talk about the experience with friends; they're thrilled when an invitation to a second such dinner arrives, and many of them get turned on to the concept of hosting a Jeffersonian Dinner of their own. Rather than producing burnout, Jeffersonian Dinners create energy.

HOW TO HOST A JEFFERSONIAN DINNER

STEP 1: PLANNING (BEGINNING FOUR WEEKS IN ADVANCE)

- Invite between eight and fifteen people who have a common interest (e.g., music and kids, innovation in education, women's health care).

- It's usually best to invite a mix of people, some of whom know one another, while others do not.

- Avoid inviting a "big kahuna"—a celebrity, powerful business executive, or political leader whose power or charisma is likely to lead others at the dinner to defer to him or her. Everyone at the dinner should feel equally free to contribute.

- If the dinner is to be focused on an objective, such as spreading knowledge of and interest in a nonprofit group, then work with the CEO of the group to tailor a topic that will interest the dinner participants.

- Choose a quiet location where the conversation can comfortably be heard, possibly a home or private room in a restaurant.

- Select an opening question that is related to the dinner theme and encourages each person at the table to tell a personal story (e.g., "Who was your favorite teacher of all time?").

- Solicit brief written biographies (100–150 words) from each participant in the dinner.

- Send out the opening question and biographies ahead of time so people will be ready to carry on the conversation.

- Select a dinner moderator—someone who has a light style but can move the conversation around and stimulate discussion.

STEP 2: DURING THE DINNER

- 7:00 p.m.: Cocktails, light conversation before seating.

- 7:30 p.m.: Moderator opens by explaining the ground rules. Most important: no talking to your neighbor, as the conversation involves the whole table.

- Ask each person at the table to respond to the opening question.

- Moderator introduces a follow-up question to link the opening answers to the general theme of the evening. This may propose a problem related to the theme that those at the table can address together. The question could be directly related to the work of the nonprofit organization, e.g., "How can we reduce teacher turnover in schools?"

- Let the discussion begin! Moderator should keep the conversation relevant, prevent side discussions from breaking up the table, and ensure that no one or two people are overly dominant.

- 9:15 p.m.: Moderator asks each person at the table to describe any ideas or thoughts he or she had during the discussion that he or she would like to follow up on, work with someone on, or just think about more.

- 9:30 p.m.: End dinner. Informal one-on-one conversations usually continue.

STEP 3: AFTER THE DINNER (WITHIN TWO WEEKS)

- Moderator or nonprofit CEO sends out a note giving the dinner participants' contact information and summarizing the follow-up points listed at the dinner's end.

- Follow up over the next few weeks, helping people connect with one another and with the nonprofit organization if desired. Nonprofit leaders may choose to set up one-on-one meetings with the dinner attendees who they thought were interested in following up.

- If you are in the midst of an ongoing campaign of some kind—or in the process of launching one—invite some of the most enthusiastic participants in the dinner to host Jeffersonian Dinners of their own.

WHEN THE UNEXPECTED HAPPENS

One of the most remarkable characteristics of Jeffersonian Dinners is the way they tend to spark unexpected results. This can happen even when the dinner itself doesn't come off exactly as planned.

In 1991, businessman Matt Goldman joined forces with old friends Chris Wink and Phil Stanton to create a unique theatrical company known as Blue Man Group. It has since grown into a multinational media and entertainment enterprise with theatrical and digital media operations across four continents, permanent live performance installations in seven cities, an ongoing theatrical tour of the United States and Canada, and a highly acclaimed show on the Norwegian Cruise Line ship *Norwegian Epic*.

Throughout their long association, Matt, Chris, and Phil have been fascinated by the interconnections between learning, creativity, and community. These interests led them to start Blue School, an innovative, experimental elementary school in New York City dedicated to the spirit of openness, creativity, and fun in learning, using a program guided by the latest findings of researchers and scientists exploring the fields of education, neuroscience, and cognition. "It's the kind of educational program we wish we'd had for ourselves and dreamed we'd have for our children," Goldman says, "a place where people feel like there is genuinely no better place to learn and to grow."

Jennifer and Jeff have become close friends with Matt, who tells the story of a Jeffersonian Dinner gone wrong—and then amazingly right. Shortly after the founding of the Blue School, Goldman and his team were hoping to attract partners who might want to help strengthen, expand, and energize the Blue School movement. In particular, they were seeking some ideas about how the school might find a permanent home in New York despite the city's ultra-expensive, ultra-competitive real estate market. In quest of allies who might help them achieve these goals, they organized a Jeffersonian Dinner around the theme of "changing education."

"Unfortunately," Goldman recalls, "we didn't have the discipline to keep the numbers down. So twelve people turned into sixteen, and sixteen turned into twenty. And after we invited our friend Eric Lewis—an amazing jazz pianist who performs under the stage name ELEW—to perform at the dinner, twenty turned into forty, and forty turned into seventy-five. It was out of control—a kind of Jeffersonian Dinner on steroids."

Despite the fact that the traditional format had been shattered, Goldman and his team went ahead with a Jeffersonian-style gathering. People gathered in the apartment that Goldman and his wife, Renee, share with their family. Everyone enjoyed a light dinner and began sharing their stories and thoughts about education, and those affiliated with Blue School talked a bit about the innovative philosophy behind its program.

But then a big monkey wrench was thrown into the evening. Although the evening had been explicitly billed (in true Jeffersonian fashion) as not a fund-raising event, one enthusiastic attendee, caught up in the excitement over the Blue School's innovative approach to learning, called out, "I want to make a donation to the school! I'm pledging $25,000—$5,000 every year for the next five years."

The room suddenly went silent. People glanced at one another, wondering whether this "spontaneous" gesture had been preplanned. Jeff Walker, one of the attendees, spoke up next. "Matt," he asked, "since money has been mentioned, how much do you think you'll need to raise in order to find a home for the Blue School?"

"Well," Goldman replied, "to do everything we'd like to do, we'd need ten to fifteen million."

The silence in the room deepened. And though the conversation about education reform eventually resumed, the mood had been permanently changed. What had been a lively, spontaneous exchange of views was now overshadowed by the question of finances—which had not been the intention of Goldman or his Blue School team members.

Goldman was feeling a bit glum the next day when he heard through the community grapevine that one of his friends was particularly upset about how the evening had unfolded. He quickly gave her a call. "Listen," Goldman said, "we did not want to turn last night's dinner into a fund-raising event. I'm so sorry you got that impression."

"I understand," said the friend. "But I have to tell you that I'm still confused about the whole thing. What was the point of the dinner? What is it that you need for this school of yours?"

"We need a building."

"Oh, is that all? Why didn't you say so?" Goldman's friend went on to explain that she knew a foreign businessman who was in the process of researching and purchasing undervalued properties on the New York real estate market. "Buying a building and leasing it to you would be right up his alley. Let me give you his number."

Goldman followed up with a call to the foreign businessman, who requested anonymity but expressed a genuine interest in helping Blue School solve its real estate challenge. He wanted to buy a number of buildings in downtown New York, and he liked the idea of making one building available to the school on a long-term lease. A savvy real estate agent quickly discovered that a historic building in the South Street Seaport district was looking for a buyer. Within a few months, the school was immersed in the process of renovating its new home, where it now conducts classes for almost two hundred happily engaged kids.

The moral of the story? You never know what kinds of serendipitous breakthroughs may occur when interesting people are brought together for a Jeffersonian Dinner—even when the dinner itself gets a little bit out of hand!

DEEPENING THE CONNECTIONS

In addition to attracting new partners, a Jeffersonian Dinner can also be a great way to enhance the connections among people who are already members of your band. Boards of directors that need an infusion of spirit and energy, for example, can often benefit from a Jeffersonian Dinner.

In some cases, people who are deeply involved in causes but teetering on the edge of burnout have been revitalized by participating in a Jeffersonian Dinner. Take our friend George, for example. We've known George for years, and he is a seasoned philanthropist. He leads a full, meaningful life that includes giving to a number of global organizations. You'll find him at the head of a table at many a gala dinner; his name appears prominently in the programs of the local symphony orchestra and opera company; he has received Man of the Year awards from more than one charitable organization. But recently George revealed something to us that caught us by surprise—that his experience of giving is often profoundly isolating.

We were a bit shocked by this revelation. Shouldn't giving be a deeply joyful act? Doesn't it make one feel more connected with one's fellow humans? So how could this wise, generous man feel isolated in the act of giving? George explained that he often feels alone after he gives because "it makes me wonder whether people see me as nothing more than a walking checkbook." "I'm happy to give," he hastened to add, "but I have a lot more to offer than just money. Only it doesn't seem as if anybody else realizes it."

George isn't the only generous supporter who has experienced this sense of flagging energy. When you sense that some of your partners are beginning to lose the spirit of excitement that originally drew them to the work, consider holding a Jeffersonian Dinner as a way of rekindling the flame.

We suggested that George organize a Jeffersonian Dinner with a few partners from his favorite nonprofit organization. The participants might include the executive director, key staff members, some fellow philanthropists, and other relevant stakeholders. For the opening question, he invited each person to tell a story of a time when he or she felt especially connected to the organization, to its work, and to its people.

How did we know this would work? Because, not too long before, we had held a dinner like this for the key board members and senior staff at Millennium Promise. We all shared stories from our visits to Millennium Villages and recalled how those experiences changed the way we viewed the world and the impact of our mission.

That dinner was one of the most powerful evenings of our lives, filled with a deep sense of community, shared experience, and passion—not to mention a true solidarity with our partners. The warmth and renewed sense of commitment generated by that evening made each of us want to delve a little deeper to discover what resources we could offer to our collaboration. The evening was an amazing cure-all for whatever feelings of isolation, burnout, or frustration we may have had—and it lit everyone in the room on fire with a renewed spirit for the mission of the project.

When you sense that some of your partners are beginning to lose the spirit of excitement that originally drew them to the work, consider holding a Jeffersonian Dinner as a way of rekindling the flame.

MAKING THE MOST OF THE ANNUAL GALA, AND OTHER COMMUNITY-BUILDING GATHERINGS

You know you've been there. A ballroom is rented, a nice dinner is prepared, and hundreds of people dress up in their formal best to celebrate and support the work of a worthy organization. Sometimes there are moments of genuine education, emotion, and inspiration mixed in with the partying: a moving speech in which the founder or the CEO shares his or her passion for the cause, a touching tribute by someone who has benefited from the good works of the nonprofit, a slide show or film that brings to vivid life the world-changing initiatives being built.

At the end of the evening, the master of ceremonies thanks everyone for coming and perhaps announces, with much fanfare, the grand total raised by the event. The crowd cheers and applauds themselves, and then disperses until the same time next year.

And in the meantime, what happens?

The answer is: not quite nothing. The money raised is, presumably, put to good use. But otherwise, precious little takes place in the gala's aftermath. And that makes it a gigantic wasted opportunity. Thousands of hours of work by organizers and huge sums of money and energy are expended, all for what amounts, in the end, to little more than a nice encounter—a pleasant, uplifting hour or two whose content and meaning are largely forgotten within a few days.

We know many nonprofit managers who sigh with relief the day after the annual gala is held. Nonetheless, many organizations do hold galas. In many cases, they play an important role in supporting the annual budget. It may not be possible to eliminate the gala from your yearly schedule; it may even be the case that the gala your organization holds is genuinely enjoyed by the majority of participants. So we aren't recommending that every non-profit organization immediately jettison the custom of the annual gala.

However, if you do hold a gala, you need to make sure it serves as the basis for creating relational, not just transactional, giving. Too many galas are superficial events that most participants forget about the moment the microphones are turned off and the wineglasses are collected. As Jennifer puts it, "When I attend most galas, I feel like part of the audience, not part of the team." Instead, you need to find ways to transform the gala into a springboard for deeper year-round relationships with your partners.

One organization that has made the annual gala into a truly effective team-building activity is the Robin Hood Foundation, which raises money to support a wide range of programs that serve the needy in New York City. Robin Hood's annual gala is a sit-down dinner for around four thousand people that raises about a third of the organization's annual budget. It's also high on the list of "see-and-be-seen" events for members of New York's boldface celebrity culture, thanks in part to the star-studded list of perform-ers and attendees it attracts: the May 2012 dinner, for example, was hosted by NBC's Brian Williams and *Saturday Night Live*'s Seth Meyers, co-chaired by New York Giants quarterback Eli Manning, and featured a musical perfor-mance by Rihanna.

Obviously Robin Hood, which was founded by some of New York's most successful Wall Street financiers, has access to resources that greatly exceed those enjoyed by most ordinary nonprofits. (Tables at the annual gala go for a cool $250,000, and the event raises between $40 million and $70 million annually.) But a big part of the Robin Hood story is the way the or-ganization surrounds the gala with supporting events that enhance its impact and deepen the connection between donors and the mission.

One of these events is the annual Heroes Breakfast, held in November, where no fund-raising takes place—attendance is free to Robin Hood partners. The purpose of the event is to honor three organizations that have done outstanding work in the fight against poverty by giving three individuals who have overcome extreme adversity the opportunity to share their stories. As you might imagine, the stories are often gut-wrenching: tales of parental abuse, rape, violence, discrimination, deprivation, and despair. It takes enormous courage for the men and women who have lived these lives to stand at a podium before a crowd of well-heeled New Yorkers and reveal the heartbreaking details—as well as the facts about how the work of Robin Hood has helped them and thousands of others like them.

Lars Jahns, an executive vice president of the foundation, explains the impact of the breakfast:

> It's easy for our message to be reduced to white noise. There are 1.8 million New Yorkers in poverty. One New Yorker in six relies on help from a food kitchen. The statistics go on and on—including the fact that Robin Hood has distributed over a billion dollars in donations. Does the persistence of poverty in New York mean that our work has failed? Not at all—because of the thousands upon thousands of lives we've transformed. The Heroes Breakfast makes those lives visible, tangible, and real.

In the course of the year, Robin Hood also hosts some forty additional events that help to further reinforce the message and deepen the connections between partners and mission. Workplace gatherings held under the rubric of Robin Hood on the Road bring experts on specific topics (drug abuse, food security, domestic violence) into the offices of corporations that have partnered with the foundation, giving employees an opportunity to delve deeply into the realities of poverty in New York, ask questions, and learn more about how they can become involved. A series of Robin Hood Unplugged breakfast conferences, held at the foundation's headquarters, gives busy executives the chance to hear about the latest findings on education, health care, or crime prevention before their ordinary workday begins. All of these meetings give the organization a chance to showcase the different programs and people devoted to the larger cause. And having different events at different times, with different focal points, for different groups of people gives a sense of momentum building up to the gala, so the gala itself feels like a convergence of a lot of different teams rather than seeing the same people telling the same stories over and over.

Some other organizations have developed similar strategies, including Berklee College of Music, currently led by our friend (and Exponential Fundraising student) Roger Brown. After honing his drumming skills in high school and by playing with bands as an undergraduate at Davidson College, and while teaching math in Kenya, Brown administered the Land Bridge food distribution operation under the auspices of CARE and UNICEF; it was the largest famine relief program ever attempted at the time. Later he co-founded Bright Horizons, which provided quality child care and early education for the children of working parents by opening facilities located near large corporations. After sixteen years at Bright Horizons, Brown became Berklee's third chief executive. His energy, creativity, and skill at forming partnerships quickly began to pay off, as indicated in part by his success in launching the first capital campaign in the history of the college.

One of the fund-raising strategies Berklee has employed with great success is what Brown calls the "micro-gala"—a fund-raising event that supplements the work of the school's annual gala, which raises between $1 million and $2 million each year. Held in the homes of individual friends of the college, the micro-galas attract forty to one hundred attendees and raise sums that are measured in the six figures, generally to support a particular Berklee initiative, such as the American Roots music program, the Berklee Global Jazz Institute, or City Music. At each event, a talented student ensemble or faculty member performs, and a handful of special items are auctioned off—musical performances or a donated collection of fine wines.

Informal and fun, the micro-galas serve as educational and community-building activities as much as fund-raisers, and they've become highlights in the annual calendar for many Berklee supporters.

At the YWCA Boston, an effective tool known as the Empower Hour has been developed. As CEO Sylvia Ferrell-Jones explains, the name plays off one of the Y's chief missions, which is to empower women and girls. Friends and supporters of the Y are asked to host Empower Hours, which may take place in an individual's home, office, or any other available venue. Ten to thirty attendees gather to learn more about a specific program of the Y—women's health, racial justice, youth leadership—and to ask questions, share stories, and find out how they can get involved.

For some who have previously been unconnected with the Y, the Empower Hour simply helps to dispel misconceptions. Ferrell-Jones observes with a smile, "There's always someone who says, 'I work out in your gym every week,' which is untrue, since we don't have a gym! They're confusing us with the YMCA." Eliminating such confusion and educating Bostonians about the mission and methods of the Y is a valuable function of the Empower Hours. And many attendees get excited about the Y's offerings and decide to become participants—some by making financial donations, others by signing up for future activities, still others by asking about volunteer opportunities in one of the Y's many community-based programs.

Replacing the grand annual gala with a number of smaller, less formal events is an effective strategy for many nonprofits. In other cases, organizations host a popular gala but fail to take full advantage of the potential for relationship building it provides. Val Broadie, another student of our Exponential Fundraising course, is working on that problem with the annual gala of the venerable NAACP Legal Defense Fund.

"We raise a lot of money with our annual gala," Val explains. "We raised $2.6 million at our gala in 2011. The year before that, it was about $2.5 million. The amount has been consistently more than $2 million over the past several of years. That's about a fifth of our annual budget—a significant amount of money that we would certainly miss if we didn't have it. And lots of our supporters look forward to the gala as an annual event. They expect to attend it every January, to reconnect with old friends and to renew their support for our organization. So the gala is here to stay, at least for the present."

However, Val and her colleagues are well aware that the gala is not being managed to its full potential:

> One of the things that we haven't done as well as we should is to leverage the relationships and the goodwill that comes from this wonderful party. So this year, for the first time ever, we reached out to establish long-term relationships with people who'd attended the dinner without actually buying tickets themselves. These are folks who were guests of others, and many of them were being introduced to the Legal Defense Fund for the very first time. So we've begun to make the effort to connect with them through mailings and emails, and to educate them about the good work we do. At the end of the year, we'll invite them to support us. And we hope we can convert some of them into individual supporters of ours, expanding our network and turning a one-night stand into a year-round relationship.

The lesson for other organizations: you don't necessarily want to cancel your annual gala, particularly if you've come to rely on it for a significant portion of your budget. (See the sidebar "Some Ways to Fix the Gala Dilemma," page 216, for a few suggestions.) But consider following the lead of Robin Hood and Berklee College by building an entire program of less-formal, more personal, more in-depth gatherings around it, which can serve to greatly strengthen the sense of partnership that the gala may spark.

SOME WAYS TO FIX THE GALA DILEMMA

Here are some creative suggestions to consider if your annual gala is falling short as a team-building tool:

- Move the gala from a ballroom into a setting that's directly connected with your work—the gym of a school you support, the dinosaur hall of a museum.
- Invite a couple of the beneficiaries of your work to sit at each table, to tell their stories and answer questions.
- Go live via satellite to a distant location (a South African village, a research station on the Great Barrier Reef) so that people can learn about your work.
- Challenge the gathering by presenting one of the biggest unsolved problems your organization faces and asking them for ideas about how to solve it.
- Ask each guest to make a two-part gift to the organization: a cash donation and an offer of some other kind of resource (the name of a best friend, access to a corporate asset, an in-kind contribution).

FUND-RAISING AS COMMUNITY BUILDING

The best kind of fund-raising event is one that fulfills several goals at once. The ideal fund-raiser (a) helps build a deeper sense of community among your partners, (b) inculcates a greater awareness and understanding of the mission of your organization, (c) helps achieve one or more of the goals for which your organization exists, and, of course, (d) generates meaningful financial support for your work.

Here's an example of a fund-raising event that accomplishes all four—and without renting a hotel ballroom, recruiting a celebrity host, or serving a single rubber chicken.

The Church of St. Barnabas is a small Episcopal parish in Irvington, New York, some forty minutes north of Manhattan. It's a modest institution, with just four employees—the rector, the assistant rector, the secretary, and the sexton, who tends the property—and 163 families and individual members. (Two of those members happen to be our co-author Karl Weber and his wife, Mary-Jo.) But this little suburban parish generates charitable donations of over $70,000 from a single event on its autumn calendar: the annual used-clothing sale. Here's a glimpse of how a traditional, usually low-key fund-raising activity has been transformed by one church into a major community-building event.

Every team member participates. When October rolls around and the clothing sale approaches, the entire parish is mobilized. Virtually every church member, young or old, finds some way to contribute. It starts when everyone cleans out their closets and totes a mountain of gently used clothing to the parish hall. Then, over a period of a few weeks, one team of parish volunteers collects, sorts, tags, labels, and displays the contributions; others design, print, post, and distribute advertising flyers throughout Westchester County; others bake desserts or cook homemade soups for sale to hungry shoppers; and still others volunteer to assist customers, pack up merchandise, and ring up purchases during the week of the sale.

Because everyone is part of the event, everyone shares the excitement (and the exhaustion) as it happens as well as the pride in the results.

People from every walk of life are welcome. Irvington and the surrounding towns are highly diverse, and that diversity is reflected in both the clothes for sale and the customers who buy them. Barely used designer dresses, suits, handbags, and overcoats are purchased at discount prices by affluent folks who love a bargain (who doesn't?); jeans, sweatshirts, sneakers, and work boots are bought by the gardeners, carpenters, and house cleaners who tend the homes of the affluent; and entire families from the county's newest immigrant groups (including Dominicans, Haitians, and Indians) turn up to shop, some of them buying a whole year's worth of clothing for Mom, Dad, and the kids. Young hipsters fill shopping bags with what they call "vintage" clothes (really just the stuff their grandparents stopped wearing years ago). Local teenagers drop in to browse through the T-shirts—and several have ended up buying like-new tuxedos to wear to the senior prom.

All these diverse customers find a warm welcome at St. Barnabas. And every year, one or two clothing-sale customers decide to begin attending "that church down the block with all the friendly people."

The work of the organization is powerfully advanced. Like most churches, St. Barnabas has made a significant commitment to supporting local charities, from the Midnight Run program (which delivers hot food, clothing, and blankets to homeless men and women in New York City) and the Medical Outreach Mission in nearby Yonkers to Irvington's own Families in Need program. Each year, everyone in the parish is invited to a post-clothing-sale dinner at which the year's proceeds are allocated to specific charities—a social event that also helps the community bond around the spirit of giving. Each year, a series of checks totaling tens of thousands of dollars is sent out from St. Barnabas to the grateful local nonprofits that have come to count on the church's support. (And as soon as the charitable checks from one year's sale are mailed out, the planning begins for the next year's clothing sale.)

If a friendly genie—or an unexpected bequest from some generous millionaire—were to suddenly provide St. Barnabas with all the money needed to fund its outreach programs for the next twenty years, it's doubtful that the parishioners would choose to cancel the annual clothing sale. The event generates so much value for the church's neighbors, creates so much positive publicity and goodwill in the broader community, stimulates so much camaraderie among the members of the parish itself, and is simply so much fun that the people of St. Barnabas would be reluctant to give it up.

Now that's what we call an effective fund-raiser.

"LET'S GO TOGETHER":
Using Travel to Bring Your Good Work Vividly to Life

One of the most powerful tools you can use to connect with people whose support you hope to win is the invitation for a shared journey. Inviting people to join you on a trip where the meaning of the cause will come to life feels far less coercive—and far more exciting—than subjecting them to yet another canned pitch. In case after case, it has proven to be life-changing.

There are a number of nonprofit organizations that routinely use the "let's go together" approach to successfully convert curious onlookers into passionate partners. Many kinds of trips are capable of transforming attitudes and behaviors, from simple two-hour visits to a local program site to dramatic week-long travels to exotic locales where an entirely new side of human existence is revealed. A few examples: the Big Apple Circus has invited donors to take a tour of the Clown Care Unit at a local hospital, where circus clowns bring laughter to sick children; MIT Media Lab sponsors a visit to their various innovation labs, enabling partners to spend the day with scientists at the leading edge of high technology; and Millennium Promise brings donors to villages in Senegal and Mali, where they meet villagers whose lives are being impacted by the organization's work.

Kenneth Watkins, director of philanthropy for the Australian Ballet, likes to use the company's international tours as an opportunity to expose donors and partners to the global reach of ballet. When we spoke to Ken in Boston, Massachusetts, during one leg of the Australian Ballet's successful 2012 tour of the United States, he described how world travel helps strengthen and deepen his partners' commitment to the company's artistic mission:

> Some of our donors have been with the ballet for a very long time, in fact, before I joined the company eighteen years ago, and of course we cherish them all. But one of my jobs is to recognize when a person may be ready to step up from one level of giving to the next, and that's where inviting them to join us on a trip can be a valuable way of enhancing the relationship.
>
> So when we can, we'll invite selected donors to travel with us to see the ballet in different parts of the world. I organize the whole trip, almost becoming a kind of tour manager, if you like. I put together a VIP tour with an appropriate price tag on it—it's the kind of trip these individuals are accustomed to taking, but with the added thrill in this case of tagging along with their favorite ballet troupe. We hire an experienced tour guide in each city who handles the detailed logistics.
>
> Our goal is to create a living, changing dynamic among the various members of our traveling party. I've found that the personalities and styles of the participants always vary enormously. A few are absolutely welded to your side, while others tend to go out and about on their own. We usually have some who are longtime supporters of the ballet, and others who are younger and new to the company. But you soon notice that everyone's watching everyone else and learning from one another. When the new people are inquisitive and ask probing questions about the company, the

dancers, their training, and their daily routines, it spurs lively conversations that the whole group enjoys.

Of course, an international journey such as the one Kenneth Watkins describes is costly and time-consuming, and it may be inappropriate for your organization. But it's possible for much shorter, simpler trips to have an equally great impact on your partners and potential partners. Lars Jahns of the Robin Hood Foundation often takes donors on visits to the organizations supported by the foundation, which are focused on alleviating poverty in the city of New York. That means they are all within a subway ride of the homes and offices of Robin Hood's supporters. Yet the glimpses of life as lived by New Yorkers in need are often as startling as if they were scenes from sub-Saharan Africa or South Asia:

There are times when I feel like a character in a Charles Dickens novel, showing people the ghosts of Christmas past, present, and future—these haunting images of how life can be for the less fortunate. We meet with ex-offenders, battered moms, homeless families, sufferers from drug abuse—the whole range of people that our programs help. I remember one man who leaned against a wall at the end of a full day of site visits, slid down to the floor, and simply whispered, "Wow. I had no idea."

Our donors are smart, knowledgeable, caring people. But it's one thing to have an intellectual knowledge that New York is a tale of two cities—the rich and the poor—and quite another to actually witness it for yourself. The result is often a deeper, more personal, even spiritual commitment by people who've come to understand for themselves what real need is like.

Robin Hood also hosts board meetings in the offices of grantee organizations, transforming otherwise routine get-togethers into opportunities to learn firsthand about the terrible social problems the foundation and its partners are helping to address.

Don't underestimate the impact that a personal visit to your organization and an opportunity to see your programs in action may have on your partners. The work you do is your everyday reality, easy to take for granted, but it may be a startling, once-in-a-lifetime experience for those whose generosity supports you. Sharing it with them in the flesh can be one of the best ways to strengthen the bond between you and to help your partners appreciate how lucky they are to be members of your team.

FOOD FOR THOUGHT

Follow-up questions and activities designed to help you get the most out of this chapter:

- Using the guidelines in the sidebar "How to Host a Jeffersonian Dinner" (pages 202–204), plan, organize, and hold your first Jeffersonian Dinner. Develop the dinner plan in accordance with the current goals of the nonprofit organization you support. After the dinner, evaluate its impact. What kind of feedback have you received? What sorts of follow-up activities have participants planned and carried out? What would you do differently to make your next Jeffersonian Dinner even more effective?

- If your organization holds an annual gala or other major social/fund-raising event, evaluate its effectiveness, measured not solely by dollars raised but by the degree to which personal connections with your organization are expanded, deepened, and enriched. What steps can you take to increase the positive impact of next year's event?

- What other kinds of fund-raising events should you consider? In particular, are there opportunities to create small, informal, thematic gatherings hosted by team members or partners that can serve as year-round opportunities for people to learn about your work and become engaged in it?

- Think about the travel opportunities that may be afforded by the nonprofit organization you support. Remember that locales and activities that may strike you as routine or ordinary may be unusual and potentially fascinating to outside supporters. Thus, behind-the-scenes glimpses of life and work in a research university, a hospital, an R&D lab, or an elementary school may prove quite intriguing and engaging to partners and potential partners. Develop a plan for using one or more of these travel opportunities to reward, excite, and motivate your partners.

9

TAPPING THE POWER OF THE AVATAR

You Become the Other

The world is so empty if one

thinks only of mountains, rivers

& cities; but to know someone

who thinks & feels with us,

& who, though distant, is close to

us in spirit, this makes the earth

for us an inhabited garden.

—Johann Wolfgang von Goethe

The fund-raising activities of international nonprofit organizations traditionally have been handicapped by the difficulty of engaging donors personally. Many would-be donors are looking for opportunities to get personally involved in the causes they favor—as volunteers, for example. This hands-on engagement gives them a stronger sense of how the funds are being used as well as a greater feeling of confidence that the money they give is reaching those in need. What's more, an individual who launches his connection to a nonprofit by donating time and energy to its programs is also much more likely to become a financial donor.

This nexus gives a big fund-raising edge to organizations such as Boys and Girls Clubs, the Girl Scouts and Boy Scouts, Habitat for Humanity, and local churches, schools, and sports leagues, all of which not only want money from donors but also have an immediate, practical need for donors' time and skills. By contrast, personal involvement by a donor in the work of an international organization such as Doctors Without Borders or the International Rescue Committee is likely to be expensive, time-consuming, and even dangerous. No wonder, according to Save the Children, that only about 1 percent of individual donations made in the United States go to international organizations.

One of the most effective new tools for connecting an individual with a cause is the avatar. It's a term we've borrowed from the world of electronic gaming, in which an avatar is the virtual representation of the player, acting on his behalf. An avatar lets us fulfill one of the deepest and most ancient of human dreams—to live someone else's life and to truly know, not just imagine, what it is like to walk in their shoes.

The secret of the avatar can allow people to relate to global nonprofits as never before. By bringing the realities of work in a distant land vividly to life in a partner's den or living room, the avatar uses technology to make the world a smaller place. It can also help bring vividness and immediacy to nonprofit work of many other kinds, whether that work is focused on health care, poverty, education, the arts, or any other field of human concern.

In this chapter, we'll look at organizations that are using the secret of the avatar to engage partners, and suggest ways that your organization can do the same, no matter what kinds of work it is engaged in.

THE AVATAR:
Marketing to the Fourth Power

Traditional nonprofit donor marketing campaigns have included three levels of marketing.

First, many organizations rely primarily on conventional advertising techniques, using both print and broadcast media and direct-marketing media, especially direct mail and email. In their appeals, they state the need or explain the cause to potential donors, and give people a number to call or a website to visit. In today's era of social media, they may send out messages on Twitter and Facebook or post videos on YouTube. Celebrity spokespeople are often employed to capture attention and give audiences an admired image to react to or identify with. The hope is that individuals will notice the messages and respond by donating money. These programs are often expensive and typically have very low response rates.

Second, some organizations use a foundational giving model, typified by the child sponsor system we described earlier. Nonprofits such as Save the Children and World Vision have had great success with this, and in recent years technology has allowed many organizations to use this model to lower their costs and increase their effectiveness. Sponsoring a child allows donors to follow an individual child through each stage of the child's life; some Save the Children donors actually stay with the child long enough to help pay for the child's secondary school and even college. However, what the child sponsor model does not allow is direct interaction with the child (for reasons that include safety and legal liability).

Third, many nonprofits focus mainly on larger donors. When funds are generated by a relative handful of major partners, it's possible for donors to enjoy personal relationships with senior members of the organization—the CEO, the executive director, a board member, or a program expert. This

enables the organization to rely on personal contact and one-on-one emotional connections to bond the donor to the cause. This typically increases
the odds of the donor giving multiple times in multiple ways, including
donations of money, time, network access, and personal attention.

Now technology is making a fourth level of marketing possible. The Internet enables us to enhance the connections between the organization and
the targets of our fund-raising strategy. The front-line professionals who are
doing the aid work can now become avatars for the organization's partners;
people who would have been several steps removed from donors because of
location can now be entirely accessible through email, blogs, Skype, and so
on. This relationship can provide the kind of long-term relationship made
possible by the child-sponsorship model while also allowing direct contact
and therefore the potential for a personal relationship, not just with a small
handful of major donors but with a large number of contributors.

This is the secret of the avatar. The basic concept is simple: Find someone in your organization whom donors can relate to, whom they might
like to support, or whom they would like to work with and follow. This
individual can become the avatar for your cause—a personal embodiment
of your work that can be used to build a connection between the potential
donor and your organization. The creation of an avatar raises the donor relationship to another level in the organization, from a relationship with the
person being helped to a relationship with the person doing the helping.

The avatar is the person many partners would love to be if their life
circumstances were different. Following the work of the avatar in real time,
as it unfolds, is the next best thing. That's why smart nonprofits are increasingly using one or many avatars to bring outside partners inside their world
and their work. In most cases, an avatar is a member of the nonprofit team
who serves as a direct, personal link to one or more outside partners. It
could be an aid worker in a developing country, a physician performing
desperately needed surgeries for children who would otherwise be unable
to receive them, or an engineer helping to build water systems or affordable

housing in a poor rural community. Partners can be linked to the avatar through any number of means, including face-to-face visits, conversations via telephone or Skype, email or Twitter bulletins, and broad- or narrowcasts of photos, audios, or videos.

There are many variations possible on the avatar system; every organization will need to adapt the concept to fit its work, resources, and donor interests. No matter how the details vary, the underlying purpose of the avatar relationship is to humanize and personalize the connection to the nonprofit organization and its cause—to help the partner feel that the avatar is a direct extension of his or her hands, brain, and heart.

One organization that has experimented with the use of avatars is Save the Children, which has been helping children around the world for decades. Traditionally, its advertising has focused on telling the story of each child—a little girl in Ethiopia, a little boy in Mozambique. Yet the organization operates through 250,000 community health workers all over the world, who travel from village to village and house to house in some of the poorest countries in the world, typically on foot, providing basic health care to the villagers and the children whom Save the Children members sponsor.

In 2010, Save the Children decided to test a new approach to telling the story of their work. The idea they came up with was to bridge the gap between partners and Save the Children's miracle-making health workers. They built a website that allowed potential donors to find out about what these community health care workers were doing each month. The workers were given cell phones to keep in touch with their supervisors, regional clinics, and Save the Children headquarters. The same cell phones also allowed the health workers to send text messages and have brief conversations with partners of the organizations as they traveled the region performing their amazing work. Jeff used this technology to follow Salif Diarra, a health care worker from the village of Satiguila, Mali, in West Africa. In one recent month, Jeff "went along" as Salif treated two children for malaria, assisted a mother in giving birth, and made a follow-up visit to that mother. Jeff found it a powerful way of sharing in work that he will never be able to perform personally—and it certainly intensified his sense of closeness and commitment to Save the Children and its mission.

As Save the Children has discovered, avatar relationships can give a donor a more visceral sense of confidence that the money he or she is giving will actually have an impact. They also demonstrate through direct communication how even a small gift can produce immediate, important results.

THE MANY FACES
OF AVATARS

Avatars have been used in the nonprofit world for quite a while, although the name is new. Consider, for example, the challenge of raising money for universities. Most development departments of universities focus their time and attention on efforts by the president and deans to raise money. That work is important, but even better results could be achieved through an additional focus on creating avatar connections between professors and donors. We've seen that some particularly successful partnerships—often leading to significant donations—have occurred as the result of a relationship between a professor who is passionately dedicated to a particular field of study and a donor with a parallel interest. The donor connects with the research, the teaching agenda, and/or the vision of the professor; he or she may be invited to visit the professor's classes occasionally to experience the energy of the learning process or drop in at the professor's lab to get a glimpse of research in action. Sometimes these relationships blossom into long-term, ongoing connections that turn into vibrant partnerships where knowledge, connections, time, and energy are exchanged as well as financial support.

The avatar concept is applicable to many other types of nonprofits as well. As the university example illustrates, avatars needn't be restricted to organizations that work on heartstring-tugging projects in exotic locales. You can easily imagine a musician at the local symphony orchestra or a curator at the art museum playing a similar role for partners of those institutions. The possibilities are limited only by your imagination. For example, perhaps your organization can consider starting a program that for one day allows partners to serve as "apprentices" to avatars who will teach them the basics of their work—research scientist for a day, museum curator for a day, music therapist for a day.

The avatar can also expand and enhance the work of organizations that are already creating strong connections between donors and recipients. For example, as we discussed in Chapter 4, DonorsChoose.org uses technology to allow donors to give to specific classroom projects that need funding in our public schools. Many of these one-time gifts lead to long-term online linkages between donors and teachers and a rich, rewarding relationship for both parties. In effect, these are avatar relationships, with teachers acting as representatives of donors through their hands-on work in the classroom.

There are a number of other online social networking websites that are focused on connecting donors to causes. They include sites such as Causes and Crowdrise (both for-profit sites). These so-called P2O (peer-to-organization) sites are focused on connecting small and medium donors to nonprofits that they and their friends are passionate about. Could these P2O sites be even more effective if they enabled donors to interact with an avatar of the cause they wanted to support?

It's easy to imagine how other kinds of nonprofits could use the avatar model. Witness.org is an amazing group, co-founded by musician Peter Gabriel, that supports individuals who use video to document human rights violations around the world. Witness.org could apply the avatar strategy by changing the emphasis of their communications from the issue of human rights to the videographers themselves, who are risking their lives to shine a bright light on repressive regimes. Perhaps a partner of Witness.org would be more likely to become a continuing donor if offered the opportunity to support an individual videographer he or she had a virtual relationship with.

The Quincy Jones Musiq Consortium has taken as its mission the task of ensuring that all children in America have access to music education while they are growing up. Naturally enough, their fund-raising message is centered on the children they want to help. What if they adopted an avatar approach? Perhaps donors would be more likely to connect over an extended period with an individual music director rather than a more general description of the need for music education, however articulate and passionate the presentation.

IMPLEMENTING AN AVATAR STRATEGY

As with any other strategy, designing and implementing an avatar approach must be done with care. You'll need to decide which individuals within the organization are best suited to serve as avatars for your donors. You'll also need to determine which technology tools to deploy in creating the avatar connections—email, text messaging, video, audio, photography, Skype, Twitter, blogging, or some combination thereof.

You'll also need to be sensitive to the personal issues that may arise. You may find that your CEO or head of development is reluctant to allow one of his staffers to establish a close, independent, personal relationship with a donor. On the other hand, a too-strong avatar may (wittingly or not) interfere with the broader strategy of the organization: it's possible that a highly charismatic individual in a particular country in Africa (for example) may end up attracting generous support for any project he personally starts . . . which may not be the highest priority of the organization as a whole. And if a particular staffer who has become a popular avatar chooses to retire or leave the organization, what happens to the donor relationships she created? So balancing the connections between the individual avatar and the overall organization can be tricky—but very important.

One approach that can be a good way to start is to make the organization's CEO or other leading spokesperson into a kind of "avatar in chief." At Jennifer's suggestion, our friend Alexander McLean, founder of the African Prisons Project, has begun assuming this kind of role with his partners. Alexander has starting writing an online travel journal every time he takes a trip to Africa. The journal enables APP's partners to share his experiences and see the continent through his eyes, glimpsing both the positive results APP's work is generating and the enormous needs still waiting to be met.

This simple approach allows APP to experiment with the avatar method in a limited, controlled fashion. It relies on Alexander—the organization's chief public spokesperson and a charismatic communicator—to serve as the personal link between partners and the work. Over time, APP may decide to expand its avatar program to include individual field workers, who could serve as the eyes and ears of donors as they work with inmates and prison staff in remote locations across Africa. If and when this happens, Alexander's experience as the organization's first avatar will enable him to serve as an effective trainer and coach for those taking on the role.

FOOD FOR THOUGHT

Follow-up questions and activities designed to help you get the most out of this chapter:

- Which individuals in your organization could serve as effective avatars? Which jobs do your staff members perform that have the greatest potential interest or appeal to donors and other outside partners?
- What kinds of technology could you use to connect one or more avatars in your organization with outside partners? Consider whether email, text messaging, blogging, Twitter, Facebook, audios, videos (on YouTube or elsewhere), photography, Skype, or other digital media could be useful tools for communicating your avatar's story and that of your organization.
- Could you create an X-for-a-day program that would allow outside partners to join your work as "apprentices"? Which of your staff members might serve as willing and effective mentors to donors eager to learn a little about the hands-on services your organization provides?

10

BUILDING AN EMPOWERED, COLLABORATIVE BOARD

*Turning an Underused Resource
into a Source of Strength*

How lovely to think that no one need wait a moment; we can start now, start slowly changing the world!

—Anne Frank

Virtually every nonprofit organization, even the smallest, has some kind of board. It may be called a board of directors, a board of advisors, or a board of trustees, or it may go by some other name. When board members are properly recruited, educated, motivated, led, and deployed, they can not only help the leadership of the nonprofit organization operate more effectively but also serve as a powerful tool for growing the support base on which the organization depends.

Unfortunately, most nonprofit boards don't operate this way. When we meet with nonprofit leaders, board woes almost always surface quickly. The issues we hear about are numerous and highly varied: "How can I get my board to provide more insight and ideas?" "Where can I recruit more energetic and involved board members?" "What can I do to engage our board in support of fund-raising?" "How can I convince board members to work on projects in between meetings?" "Is there a way to rein in the one or two board members who dominate every conversation with their pet projects?" "How can I get our board chairman to be a more dynamic leader?"

Our Exponential Fundraising students frequently share such problems with us. One student told us, "We have a large board with many smart members and a strong chairman. But getting them to focus on big issues is a challenge. We're in the process of redesigning our headquarters space, and the board recently spent an entire hour debating the location of an internal staircase. It's a waste of time, especially when there are so many more important problems they could be tackling."

Another reported, "We have a board that's very engaged in overseeing our programs, but they've never helped with fund-raising, which is a big area of need. Nor have they taken a big step back to analyze our overall strategy, where we could use real help. I wonder how to get the board to direct its energies where they're most needed."

Still another said, "I work for a long-established nonprofit with a board that never had term limits. As a result, we have some members who have been in place forever—forty years or more. Most are retirees with lots of time on their hands who seem to regard board membership as an opportunity to socialize with old friends rather than a serious commitment."

The stories vary, and they're matched by stories of frustration told by board members themselves. For every organizational CEO who complains, "During board meetings, our members seem to focus on trivia," there's a board member who moans, "Our meetings never seem to grapple with the big issues facing the organization."

The varied complaints all point to the same basic problem: boards that are fundamentally disconnected from the work of the nonprofit, or (in some cases) connected in a dysfunctional way that hampers and stymies rather than supports and energizes the management team.

How can you fix this problem? The discussion needs to start with one basic question that is often overlooked—namely, what is a board for in the first place? In one recent class, a student launched the conversation by saying, "There are four things I want from my board: work, wisdom, window dressing, and wealth." That is, this student expects her board members to tackle specific, concrete tasks on behalf of the organization (work); to offer worthwhile ideas, advice, and feedback concerning the organization's strategies and programs (wisdom); to lend a bit of prestige through their own fame and reputations (window dressing); and to assist with fund-raising efforts as well as making personal donations to the organization (wealth).

These "four Ws" aren't a bad start at delineating the possible contributions that board members can make to your organization's success. A fifth goal we'd add to the list is networking: the readiness to share contacts with other people who may have valuable resources to offer the organization. But of course a mere list of goals has the danger of making the task of board leadership feel mechanistic, a matter of ticking off items on a checklist. Like all other forms of teamwork, board relationships need to be open-ended, joyful, spontaneous, and ever changing—true partnerships like those we've described throughout this book.

If you want to strive for this kind of connection with your board members—and in the process turn your board from a deadweight into a dynamic source of ideas, resources, and energy—you need to begin by exploring the question of *what kind of board* your organization needs. That's the topic we'll tackle in the next few pages. As you read, consider the challenges your organization faces, and think about which of the varying board structures we'll describe might be right for you. Later in the chapter, we'll explain some strategies for rebuilding your board (if necessary) to bring it closer to the ideal form you envision while also leaving it open to the free play of emotional, psychic, and spiritual energy that is essential to all true partnerships.

THE UNIVERSE OF BOARDS:
Structures, Styles, and Cultures

As a longtime executive in the world of private equity as well as an engaged philanthropist, Jeff Walker has served on many boards of both for-profit and nonprofit organizations. The experience has taught him the importance of recognizing the variety of management and leadership styles represented by various board types. Among the most significant challenges for the nonprofit leader who wants to make her board more effective is to recognize what kind of board she has, decide whether it's the right kind for the organization, and then think long and hard about whether and how to try to institute changes.

Many board members come to the nonprofit world after years of successful experience in for-profit companies. Having worked effectively with for-profit boards, they assume they know all about the proper role of the board. But it's a mistake to try to import communication, organization, and structural tools wholesale from the for-profit board to the nonprofit board. This is not to say that boards of various kinds can't learn from one another—just that this learning must be conducted in an atmosphere of respect for the cultural and social differences among board types.

Here are some of the most common types of boards found in both for-profit and nonprofit organizations.

Structure #1: The Informal Board Many small to midsized organizations, especially those that are fairly new, are managed by an *informal board*. In this kind of organization, whether for-profit or nonprofit, the founder tends to dominate the management team. (In the very early stages of growth, the founder may actually be the sole employee as well as the head of management.) As a natural consequence, the informal board is generally made up primarily of close friends and relatives of the founder of the organization. Over time, outsiders may join the board, but they usually serve mainly as informal advisors to the founder, who basically retains complete control of the organization.

The members of an informal board may have widely varying credentials and expertise; some may be deeply committed to the work of the organization and highly knowledgeable about it, while others may be board members merely because of their family connection or their friendship with the founder. Thus, it is sometimes the case that informal boards serve as little more than a rubber stamp for decisions made by the CEO, president, or chairman, contributing little concrete value in terms of intellectual or managerial prowess.

Structure #2: The Fiduciary Board As successful organizations evolve, they outgrow the informal board structure in favor of a less cliquish and more professional type of board. In time, many develop what we call a *fiduciary board*, so called because its members are supposed to have a fiduciary relationship to the organization—that is, they are expected to serve as responsible overseers for the use of funds and other resources by management, even intervening if necessary when management makes serious mistakes.

In a for-profit company, the fiduciary board represents the interests of owners (shareholders). The board views management primarily as a tool wielded by the board in pursuit of business goals, especially profit; the CEO and other executives serve at the pleasure of the board and are liable to be replaced as necessary. (This can happen even when the CEO is the company founder; needless to say, it's a bitter pill for him or her to swallow, and often represents a crucial inflection point in the history of the business.)

Board members are selected because of the skills, knowledge, experience, and contacts they bring to the assignment; they may include veteran business leaders, bankers and other financial experts; scientific, technical, or academic luminaries; and distinguished figures from government and the nonprofit sector. The board's operations are usually rather formal and in fact may be governed by strict rules and regulations, especially in the case of publicly traded companies. Management generally makes formal presentations to the board concerning proposed strategies, which are approved or disapproved, often after serious and probing discussion. Between meetings, in-depth conversations between board members and members of the management team may be rare, and the relationship between the two groups is governed by formal rules; hence the "wall" between the two in the chart "Types of Boards" (page 247).

In the nonprofit world, fiduciary boards are especially common in large, mature organizations, such as universities, major arts organizations, and hospitals. The fiduciary board of a large nonprofit usually has the same kind of arm's-length relationship with management as in the for-profit world. The CEO or president and other leaders of the nonprofit often make formal presentations to the board, which passes judgment on the strategic plans and other programs proposed by management.

The fiduciary board does not represent "owners" or "investors," since these groups don't exist in the case of nonprofit organizations. However, it may include major donors to the nonprofit, whose relationship to the organization is somewhat parallel to that between investors and company (since, like investors, they provide the funding on which the organization depends). Large nonprofits in the world of culture, education, and the arts are often managed primarily by donor boards. In many cases, the members of donor boards are distinguished mainly by their wealth and by the success they've enjoyed in business, finance, or other fields. This means such boards are often dominated by individuals who may or may not be deeply knowledgeable about the work of the nonprofit they nominally direct.

When Jeff served as a member of one such board, he was the youngest member of the group by a wide margin, even though he was already in his fifties at the time. That particular board labored under the handicap of a rule that the organization's development staff—that is, its fund-raising experts—were actually *forbidden* to speak with board members, perhaps out of a misguided belief that "church and state" (that is, the management of the organization and its financial side) could and should be separated. This led to frequent misunderstandings and missed opportunities to strengthen the organization's financial state. (Needless to say, Jeff wouldn't recommend such a rule to other nonprofits!)

Structure #3: The Active Board The third category of board found in both for-profit and nonprofit organizations is the *active board*. We've seen nonprofit boards whose members did almost nothing to justify their positions: a few times a year they attended meetings that they treated mainly as social occasions, shared a meal or two, swapped stories with one another, and routinely approved virtually every report or plan without asking probing questions or offering any substantive advice. On the other hand, we've also seen boards that pushed the idea of engagement to excess—where the chairman of the board had such a strong-willed, dominant personality (as well as the requisite time, energy, and inclination) that he actually micromanaged the daily operations of the organization, with or without the acquiescence of a weak-willed, inexperienced, or ineffectual executive director.

The active board avoids both of these dysfunctional extremes. It provides the leadership with many extra sets of eyes, helping the leaders to see the organization and its challenges from the perspective of a team of sympathetic outsiders with deep, sophisticated knowledge of the world in which it operates. And, when necessary, the active board is ready and able to replace an ineffective leader for the good of the organization. In the for-profit world, this type of board is often made up of major investors who have the knowledge, background, and interest to take a hands-on approach to the strategic and management challenges faced by the company—in fact, they may have bought stakes in the company primarily because they saw an opportunity to improve the operations of a poorly run business and thereby multiply the value of their shares. Sometimes the active board and the company management have overlapping members. But even when this is not the case, the wall that separates board and management in the case of a fiduciary board is basically nonexistent with an active board.

In the nonprofit world, the active board is made up of individuals who want to take a hands-on role in helping to guide and support management and who have the knowledge and skills to do so. Sometimes they are major donors who are eager to track the social benefits being generated by their gifts. In this respect, they are closely parallel to the investors in a private equity or venture capital fund. In fact, they often describe their gifts as "investments" and demand metrics as a way of ensuring a "return on investment" (although it takes the form of lives saved, environmental problems averted, schools built, or families lifted out of poverty rather than profits earned or share prices increased).

Other Variations Many nonprofits have seen the value in having a number of specialized advisory boards, each representing a different set of stakeholders and enhancing the work of the organization in a different way. For example, there may be a donor board, a board of experts in the program areas touched by the nonprofit, a board made up of representatives of other organizations that partner with the nonprofit, a board representing the groups that benefit from the nonprofit's work, a scientific board, a strategy board, and so on. Some may be standing boards with a permanent role; others may be ad hoc boards created to tackle a short-term problem and then vote themselves out of existence. Helping to keep these multiple boards energized, actively engaged, and communicating productively with the leadership of the nonprofit organization is a big, complicated, and time-consuming job—but the benefits can be huge. Later in this chapter, we'll talk more about some of the various kinds of boards nonprofits have launched and the ways in which they've enhanced their work.

Think about the nonprofit organization you care about most, whether you serve it as a manager, an employee, a board member, a volunteer, a donor, or in any other capacity. Which type of board(s) does the organization have? (See the chart, "Types of Boards," on page 247, for a visual template and brief summary of the three board models we described above.) What kind of relationship exists between the board and the management? How well does the board seem to be serving the organization's short-term and long-term needs? These are important questions whose answers can have a profound impact on the future of your cause.

STRUCTURING YOUR BOARD

There are a number of other ways to consider the form and structure of the ideal nonprofit board for your organization. One issue is size. Research has shown that groups of six to ten are the ideal size for most kinds of problem-solving and organizational tasks. Groups smaller than this generally have gaps in knowledge, skill, and personality types, while groups that are significantly larger are unwieldy and difficult to manage. Thus, if we were creating a nonprofit board from scratch, we'd recommend six to ten members as the best size.

The reality, however, is that most nonprofit boards include significantly more members than this. In many cases, that's unavoidable and possibly desirable. The work of the organization may be so complex that it demands

TYPES OF BOARDS

	FOR-PROFIT	NONPROFIT
INFORMAL	 In a small, often family-owned business, the founder and manager are usually one and the same (shaded circle) and are advised by an informal board of friends and relatives.	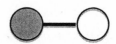 In a small nonprofit, the founder and manager (or executive director) are usually one and the same (shaded circle) and are advised by an informal board of friends and counselors.
FIDUCIARY	In a public company, there is an arm's-length relationship and often a formal wall of separation between management (shaded circle) and board. Board represents shareholders and uses management as a tool for achieving financial goals.	 In many large nonprofits, such as universities and major arts institutions, there is an arm's-length relationship and often a formal wall of separation between management (shaded circle) and board. Board represents major donors; meets infrequently and often receives formal presentations from management about strategy and plans.
ACTIVE	Management (shaded circle) and board meet frequently and informally. Board represents investors and may have overlapping membership with management. Especially typical of boards that are backed by venture capital and private equity funds.	Management (shaded circle) and multiple boards meet frequently and informally. Boards represent donors, expert advisors, community partners, beneficiary groups, and other stakeholders. Typically found in growing social enterprises and impact investments.

a board with expertise in a wide array of subjects; there may be important stakeholder groups that need to be represented; there may be major donors with talent and ideas to contribute who should be included; there may be prominent individuals with powerful connections to the organization or enormous prestige to offer. Once you start adding board members to address concerns like these, you quickly discover that the group has grown from eight or nine to twelve, fifteen, or even more.

This isn't the end of the world, as you can tell simply by looking at the nonprofits that have operated successfully with boards of this size. However, once the number of board members reaches fifteen or more, it's generally necessary to add an additional management layer through the use of board committees.

Board committees are subgroups charged with specific areas of activity. The committees generally meet separately from the overall board, often more frequently, and report their findings and recommendations to the board for its approval. A committee structure is an ideal way to combine the benefits of a large, inclusive board with the practicality of small teams of six to ten members.

Such committees are familiar from the for-profit world, where most boards feature an executive committee (a small group of key leaders who can tackle urgent problems that may arise between meetings of the whole board or may demand detailed, hands-on involvement from a few people); a finance committee and/or an audit committee (with special responsibility for studying the numbers); and a nominating committee (whose chief role is to recruit new members for the board itself).

Nonprofit boards may also choose to create other kinds of committees that often take on special importance. The most crucial is the development committee, whose focus is fund-raising. If your board boasts a number of members with particularly large and well-maintained networks of friends and colleagues, these individuals may be great candidates for your development committee, since they may be able to mobilize large portions of their personal networks around your cause. The development committee's jobs may include meeting monthly with the organization's head of development to review the current list of top donor prospects and formulate strategies for soliciting them; participating in fund-raising calls with the CEO, development director, or other staff members; and playing a liaison role in engaging the rest of the board members in the fund-raising process.

Specialized committees can be a great way of attracting talent to the board. For example, if you know a human-resources expert who could help your organization solve its chronic staffing problems, a great way to entice that person to join the board can be to offer membership or even the chairmanship of a special committee dedicated to that issue. You may also choose to allow board committees to include members who are not members of the overall board but have special expertise that you want to take advantage of. The committee structure can be a way of expanding your organization's network of partners without creating a massive, difficult-to-manage central board. At many organizations, most of the real work is done by board committees, with the full board serving mainly to ratify the committees' activities with its formal imprimatur.

Your board committee structure can be as flexible and creative as you like. Whenever a problem or opportunity arises that needs a rapid infusion of talent and energy, consider appointing a special committee to tackle it. (You might call a committee focused on a single short-term project, problem, or initiative a "task force" to distinguish it from a standing committee.) Many such ad hoc committees or task forces have sprung into action around short-term challenges, solved them effectively, and then voted themselves out of existence, all within six months—and in the process accomplished more tangible good than the full board did during the entire year.

Committees can even help solve other common board problems. One of Jennifer's students created an ad hoc board committee as a way to channel the energy of a particular member who was behaving in dysfunctional ways—for example, continually redirecting discussions to focus on his own pet interests. The committee was designed to launch a project tailored specifically to address Mr. Dysfunction's concerns. As chair, he named several of his buddies to the committee; they met on and off for a year, mapped out strategy for the project, raised a million dollars to pay for it, and peacefully disbanded. Jennifer's student says, "The specially created committee made good use of Mr. Dysfunction while controlling his energy, like the containment vessel at a nuclear plant."

Still another option, as we've seen, is to create an array of boards to serve various functions. Some nonprofits, for example, have a board made up of subject-matter experts (often called the advisory board) and another with responsibility for overall management of the organization (the board of directors proper). Many organizations that are national or global in scope establish regional or local boards whose job is to oversee, advise about, and energize activities in their own area. This is an ideal way to engage people who are interested only in the work that is happening in their town or state, as well as people who may not have the time or ability to travel to a distant city for the quarterly meetings of a national board. Other organizations have "youth boards" made up of younger partners who can help them attract, communicate with, and address the interests of people in their twenties and thirties (as opposed to the older cohorts who generally make up the typical board). Local boards and youth boards often serve as training grounds for talented people who eventually move up to the main board.

Sometimes an organization needs a kind of board that doesn't fit any of the conventional categories. Matt Goldman of Blue School is particularly proud of the organization's advisory board, which includes a number of distinguished experts on child development and education as well as leaders from other relevant fields. Education expert Ken Robinson conducts in-service training programs for Blue School teachers and staff members whenever he is in the New York area. Dan Siegel, author of *The Whole-Brain Child*, has provided a four-day mind/sight training program for the Blue

School community. Larry Cohen, author of *Playful Parenting*, visits with Blue School family members and leads wild, wonderful, vigorous play sessions in a specially padded room, helping moms and dads learn new ways of interacting with their kids. And David Rockwell, the noted architect who designed the renovation of Blue School's classroom building and subsequently became another member of the advisory board, has embarked on a three-year study examining how the spaces in which kids play and work affect the ways they learn—using Blue School itself, of course, as his lab.

The education nonprofit Blue Engine (no relation to Blue School) has a typical board of directors, which (as of early 2013) has six members. But founder Nick Ehrmann has discovered that a significantly larger number of people want to be part of the team. To accommodate them, he developed something he calls the Board of Engineers, a play on the organization's name. Nick explains:

> The Board of Engineers fills the gap between a traditional board of directors and a loosely affiliated board of advisors. It includes forty members, all young professionals from their mid-twenties to their mid-thirties, who want proximity to our work and knowledge about the problem and our proposed solution. They also want to be able to hang out with peers whom they are inspired by and whom they respect. Serving on our Board of Engineers offers them an opportunity to do just that.
>
> To be eligible to join the Board of Engineers, you have to pledge a minimum gift of $1,000 per year. In return, you get to help us plan ways for you and your peers to get involved. We're creating special task forces that will make use of people's particular skills. We're creating opportunities for Engineers to visit schools, to talk with the teachers who are working with high-risk students, and to organize and host unique fund-raising activities. The Board of

Engineers offers us a way to organize and channel incoming ideas and partner involvement into a structure that's mutually beneficial. It's about partnership, not a one-way ticket.

As these examples suggest, the number and kind of boards you can establish are limited only by your imagination, the needs of your organization, and the time your leaders have to work with the board members. Specialized boards can be a great way of expanding your team of partners, engaging fresh energies and ideas from a wide variety of sources, and "auditioning" new talent for a possible role on the main board at some time in the future.

GETTING THE RIGHT PEOPLE ON YOUR BOARD

One of the major board challenges facing nonprofit managers is how to attract excellent, committed, energized board members—and discourage the other kind. The worst are what we refer to as "big hat, no cattle" board members—those who do the least, talk the most, and inevitably seem to think they are the smartest people in the room. They must be weeded out, and fast.

Unfortunately this is easier said than done, particularly if you have recently joined a nonprofit organization or have inherited a board that you have not personally helped to recruit or train. If your organization has a tradition that board seats are held in perpetuity, it can be especially difficult to "fire" unproductive members (or induce them to resign). The problem seems to be particularly challenging for nonprofit organizations, which are often staffed with people who are conflict-averse.

One way to mitigate or avoid this problem is by implementing a policy of regular rotation of board seats. Set specific terms (three years is a practical length), limit the number of successive terms that a member may serve, and stagger the appointments so that a predictable fraction of the membership is set to retire every year. This provides continual opportunities to refresh the team, introduce new blood, and quietly separate from members who haven't been pulling their weight.

Sometimes, however, the need to force one or more resignations as part of a general renovation of the board is unavoidable. A board whose culture has become seriously dysfunctional may need a major overhaul, which generally requires turning over at least three board seats to new members. (Changing just a single member is unlikely to have the desired impact, while three new members who have been primed to model the new attitude and behavior needed to revitalize the board can work together to trigger an overall cultural shift.)

When an organization is faced with this necessity, the CEO or president of the organization shouldn't have to bear the burden of soliciting resignations—this is a job for the board chairman. Obviously it must be handled in privacy and with plenty of respect and dignity. The language used should emphasize the positive changes being sought rather than the problems or failures that require fixing: "We're going to ask you to cycle off the board because we're looking for a different set of skills right now," for example. If you handle these transitions with tact, it's often possible to retain the departed board member as a friend and partner of the organization.

The other side of the coin, of course, is the challenge of recruiting first-rate board members to replace those who have departed. Many nonprofit founders, CEOs, and other leaders find this task intimidating. One of Jennifer's students bemoaned the difficulty of identifying potential board members, saying, "Most of the philanthropists I know already have their favorite cause—how can I find some who will embrace mine?"

The job can be difficult—but don't make it more difficult than it needs to be. Start with your list of major donors. One central purpose for most boards is to provide a way of allowing important partners to become part of your leadership team. Many of those who provide significant financial support—though not all—also have a rich array of networks, experience, knowledge, insights, and ideas to offer that your organization can surely benefit from.

When compiling your list of board-member candidates, avoid making needless assumptions. If you Google the name of a potential board member and find it publicly linked with one or more charitable causes, don't jump to the conclusion that Mr. A or Ms. B is "taken." People may make gifts or even agree to serve on a board for many reasons, not all of them related to a profound personal commitment. It's almost always worthwhile to propose an open-ended conversation. You may well discover that the person at the other end of the sofa has an untapped passion that links directly to your work.

John Megrue, who has helped develop more than his share of excellent boards, advises recruiters to "gang-tackle" the job—solicit plenty of help from allies and partners inside and outside the organization. Ask your board chair, your committee chairs, your CEO, and any well-connected donors and partners who are not already board members if they can recommend anyone who is seeking a new challenge and may have the right temperament, energy level, and values. Look for people who are at stages in life when they may be ready to engage—people about to retire from business life, thirty-something professionals eager to supplement their work with a rewarding outside activity, parents whose children are moving on to college. These are times when many people are ready to shift to something new.

The task of recruiting a board chair is especially important, of course. The board chair needs all the characteristics that mark an excellent board member, and then some. In addition to being hardworking, open-minded, resourceful, diplomatic, energetic, and dedicated—which every board member should be—the board chair also needs strong leadership and communication skills. Also essential: the "managed ego" required to maintain positive relationships with a roomful of smart and strong-willed individuals, each with his or her own deeply held philosophy of life. When the chips are down, the chair should be capable of rallying the other board members behind a vital initiative or a tough decision, even when there may have been honest disagreements leading up to that decision.

The board chair also needs to be prepared to take on a significant time commitment. The best chairs devote between 15 and 20 percent of their time to the organization. (Much less than this is inadequate and is likely to leave vital tasks untended; much more may be excessive and may lead to micromanaging that trespasses on the prerogatives of staff.) The chair should be capable of a close, trusting relationship with the CEO, president, or executive director of the organization. Occasional arguments between the two are fine—in fact, they often reflect a healthy atmosphere in which new ideas can be tested and challenged appropriately. But the chair and the CEO should be partners with strong mutual respect who are able to call on each other in good times and bad, knowing they share both values and dedication to the mission of the organization.

Once you've recruited a great board chair, take full advantage of his or her talents—but don't abuse the chair through a protracted term in office. In our experience, two to three years is about the right length of time for any one person to fill the job. By the end of a three-year term, the chair's creative energies are likely to be flagging, and his or her roster of valuable contacts has probably been largely depleted. That's a good time to put a new person at the helm—preferably a current board member who has been preselected for the job and groomed during a year-long apprenticeship working closely with the previous chair.

Finally, once the new chair is in office, find a good role for the chair emeritus, depending on his or her skills and preferences. The ex-chair may want to head up a special initiative, chair your upcoming capital campaign, or become a freelance voice for the organization, giving supportive speeches, interviews, and presentations while being careful not to steal the spotlight from current leadership.

Recruiting great board members is an ongoing challenge for most nonprofits. Fortunately, moving your board in the right direction tends to produce a positive spiral effect. The more you seek out fully committed individuals to serve on your board, the more actively engaged the board will become; as the board takes on increasingly interesting, challenging, and creative work, the more it will tend to attract smart, talented, energetic people. Great board members prefer to recruit others like themselves. Set the right tone and start the ball rolling, and good results will begin to accumulate.

One last point about recruiting board members. Some organizational leaders worry excessively about demographic diversity on their board. They devote a lot of time and energy to identifying and wooing the "right" proportions of women, minority-group members, people with for-profit or nonprofit experience, and so on. Diversity is important, but it's not a matter of checking off boxes on a census form—intellectual and psychological diversity is far more significant. (A board filled with members who think exactly alike is worth little more than a single advisor with the same suite of ideas.) And more important still are the passion, energy, and willingness to work together that your board members bring to their assignments.

So put together a board that is diverse in terms of race, ethnicity, and gender if you can. But a board that really *works* is much more essential—and rarer.

GETTING THE GREATEST VALUE FROM YOUR BOARD

But how do you work with the board so as to elicit the greatest possible contributions from its members? Here are some suggestions, based on Jennifer's and Jeff's observations as advisors to nonprofit organizations as well as their extensive experience as board members themselves.

First, *set goals for board members—and make them personalized and explicit.* Jeff suggests a biennial one-on-one conversation between the board chairman and each board member that is very much like the annual performance review that most business managers are expected to conduct. The board chairman should ask, "What are you planning to contribute in the next couple of years? What projects would you like to undertake? Which programs would you like to participate in? Is there a board committee you'd like to join, or a new committee you'd like to start? How many potential new partners can you introduce to our organization? What new corporate connections can you make for us? What other objectives shall we set for you for the next twelve months?" By the end of the conversation, a specific list of goals should be agreed upon, to be confirmed in writing within a few days. And, yes, the list should include a financial goal, representing funds that the board member will personally donate, raise from acquaintances, or both.

Your organization's internal staff, from the CEO on down, also needs to be prepared to participate in the board's goal-setting process. You probably don't want the CEO or another staff member to attend the goal-setting meetings; those are best left as private conversations between the board members themselves. But the staff should be aware of the goals that are being set, should be able to suggest ways to make the goals supportive of the organization's overall strategy, and should be prepared to work with the board members in pursuit of their goals. One smart strategy used at many well-run nonprofits is to assign a particular staff member the job of serving as board liaison, ready to answer questions posed by board members, make connections to other staffers, and perform basic research tasks that may be helpful.

When creating a goal-setting system for your board members, don't forget about your board committees. These, too, should have explicit goals, with the committee chairs running the process of establishing goals (with input and approval from the board chairman) and taking responsibility for ensuring that the goals are met.

Second, *involve every board member in fund-raising*. This starts with making sure that all of your board members are themselves financial supporters of the organization. This may seem like an obvious step, yet surprisingly few non-profits are diligent about pursuing it. In an August 2011 survey of nonprofit executives, fewer than half of those surveyed reported meaningful board support for their fund-raising efforts.[15]

We can look at these data points as discouraging, since they reflect the disappointingly low level of participation by most of today's nonprofit boards in fund-raising; or we can view them as encouraging, since they suggest the enormous potential waiting to be realized, if only we can energize our boards as active participants in the task of mobilizing resources.

Of course, bringing board members into the job of fund-raising must be handled with sensitivity, tact, and judgment. If your board has previously not been required to help with fund-raising or even to make individual donations, you may experience pushback and even resentment from some members over this new request. You may need to implement the new expectation gradually, perhaps creating special grandfather exceptions for some older members who may find it difficult to meet that expectation. If the financial situations of board members differ greatly, a one-size-fits-all minimum donation may not be appropriate. Nor does every single member

---

15 *Daring to Lead: A National Study of Nonprofit Executive Leadership*, http://daringtolead.org/wp-content/uploads/Daring-Brief-3-080511.pdf.

of the board need to be fearless and highly effective at raising funds from friends and acquaintances. (Consider setting a lower bar for the personal donation from those who are especially good at making The Ask—and of course invite them to join your development committee.)

If your current board is not sufficiently in synch with this role, you need to take steps to begin to fill this gap. Start by visiting with each individual board member to seek understanding and support of the need to enhance the board's involvement. This is both a listening and briefing assignment. In addition to the board chairman, we suggest involving your CEO and a few key staff members in these briefings so that the board member sees a team of leaders and does not identify everything with the CEO only. This both preserves and enhances his or her leadership role.

In these discussions, communicate the strategic approach you are taking and the progress you are making to craft a vision and case for your future. Most important, suggest raising the expectations for the board, both as individuals and as a vitally important leadership team. Make it clear that the board's job is not simply to admire and approve the staff's brilliant plan, but to take ownership of it and back it with their own energy and commitment. Remember that the depth of each board member's personal relationship to the organization will drive fund-raising to a significant degree and will be the core of your fund-raising success.

REENERGIZING A BOARD:
Two Stories of How It's Done

One of Roger Brown's most important—and challenging—goals as the president of Berklee College has been to energize his large board of trustees (with no fewer than thirty-five members) and encourage them to begin offering all the enormous benefits they are capable of providing. His first step was to simply initiate a well-planned program of open dialogue with them:

> We had the membership committee interview every single board member, in person if possible, using a simple interview guide that we created: *What have you enjoyed about your Berklee experience? What could be better? Where do you think the college is doing a good job? Where could the college do better? How do you think Roger could do a better job? And what would you like to do? How do you think you could contribute to the next phase of Berklee's story and elevate your own participation in your game?*
>
> After each interview, the committee members wrote up a descriptive three-to-five-page report, and the head of the membership committee created a white paper where he summarized all the results, especially the recommendations for future actions by the various board members. That white paper became the basis for my response to the board.

Of course, evaluating and then synthesizing the ideas and suggestions of thirty-five different board members is no easy task. "The terrifying thing about this process," Brown says with a chuckle, "is that when you ask thirty-five different people for their opinions and ideas, you get thirty-five hundred responses!" Brown's method for handling this is what he calls "a bit of jujitsu." In a thirty-minute talk to the board, Brown observed:

> The number-one thing I heard from all of you is that we need to be better focused—to target our resources at a few things we want to do with excellence, and not to be distracted by shiny objects to the right and left of the path. That means that we won't be able to act on all of the brilliant ideas you gave me. If we're going to be focused, we can't do everything. So this morning we're going to

present our strategy, as best as I can define it, and we're going to work hard to stick to it and avoid being distracted by projects that aren't part of that strategic path.

"The board members understood what I was saying and they really appreciated my honesty about it," Brown reports. "It was very liberating for me personally to admit that I can't do everything people might like me to do, and I think it allowed me to be more fearless about really listening to what everyone had to say."

The next stage of the process was a careful review of each board member's interview, analyzing the interests, preferences, likes, and dislikes noted. This review serves as the basis for a goal-setting meeting with the board member—a personal conversation with Brown at which targets were laid out and commitments made. "They've all been great meetings," says Brown.

One trustee had initially commented, "You're asking us all to contribute more of our time and energy. But I'm giving you all I can give." I think that was really a positive moment. Prompting honest discussions like this is really a valuable part of the process. And what I've found is that, over time, even people like that board member, who were skeptical about their ability to commit more time and energy, have gradually gotten on board. It's the magic of raising expectations. We're saying, "We're all going to raise our game here," and people respond to that, especially once they've gone through a process where everybody has their say.

Energizing the board at Berklee College is still a work in progress. "I don't pretend we've got it all figured out," Brown says. "But I think the vibe, the karma of the board is very good. Now many of our members are saying that Berklee is the most fun and interesting board they've ever been on. I think that tells us we're on the right path."

Vanessa Kirsch is founder and managing director of New Profit, Inc., a "venture philanthropy fund" that pools money from a number of donors to help innovative social entrepreneurs and their organizations address some of America's biggest challenges in education, workforce development, public health, and poverty. Their distinguished list of grantee organizations includes such famous names as Teach for America, Kipp Schools, Year Up, and Peer Health Exchange. In addition to financial backing, Kirsch and her team provide the organizations they back with research and analysis, management advice, technical support, vital networking opportunities, and other kinds of help. Through a partnership with Monitor, the well-known consulting company, New Profit is able to offer social entrepreneurs access to expertise that might otherwise cost millions of dollars. (Jeff Walker is a member of New Profit's board and an avid supporter of its work.)

When New Profit was launched in 1998, its board consisted entirely of major donors who viewed themselves as nonprofit "investors" keeping an eye on the use of their money. Their relationship to the organization followed a simple hub-and-spoke system, with Kirsch at the center of the wheel. This worked well enough when the organization was relatively small and simple, but over time it became more and more unwieldy.

By 2011, it was obvious to Kirsch that a more professional system for organizing the board and making use of its insights would be tremendously valuable. With help and advice from Jeff, she and her team of staffers worked with board chairman Josh Bekenstein to create such a system. Using an approach similar to the one put in place at Berklee College, a team of board members interviewed all the other members, created written reports summarizing the feedback and suggestions, and crafted a committee structure to assign specific sets of responsibilities to board members who had expressed interest in taking them on. The goal has been to encourage board members to be more actively engaged in the daily workings of New Profit and the entrepreneurs it supports, and to provide them with a platform for doing so efficiently and effectively.

However, Kirsch soon discovered that introducing dramatic change is often challenging in itself. In September 2011, several months into the process of reshaping the board, Kirsch attended a board meeting at which she announced her plan to hire a new managing director to help her run the organization—an experienced nonprofit manager she'd known for twenty years, named Tripp Jones. Kirsch was stunned to discover that the board wasn't content to simply rubber-stamp her choice (as they would have been at any previous time in the history of New Profit).

"We'd wakened a sleeping giant!" Kirsch recalls.

All of a sudden, they wanted to be engaged, and that meant engaged in *everything*—including the hiring of Tripp. Some immediately agreed with the idea. Others wanted to learn more about him. Still others said I should hire a recruitment firm and conduct a nationwide search—which I knew meant that I'd lose Tripp as a candidate. The meeting was loud and confusing, with board members interrupting me and one another. I was so surprised and upset I actually walked out of the meeting at one point and burst into tears!

The disagreement was soon resolved: Kirsch was able to hire Jones, and he is now a valuable part of the New Profit team, just as she expected. But this contentious meeting was a wake-up call for the board members and for Kirsch and her management team. They all realized that while a structure for organizing interactions with the board was being built, a culture of norms for communication and decision making had yet to be developed. Now the creation of that culture has become a central focus of everyone in and around New Profit.

"We're finding our way together," Kirsch reports. She describes a recent experience in which a board member who'd been asked to interview a candidate for a new job opening abruptly dismissed the candidate with the words "You're not a good fit"—unintentionally short-circuiting the process in which Kirsch and other team members should have had input. Later the same day, Kirsch and the board member spoke on the phone about the misstep, and the board member quickly apologized: "Oh my gosh, I didn't realize I was stepping over the line. It won't happen again."

The job of engaging board members more deeply in the work of the organization, and then developing effective ways to make the expanded team work smoothly and effectively together is time- and energy-intensive. Kirsch reports that she now talks to one or another board member an average of two or three times per day. What's more, at least eight or nine other staffers at New Profit have had their job descriptions revised to include some responsibility for interactions with board members. "Yes, it's a lot of work," Kirsch observes.

> But it's incredibly valuable, too. I think our staff members are able to do a better job because of the constant conversations with the board. After all, the board members are our donors. That means they're investors in our mission—and "investor" is another word for "customer." And just as in any business, understanding the customer's perspective and applying it intelligently in your everyday job is one of the most important things anyone can do.

Think about the story of New Profit when you're wondering how you can do a better job of energizing and engaging your board. There are few more valuable steps you can take to improve the flow of resources into and through your organization—but make sure you're prepared to handle the challenges that may arise once you've wakened the sleeping giant.

In our experience, managers at practically all nonprofit organizations say that they wish they could get greater contributions of talent, energy, and creativity from their boards. At the same time, practically all nonprofit board members say they feel underappreciated, underinvolved, and underutilized. The problem is that the smart, articulate leaders on both sides of this divide find it difficult to communicate these feelings to one another and then explore the enormous areas of overlapping wishes where so much great work is possible.

One big benefit of the engagement process we've just described in the Berklee and New Profit stories is that it provides a simple vehicle for launching such conversations and making them productive. When necessary, it can also provide a straightforward and relatively painless way to counsel particular board members off the board. Rather than requiring a board chairman to single out an ineffective member for an embarrassing "firing," it creates a universal set of rising expectations for all board members. This makes it easy for an individual member to say, "I understand the new direction you're taking, but I'm just not able to increase my commitment to the same extent," and then step down from the board with no recriminations or hurt feelings on either side.

KEEPING YOUR BOARD FOCUSED AND POSITIVE

Recently, a friend who is the executive director of a very large nonprofit based in New York City said that she's frustrated with her board. She was lamenting that she can't get them to give and do more. The solution she considered is to find new trustees and weed out the ones who aren't performing. This is a common reaction to an unfortunately common concern.

Our response to this challenge is quite different from our friend's.

Instead of rushing to make changes to the board's makeup, ask yourself: *Exactly what are we doing to motivate our board emotionally?*

Our experience suggests that most organizations drop the ball here. We fail to invest time and energy in this vital matter of motivation, and so we miss out on enormous opportunities to create engaged, highly productive boards.

To address this issue, we need to start by going back to basics. What moves us humans to do things, especially in the sphere of social action? Remember, it's not a matter of persuasive ideas or even powerful arguments. *What generally moves us to action is a fundamental, emotional belief that we can truly make a difference*—that our work is going to have a meaningful impact on the lives of others and the world around us. Emotions wake us from autopilot and remind us why we're here, what is possible, and what we might accomplish together.

Against this backdrop, here's an idea that delivers reliable results. At your next board meeting, before tackling the prepared agenda, go around the room and ask each board member to describe the moment when he or she realized that your organization could fundamentally make a difference in the world. (You may recognize this technique as being borrowed from the Jeffersonian Dinner, as described in Chapter 8.) These memories will help them access their internal sources of possibility, inspiration, and imagination. And each story will be woven into the other stories in the room in a way that will stir people to find the capacity to act together in new and powerful ways.

Helping your board members rediscover the personal stories locked inside them will go a long way to engaging them and motivating them to action. A similar exercise can work wonders with other groups of partners as well—for example, consider using it at your organization's next staff meeting as a way of fending off the ever-looming threats of cynicism and burnout.

Sometimes the mood of the board—and its effectiveness—fluctuates in reaction to external circumstances. One key responsibility of leaders is to maintain the flow of positive emotional energy, even at times when doing so is difficult. Every organization has its problems and its moments of crisis, big and small. When these tough times strike, it's up to the leadership—the board chairman, the more experienced board members, and the CEO or other staff members—to set the example of a calm, upbeat, realistic, but determined attitude. Even if two or three of your board members become querulous, don't get defensive. Instead, send the message "We will get through this," treating setbacks and problems as "potholes" or "roadblocks" that you will get over or around with the help of your team. When leaders tackle challenges with resolve and confidence, things usually work out well—and their followers, including board members, develop greater confidence as a result.

Jeff and Jennifer have seen firsthand the ability of a strong-minded leader to shape the mood and attitude of a group. During a retreat designed to help energize and engage the members of the board of an organization involved in global development, a leading staff member took the floor and delivered a long, pessimistic diatribe about the state of the world's economy and its political and social systems. Much of what the staff member said was accurate, but there was little that our organization could do to directly address these systemic problems. So as the diatribe continued, the mood in the room became increasingly gloomy, threatening to derail the very purpose of the retreat.

Fortunately, John Megrue was also present at this retreat. When the staff member's presentation ended, Megrue stood up and offered a response, beginning with the words, "This is exactly why the work we're doing here is the most important work that any of us could possibly be doing." He went on to model *positive* energy with as much conviction and strength as the staff member had modeled negative energy, demonstrating by example something that Megrue himself likes to call "the power of the made-up mind." The mood of the meeting totally changed, and when Megrue sat down, the staff member himself stood up and reframed his earlier comments in a more positive light.

When the retreat resumed, the level of energy and creativity among the group was remarkably high.

WHEN A BOARD MUST BE REBUILT

Occasionally a board needs a major overhaul rather than a mere tweaking. When that's the case, the process requires creativity and strategic insight as well as tact and sensitivity.

Our friend (and Jennifer's student) Sarah Holewinski is executive director of Center for Civilians in Conflict, an organization dedicated to improving the protection of civilian populations who are caught up in armed conflicts around the world. The organization was founded in 2003 by Marla Ruzicka, a courageous humanitarian who was tragically killed by a suicide bomber on Airport Road in Baghdad in 2005 while working as an advocate for Iraqi families.

In 2006, Holewinski took over the organization, which was then known as CIVIC. She inherited a board that had been designed to meet the needs of a fledgling nonprofit whose main initial challenge was to define its mission. "Ruzicka called upon her friends at Human Rights Watch to serve on the board," Holewinski explains.

They were tremendous policy advocates, really smart and very knowledgeable. But by the time I became involved, our needs had evolved. We'd defined our mission and were ready to expand and grow. However, the eight members of the existing board were not experts in organizational governance, they weren't involved in fund-raising, and they had no special access to resources. So with our organizational needs changing, we needed to redesign the board completely.

Of course, a complete overhaul of any existing institution is easier said than done. Holewinski spent two years trying to develop a plan for the transition. It wasn't hard to draw up a list of the kinds of people she wanted to recruit for the new board—men and women who could help with governance and policy issues, assist Holewinski with organizational strategy, provide access to funding and other resources, and help serve as public faces and voices for the organization and its mission. But convincing such people to join the board was another matter. "With a fledgling organization," Holewinski says, "no one at a high level of expertise and credibility wants to be the first to join the board. It's understandable—they don't want to have to take on the heavy lifting all by themselves." So Holewinski spent months wooing some of the most likely candidates, without success.

A conversation with Jennifer helped Holewinski solve the puzzle:

Jennifer told me, "You've already got all the people you need. It's just a matter of reaching out to them and asking the right questions and figuring out how they can help you." And so I began asking, "Who do we have? Who can help us with this challenge?" And I thought of Aryeh Neier, who was then the president of the Open Society Foundations. He's a mentor of mine and had been a respected supporter of our organization for years. I realized that Aryeh could be the key to the equation.

Aryeh Neier had the kind of credibility in the international human rights community that Holewinski and her organization were seeking to build. He also had a network that included practically all of the people who would be ideal members for Holewinski's redesigned board. Thinking outside the box, Holewinski approached Neier with an unusual request. She presented him with her list of board candidates and asked Neier to host a luncheon for the entire group.

Neier agreed, and the strategy worked like a charm. Attracted by Neier's reputation, all the invitees attended the luncheon in January 2012, at which they met Holewinski (in some cases for the first time) and learned about the center's work on behalf of endangered civilians. Impressed, many of them responded favorably to Holewinski's request that they consider joining her board. By early summer, she was in the process of formally reconstituting the board to include nine new members (along with two holdovers from the existing board).

The luncheon also produced some unexpected ancillary benefits. One of the experts Holewinski had been trying to recruit for her board was the journalist Sebastian Junger, author of The Perfect Storm as well as War, which deals with the conflict in Afghanistan. "I had asked him for several years in a row," Sarah recalls. "He said, 'No, no, no, I've got too much to do.' But when he heard about this lunch and about the amazing people who attended, he could see that there was a real growth of legitimacy and credibility and interest in the organization. We talked later, and he has since joined our board."

Holewinski is also working to handle the transition from the previous board to the new one with sensitivity. To recognize the years of valuable service provided by the former board members (and to keep them involved in years to come), she is creating an emeritus board. Members of this board will no longer have governing responsibilities; however, they will continue to receive informational updates about the organization, and their ideas and input will continue to be sought and valued.

The board transition for the Center for Civilians in Conflict is now nearly complete, but the board work for Sarah Holewinski is far from over. She admits that getting to know all her new team members, working with them to benefit from their wisdom, energy, and connections, and reshaping the organization to take advantage of their insights is time-consuming and occasionally exhausting. But the benefits she anticipates are enormous.

Build a truly great board, and the value it generates will more than outweigh the work it demands.

FOOD FOR THOUGHT

Follow-up questions and activities designed to help you get the most out of this chapter:

- Review the discussion of board types (pages 241–246). Which type of board best describes the one your organization now has? How well is the current board structure serving your needs? Does it make sense to consider starting a transition to a different board type?

- Does your board currently make use of special committees to tackle particular problems? If so, is the list of existing committees suitable for your organization's needs? If not, what kinds of committees might be worth creating to supplement the work of the board as a whole?

- Are there any useful functions not being served by your current board that might be filled by a second board? For example, could your organization benefit from an advisory board, a board of experts, a youth board, a regional or local board, or some other kind of specialized board?

- Do your organization's board members currently set and pursue annual goals for fund-raising and other activities? If not, meet with your board chair to discuss the possibility of creating a goal-setting system as an important step toward improving the productivity of your board and its members.

- How fully engaged are your board members? Do they participate actively in meetings? Do they contribute ideas, questions,
  contacts, and suggestions between meetings? If your board
  members are less than fully involved, talk with them to uncover
  the reasons and develop a plan for energizing their interests
  and talents on behalf of the organization. And consider assign-
  ing one or more staff members to maintain communication with
  board members on a regular basis.

EPILOGUE

WHAT DOES SUCCESS LOOK LIKE?

When you reach the top, keep climbing.

—Zen proverb

There are times when work in the nonprofit arena feels thankless, exhausting, and never-ending. The problems we choose to tackle are so vast, the complications so limitless, the issues so complex. And problems such as poverty, disease, pollution, ignorance, bigotry, and violence are so pervasive and so persistent that it can be difficult to even imagine a true solution—an answer to the challenge that is more than a mere Band-Aid or a finger in the dike.

So for those of us who've chosen to make these epochal problems our life's work, what does success look like? Does it look like a world where the more serious human problems have been vanquished once and for all?

Not really. As most of us recognize, such a world is a pipe dream unlikely ever to be achieved. But there's a vision of success that's far more realistic—one that can inspire our continuing efforts despite the challenges and obstacles we encounter practically every day.

Success looks like a world where millions of people have gained a deeper understanding of the problems faced by their peers halfway around the planet—and have learned to care about those problems and even contribute to the solution.

It looks like a world where leaders of hostile faiths can come together around a shared sense of compassion and responsibility, join forces to save the lives of hundreds of thousands of children, and then begin to explore the potential for similar joint efforts against other mutual foes, from malnutrition to AIDS.

It looks like a world where political leaders from dozens of countries can put aside their jealousies and disputes and make common cause in the name of relieving human suffering for millions of their people.

And it looks like a world where all these things are possible, in part, because one man or woman decided to try to make them happen—and reached out across barriers of nationality, race, religion, prejudice, self-interest, and flawed assumptions to create a team that would work together in a spirit of openness and generosity to turn vision into reality.

That, to us, is what success looks like. Success is not a large and powerful organization, a collection of awards and trophies, or even a series of encouraging metrics recording improvements in some social problem (hunger, disease, poverty). Rather, success is a dynamic, fluid condition of ever-increasing openness, creativity, and power, which enables nonprofit organizations and those who lead and support them to continually evolve, change, and grow, bringing hope and better lives to people around the corner or around the world. It's a journey of discovery that never ends.

Our hope—and our deeply held belief—is that success on these terms will be within reach for every leader, team member, and partner who reads this book and takes its message to heart. You're invited to join us in a never-ending relationship centered on change, growth, and discovery . . . a conversation in which the future of our communities, and even of all humankind, may be invented.

RECOMMENDED RESOURCES

Books

Csikszentmihalyi, Mihaly. *Flow: The Psychology of Optimal Experience*. New York: Harper Perennial, 2008.

Ganz, Marshall. *Why David Sometimes Wins: Leadership, Organization, and Strategy in the California Farm Worker Movement*. New York: Oxford University Press, 2010.

Hyde, Lewis. *The Gift: Imagination and the Erotic Life of Property*. New York: Vintage Books, 1979.

Needleman, Jacob. *Money and the Meaning of Life*. New York: Doubleday, 1994.

Panas, Jerold. *Asking: A 59-Minute Guide to Everything Board Members, Volunteers, and Staff Must Know to Secure the Gift*, Revised Edition. Medfield, MA: Emerson & Church, 2013.

Salamon, Julie. *Rambam's Ladder: A Meditation on Generosity and Why It Is Necessary to Give*. New York: Workman, 2003.

Salzberg, Sharon. *Lovingkindness: The Revolutionary Art of Happiness*. Boston: Shambhala, 2002.

Twist, Lynne. *The Soul of Money: Reclaiming the Wealth of Our Inner Resources*. New York: Norton, 2006.

Tierney, Thomas J., and Joel L. Fleishman. *Give Smart: Philanthropy That Gets Results*. New York: PublicAffairs, 2012.

Vanier, Jean. *Becoming Human*. Toronto, ON: House of Anansi, 2008.

Blogs

Andresen, Katya. *Katya's Non-Profit Marketing Blog.* http://www.nonprofitmar
ketingblog.com.

Bornstein, David. *Opinionator* (New York Times blog). http://opinionator.blogs
.nytimes.com/author/david-bornstein/.

Dichter, Sasha. *Sasha Dichter's Blog.* http://sashadichter.wordpress.com.

Godin, Seth. *Seth's Main Blog.* http://sethgodin.typepad.com.

Kanter, Beth. *Beth's Blog: How Nonprofits Can Use Social Media.* http://www.beth
kanter.org/welcome/.

LinkedIn For Good. *LinkedIn Blog.* http://blog.linkedin.com/topic/linkedin
-for-good/.

Grant, Adam. *Give and Take: A Revolutionary Approach to Success* (blog). http://www
.giveandtake.com/Home/Blog.

Huffington Post. *Huffpost Impact* (blog). http://www.huffingtonpost.com/
impact/.

Philanthropy Journal. *Inside Philanthropy: A Blog on Philanthropy and Nonprofit News
and Issues.* http://philanthropyjournal.blogspot.com.

Stanford Social Innovation Review. *Blog.* http://www.ssireview.org/blog/.

COURSE IN
Exponential Fundraising Participants
(NOT LISTED ELSEWHERE):

Jeremy Barnicle
CHIEF DEVELOPMENT
OFFICER/ CHIEF
COMMUNICATIONS OFFICER,
MERCY CORPS

Richard Buery
PRESIDENT AND CHIEF
EXECUTIVE OFFICER, THE
CHILDREN'S AID SOCIETY

Charles Best
CEO, DONORSCHOOSE.ORG

Sasha Chanoff
FOUNDER AND EXECUTIVE
DIRECTOR, REFUGE POINT

John Maeda
PRESIDENT, RHODE ISLAND
SCHOOL OF DESIGN

Sylvia Ferrell-Jones
PRESIDENT AND CEO, YWCA
BOSTON

Alexander McLean
DIRECTOR GENERAL,
AFRICAN PRISONS PROJECT

Suzanne Helm
VICE PRESIDENT,
DEVELOPMENT COUNCIL ON
FOREIGN RELATIONS

Joi Ito
EXECUTIVE DIRECTOR, MIT
MEDIA LAB

Valerie Broadie
DIRECTOR OF DEVELOPMENT,
PLANNED PARENTHOOD OF
METROPOLITAN WASHINGTON

David Angel
PRESIDENT, CLARK
UNIVERSITY

Chris Balme
CO-FOUNDER AND CEO,
SPARK

Adam Braun
FOUNDER / EXECUTIVE
DIRECTOR, PENCILS OF
PROMISE

Barbara Bush
CEO AND CO-FOUNDER,
GLOBAL HEALTH CORPS

Esther Cohen
CHIEF OPERATING OFFICER,
EPISCOPAL RELIEF &
DEVELOPMENT

Erica Di Bona
BOARD MEMBER AND
TRUSTEE, RHODE ISLAND
SCHOOL OF DESIGN

Ingeborg Haavardsson
EXECUTIVE DIRECTOR, PRE
PEACE RESEARCH INSTITUTE
OSLO

Lars Jahns
SENIOR VICE PRESIDENT,
ADVANCEMENT ROBIN HOOD

Jordan Kassalow
FOUNDER AND CEO,
VISIONSPRING

Kathryn (Kate) Roberts
FOUNDER AND VP,
YOUTHAIDS/PSI

Sarah Holewinski
EXECUTIVE DIRECTOR, CIVIC

Kenneth Watkins
DIRECTOR OF PHILANTHROPY,
THE AUSTRALIAN BALLET

Robert (Bob) Weiss
VICE CHAIRMAN AND
PRESIDENT, X PRIZE
FOUNDATION

Audrey Levitin
DIRECTOR OF DEVELOPMENT,
INNOCENCE PROJECT

Spencer Kympton
CHIEF OPERATING OFFICER,
THE MISSION CONTINUES

Geoffrey MacDougall
PARTNERSHIP LEAD, HEAD
OF DEVELOPMENT, MOZILLA
FOUNDATION

Sydney Morris
CO-FOUNDER AND
CO-CEO, EDUCATORS FOR
EXCELLENCE

Reid Saaris
EXECUTIVE DIRECTOR, EQUAL
OPPORTUNITY SCHOOLS

Michael Schreiber
MANAGING DIRECTOR,
GBCHEALTH

Laura Segura-Mueller
DIRECTOR, ALLIANCES, X
PRIZE FOUNDATION

Lawson Shadburn
CHIEF OPERATING OFFICER,
TURNAROUND FOR
CHILDREN, INC.

Lorna Solis
FOUNDER AND CEO, BLUE
ROSE COMPASS

William Spear
PRESIDENT, FOUNDER,
FORTUNATE BLESSINGS
FOUNDATION, INC.

Louise Walsh
DIRECTOR, ARTSUPPORT
AUSTRALIA

Christina Williams
DIRECTOR OF DEVELOPMENT
AND FINANCE, MIT MEDIA LAB

Patrick Willingham
EXECUTIVE DIRECTOR,
PUBLIC THEATER/
SHAKESPEARE IN THE PARK

Mark Arnoldy
EXECUTIVE DIRECTOR, NYAYA
HEALTH

Blakely Braniff
DIRECTOR OF DEVELOPMENT,
BLUE SCHOOL

Amy Clark
PARTNERSHIPS LEADER,
ASHOKA UNITED STATES

Andrew Cyr
ARTISTIC DIRECTOR/
CONDUCTOR, METROPOLIS
ENSEMBLE

Sol Echeverria
EXECUTIVE DIRECTOR, CALI
FOUNDATION

Debra Eschmeyer
CO-FOUNDER AND VICE
PRESIDENT OF POLICY AND
PARTNERSHIPS, FOODCORPS

Zack Exley
CHIEF REVENUE OFFICER,
WIKIMEDIA FOUNDATION

Giyoun Kim
ACTING EXECUTIVE
DIRECTOR, ASIAN FORUM
FOR HUMAN RIGHTS AND
DEVELOPMENT (FORUM-ASIA)

Debra Montanino
CHIEF DEVELOPMENT
OFFICER, COMMUNITIES IN
SCHOOLS

Alexis Morin
CO-FOUNDER AND
CO-EXECUTIVE DIRECTOR,
STUDENTS FOR EDUCATION
REFORM

Lucia Nadar
EXECUTIVE DIRECTOR,
CONECTAS DIREITOS
HUMANOS

Ben Paul
PRESIDENT AND CEO, AFTER-
SCHOOL ALL-STARS

Vivian Newman Pont
DEPUTY DIRECTOR,
DEJUSTICIA

Carolyn Ramo
EXECUTIVE DIRECTOR,
ARTADIA

Edwin (Ed) Rekosh
EXECUTIVE DIRECTOR,
PILNET: THE GLOBAL
NETWORK FOR PUBLIC
INTEREST LAW

Joel Rose
CO-FOUNDER AND CEO,
NEW CLASSROOMS
INNOVATION PARTNERS

Seth Rosen
MANAGING DIRECTOR OF
DEVELOPMENT, GAY MEN'S
HEALTH CRISIS

Eric Stowe
FOUNDER & DIRECTOR,
SPLASH

Jill Vialet
CEO/FOUNDER, PLAYWORKS

Christine Wilson
FOUNDER/BOARD
VICE CHAIR, ANTIGUA
INTERNATIONAL SCHOOL

Jocelyn Wyatt
EXECUTIVE DIRECTOR,
IDEO.ORG

Rhode Island School of Design (RISD), 83–84

Rihanna, 211

Rmo, Carolyn, 280

Roberts, Kathryn (Kate), 279

Robin Hood Foundation, 22, 211–213, 215,
221–222

Robinson, Ken, 250

Rockwell, David, 251

Rodriguez, Alfredo, 63

Rose, Joel, 280

Rosen, Seth, 280

Ruzicka, Marla, 268

Saaris, Reid, 279

Sachs, Jeff, 90, 126

"Sages and Scientists" conference, 2–3

Saint-Exupéry, Antoine de, 172

salesmanship, 125
  myths about, 174, 176

Salk, Jonas, 3

Salzberg, Sharon, 40, 149–150

Sanskrit classics, 45

Save the Children, 227, 228, 230–231

scarcity, doctrine of, 31–32, 35, 42

Scharmer, C. Otto, 87

Schreiber, Michael, 279

second meetings, 156, 166

Segura-Mueller, Laura, 279

self, story of, 49–51, 57–60, 125, 142–143,
184, 199

self-actualization, 75

self-esteem, 29, 35

self-nurturing, 104

Seneca, 156

senses, stories and, 46, 64

sensory details, 59

Shadburn, Lawson, 280

Shaw, George Bernard, 68, 98

Siegel, Dan, 250

SIM challenge, 169, 170

SixDegrees.org, 117

sleep, 104

Smith, Margaret Bayard, 197

social media, 7, 111–117, 122, 228–230, 232,
233, 235

Solis, Lorna, 280

solitude, importance of, 104

Soros, George, 143

Spear, William, 280

standing boards, 245

Stanton, Phil, 205

"Story of Stone Soup, The," 68–69

storytelling, 44–65, 125, 183
  to groups, 62–64, 65
  importance of, 45–47
  overcoming excuses, 52–57
  with power, 48–52
  public narrative concept, 48–52, 57–61, 64,
    184–185, 199
  senses and, 46, 64

Stowe, Eric, 280

strategy statement, 119

success, vision of, 274–275

synergy, 88

Teach for America, 262

Terkel, Studs, 54

term limits, 239, 253

testimonials, 47

*Theory U: Leading from the Future as It Emerges: The
  Social Technology of Presencing* (Scharmer), 87

Thomas Jefferson Foundation, 195

Tierney, Thomas J., 179

timing, The Ask and, 180–182

traditional fund-raising, 8, 35–36, 125

transformational giving, 6, 8–12, 23–25, 34,
  36, 124, 127, 142–143

transparency, 33, 56, 100, 102, 107, 121, 125,
  128–131, 146

travel opportunities, 6, 219–222, 223

Twitter, 112, 113, 117, 228

Uganda, 109–111

uncertainty, sense of, 22

Uncharitable (Pallotta), 179

United Jewish Communities, 116

United Nations, 91, 142, 213

U.S. Agency for International Development,
  92

United Way, 116

universities, avatar concept and, 231

unknown, fear of, 33, 35, 42

us, story of, 49–51, 57, 125, 184, 199

Value Mentors, 73–74

values, 73–78, 82–85, 95

verbal learners, 63

Vialet, Jill, 280

visual learners, 63

vulnerability, as strength, 132

Jennifer McCrea has twenty-five years' experience as a fund-raiser for a broad array of nonprofit organizations. She started her career in the field of higher education, raising funds for Case Western Reserve University and serving at Washington University in St. Louis during their multibillion-dollar campaign. She was also Vice President for Development at Dickinson College.

More recently, Jennifer has worked as a consultant, coach, and advisor to CEOs, fund-raisers, and board members from a wide variety of organizations, including Millennium Promise, Acumen Fund, DonorsChoose.org, Grameen America, Teach for America, Witness, Columbia University, Quincy Jones Foundation, Comic Relief, X Prize Foundation, VH1 Save the Music Foundation, Rhode Island School of Design, Creative Commons, and many others.

Jennifer is a Senior Research Fellow at the Hauser Center for Nonprofit Organizations at Harvard University, where she designs and leads the course Exponential Fundraising. She is also a Henry Crown Fellow at the Aspen Institute; serves as an advisory board member of the MIT Media Lab, Berklee

College City Music program, and the Blue School; and is a co-founder and board member of the Quincy Jones Musiq Consortium.

Jeff Walker came to the world of philanthropy from a successful career in business. After earning his MBA at Harvard, Jeff went to work at Chemical Bank, and in 1983 he and a partner got permission to set up the bank's first venture capital unit. Chemical Venture Partners ended up performing spectacularly for the bank, earning over 20 percent returns a year and growing the portfolio to more than $12 billion, with successful niches in media, entertainment, consumer products, energy, health care, and manufacturing. This formula worked well over a twenty-four-year period and through eight mergers, as the business evolved from JPMorgan Partners to the independent firm CCMP Capital.

Throughout his business career, Jeff devoted a portion of his time to nonprofit leadership. In 1998, he co-founded a nonprofit called NPower (www.npower.org). Over the past thirty years he has served on the boards of dozens of nonprofit organizations, including Monticello, the University of Virginia McIntire School, the Wilton School Board, the Big Apple Circus, Millennium Promise, the Berklee College of Music, and many others. Jeff retired from private equity in 2007 and began working on bringing his active investor skills to the nonprofit and social enterprise space. He also went on to work for two years as an executive in residence at Harvard Business School and to teach a seminar at the Harvard Kennedy School on applying private skills to the nonprofit world. He is currently working in global health with the MDG Health Alliance and at the University of Virginia with the Center for Contemplative Sciences. He also mentors many social entrepreneurs and sits on a number of advisory boards, including the MIT Media Lab, Witness, the Blue School, the Tibetan Village Project, and Ideo.org.

Karl Weber, the third member of the author team, is one of today's leading writers and editors of serious nonfiction. He specializes in the topics of business, politics, and current affairs, and has a series of critically acclaimed and bestselling books to his credit.

Karl's recent projects include the *New York Times* bestseller *Creating a World Without Poverty* (2008), co-authored with Muhammad Yunus, winner of the 2006 Nobel Peace Prize, and its sequel, *Building Social Business* (2010); *The Triple Bottom Line*, a guide to sustainable business, co-authored with Andrew W. Savitz (2006); and the companion books to the films *Food Inc.* (2009), *Waiting for "Superman"* (2010), and *Lincoln* (2013), which Karl edited.

To join our Generosity Network, sign up for our newsletter, and discover additional resources that can help you grow as a nonprofit leader and team builder, visit us at www.thegenerositynetwork.com.